Colección Támesis

SERIE A: MONOGRAFÍAS, 277

A COMPANION TO JORGE LUIS BORGES

STEVEN BOLDY

A COMPANION TO JORGE LUIS BORGES

TAMESIS

First published 2009 by Tamesis, Woodbridge
Paperback edition 2013

ISBN 978 1 85566 189 9 hardback
ISBN 978 1 85566 266 7 paperback

Transferred to digital printing

Tamesis is an imprint of Boydell & Brewer Ltd
PO Box 9, Woodbridge, Suffolk IP12 3DF, UK
and of Boydell & Brewer Inc.
668 Mt Hope Avenue, NY 14620–2731, USA
website: www.boydellandbrewer.com

A CIP catalogue record for this book is available
from the British Library

The publisher has no responsibility for the continued existence or accuracy
of URLs for external or third-party internet websites referred to in this book,
and does not guarantee that any content on such websites is,
or will remain, accurate or appropriate.

This publication is printed on acid-free paper

CONTENTS

FOREWORD

This Companion to Jorge Luis Borges has been designed for keen readers of Borges whether they approach him in English or Spanish, within or outside a university context. It takes his stories and essays of the forties and fifties, especially *Ficciones* and *El Aleph*, to be his most significant works, and organizes its material in consequence. About two-thirds of the book analyses the stories of this period text by text. The early sections map Borges's intellectual trajectory up to the fifties in some detail, and up to his death more briefly. They aim to provide an account of the context which will allow the reader maximum access to the meaning and significance of his work. They provide a biographical narrative developed against the Argentine literary world in which Borges was a key player, the Argentine intellectual tradition in its historical context, and the Argentine and world politics to which his works respond in more or less obvious ways.

I have been reading Borges, and criticism on him, for many years, and have probably come to consider as my own those thoughts I absorbed early on from Ronald Christ, Dunham and Ivask's *The Cardinal Points of Borges*, Donald Shaw, the *Cahiers de L'Herne* collection, and others. On writing my Companion I have mined Edwin Williamson's *Borges. A Life* thoroughly for biographical information, and have not found space to acknowledge every last scrap I have used. Something similar goes for Evelyn Fishburn and Psiche Hughes's invaluable *A Dictionary of Borges*, which I have consulted over a much longer period. For many, Borges is already an integral part of their mental make-up, while others are just facing their first puzzlement and excitement at his stories; I hope to have provided extra focus or useful guidance for both groups.

I thank Stephen Hart as General Editor of Tamesis, and Ellie Ferguson as Managing Editor, for their graceful forbearance in nudging me into what has been a most rewarding and enjoyable project.

ABBREVIATIONS

I have cited Borges from the following editions, and will use the abbreviations indicated:

In Spanish

Inq	*Inquisiciones* (Madrid: Alianza, 1998)
TE	*El tamaño de mi esperanza* (Madrid: Alianza, 2005)
IA	*El idioma de los argentinos* (Madrid : Alianza, 2000)
OP	*Obra poética 1923–1967* (Buenos Aires: Emecé, 1969)
Al	*El Aleph* (Buenos Aires: Emecé, 1969)
I	*Obras completas*, vol I (Buenos Aires: Emecé, 2004)
II	*Obras completas*, vol II (Buenos Aires: Emecé, 2004)
III	*Obras completas*, vol III (Buenos Aires: Emecé, 1989)
OC	*Obras completas en colaboración* (Buenos Aires: Emecé, 2001)
TR I	*Textos recobrados 1919–1929* (Buenos Aires: Emecé, 2002)
TR II	*Textos recobrados 1931–1955* (Buenos Aires: Emecé, 2002)
TC	*Textos cautivos: ensayos y reseñas en* El Hogar *(1936–1939)* (Barcelona: Tusquets, 1986)
BP	*Biblioteca personal* (Madrid: Alianza, 1988)

In English

F	*Fictions*, trans. by Andrew Hurley (London: Penguin, 2000)
A	*The Aleph*, trans. by Andrew Hurley (London: Penguin, 2000)
TL	*The Total Library. Non Fiction 1922–1986*, ed. by Eliot Weinberger (London: Penguin, 1999)
SP	*Selected Poems*, ed. by Alexander Coleman (London: Penguin, 2000)
CF	*Collected Fictions*, trans. by Andrew Hurley (New York: Penguin, 1998)
Com, Aut	'Commentaries' and 'An Autobiographical Essay', in *The Aleph and Other Stories, 1933–1969*, ed. and trans. by Norman Thomas di Giovanni (London: Jonathan Cape, 1971)

Other Works

B	Daniel Balderston, *Out of Context* (Durham and London: Duke University Press, 1993)
FH	Evelyn Fishburn and Psiche Hughes, *A Dictionary of Borges* (London: Duckworth, 1990)
MF	José Hernández, *Martín Fierro* (Madrid: Cátedra, 1990)
S	George Bernard Shaw, *Back to Methuselah*, in *Collected Plays with their Prefaces* (London: Max Reiharde, The Bodley Head, 1972)
V	María Esther Vázquez, *Borges: esplendor y derrota* (Barcelona: Tusquets, 1996)
W	Edwin Williamson, *Borges. A Life* (New York: Viking, 2004)

I
CONTEXT

Perspectives

Borges is a world of complex and paradoxical perceptions and dimensions. He can be seen as an author of purely archetypal literary texts; as a bookish and almost unreal individual; as a harbinger of major trends in structuralist, post-structuralist and post-modern thought; as a cosmopolitan, universal writer; as an essentially Argentine author deeply concerned with both his country's literary classics and its history; as a writer engaging with the historical and ideological issues facing the Western world from the twenties to the Cold War. A glance at a number of these dimensions may serve as a preliminary and impressionistic introduction to the phenomenon of Jorge Luis Borges. An essay, 'The Argentine Writer and Tradition', will serve to introduce Borges's use of paradox and polemics, his preoccupation with cultural transmission and translation, his quirkily irreverent use and misuse of others' texts, and his thoughts on the status of Argentine, and Latin American, culture.

Read in France in the early fifties in the translation of Roger Caillois, or as *Labyrinths* in the USA in the sixties, the stories of *Ficciones* and *El Aleph* seemed almost eternal, rounded, and mysterious: perfect intellectual fables without precedent or provenance. Symptomatically, Caillois excised texts with specifically Argentinian themes, such as 'The South', 'El Sur', from his edition.[1] The truth is that they emerge, miraculously but laboriously, from the vast nebula of Borges's previous production, firmly grounded in the literary and political reality of Buenos Aires: poetry, literary and political polemics, four published collections of essays, intense if eclectic reading of the 1911 *Encyclopaedia Britannica*, and the endless slog of literary reviewing over two decades. Borges edited journals such as *Proa* and *Prisma*, produced a string of influential anthologies (of *ultraísta* poetry, of fantastic literature, of detective fiction), penned endless short introductions to world literary figures in the pages of the popular women's magazine *El Hogar*, and reviewed an inconceivable number of texts in the pages of journals as diverse as *Nosotros* and *Martín Fierro*. Borges was a professional reader before he

---

[1] See Jason Wilson, *Jorge Luis Borges* (London: Reaktion, 2006), 123.

became the successful story-writer, and these two dimensions are inseparable in his thought and literary practice. The stories emerge as a genetic mutation almost, when the literary review becomes story, mystical quest and metatextual game in 1939, with 'The Approach to Al-Mu'tasim', 'El acercamiento a Almotásim'.

Similarly, from photographs and physical descriptions of Borges, there emerge for me two very different figures. A 1939 photograph with Haydée Lange shows a bearded and thick-set Borges with a Basque beret hiding scars from a recent head wound, and a tightly stretched double-breasted suit. On the back, he wrote: 'Wounded Tapir', suggesting a man ill at ease with his body, alienated and alone (V 165). He might almost have written 'wounded minotaur'. Leopoldo Marechal, a one-time friend and literary collaborator, who had become hostile to Borges over disagreements on nationalism, Irigoyen, and Peronism, described his avatar Luis Pereda in his 1949 novel *Adán Buenosayres* as 'theoretical defender of local colour … a man as stocky and lurching as a blind wild boar'.[2] In photographs of the final decades of his life, however, a blind, white-haired, stylized Borges, face turned upward towards the light, hands resting on a cane, is classical, seraphic almost, a twentieth-century Homer: 'a blind old poet serenely facing the world of shadows'.[3]

Beatriz Sarlo, who has done more than most to situate Borges in the cultural reality of Argentina and Buenos Aires, comments that he has become 'a cult writer for literary critics who discover in him the Platonic forms of their concerns: the theory of intertextuality, the limits of the referential illusion, the relationship between knowledge and language, the dilemmas of representation and of narration' (Sarlo, *Borges*, 5). He has been seen as the inspirer of the systems of Foucault's *Les Mots et les choses* (1966), of Roland Barthes's 'death of the author' (1967), and even, in his labyrinthine libraries and endless recombination of references, as precursor of the world-wide-web. Borges is all this, but it is a vision which should be tempered by studies such as those of John King in *Sur*, who situates Borges in the context of Argentinian literary journals, and Daniel Balderston, in *Out of Context*, who brings out the precise and complex sources behind seemingly abstract or playful pieces: his detailed use, for example, of Indian and Irish history, and the historiography of the two World Wars. A certain Argentine left, of course, has painted Borges with broad brush-stokes as a product and cham-

---

2   'criollista teórico … hombre fortachón y bamboleante como un jabalí ciego' (*Adán Buenosayres*, 163).
3   'un viejo poeta ciego, enfrentando, erguido, el mundo de la sombra' (V 215).

pion of a reactionary upper middle-class establishment.[4] More recently, his stand against fascism has been considered in detail.[5]

In Fanny Haslam, Borges has an English grandmother, and in Guillermo Borges, an anglophile father; and after a period in the twenties of *nacionalismo criollo*, a literary championing of the aesthetics of the Buenos Aires suburbs, largely suppressed by the author during his lifetime, he published articles and many of his best stories in the pages of the cosmopolitan and patrician journal *Sur*, a local version of the *Nouvelle Revue Française* or Ortega y Gasset's *Revista de Occidente*. This, together with the fantastic and philosophical dimensions of his work, attracted accusations from the nationalist right that he was 'extranjerizante', tending to the foreign and European. The Cuban socialist Roberto Fernández Retamar, while hostile to Borges's project and social class, sees him not as European, but as the final vestiges of a colonial Latin American: 'his writing ... is more like a reading. Borges is not a European writer: there is no European writer like Borges. ... Apart from a few literature professors who receive a salary for it, there is only one sort of person who knows European literature truly and comprehensively: the colonial.'[6] Retamar could have found a less choleric version of this analysis in Borges's own essay 'The Argentine Writer and Tradition', 'El escritor argentino y la tradición', delivered as a lecture in 1951, published in *Sur* in 1955 in the final months of Perón's regime as a rebuttal of nationalist literature, and finally included in later editions of *Discusión*, originally published in 1932.

The piece is an example of Borges at his polemical and paradoxical best. His starting point is José Hernández's narrative poem *Martín Fierro*, the two parts of which came out in 1872 and 1879, and which recounts the ill treatment of the *gauchos*, *mestizo* cowboys, at the hands of the government in a stylized, literary version of the *gaucho* dialect. Often seen as the canonical Argentinian text, it had become a literary and ideological battle ground. Leopoldo Lugones, the grand patriarch of Argentinian poetry during Borges's youth, a late example of the *modernismo* of Rubén Darío, who moved later in

---

[4] Typical of such criticism is David Viñas, in *De Sarmiento a Cortázar* (Buenos Aires: Siglo Veinte, 1971)

[5] See, for example, Annick Louis, *Borges ante el fascismo* (Oxford: Peter Lang, 2007).

[6] '[su] acto de escritura ... se parece más a un acto de lectura. Borges no es un escritor europeo: no hay ningún escritor europeo como Borges. ... Fuera de algunos profesores de filología que reciben un salario por ello, no hay más que un tipo de hombre que conozca de veras, en su conjunto, la literatura europea: el colonial' (Fernández Retamar, 117–18). For an interesting discussion of Borges's Argentinianness, see Sábato's novel *Sobre héroes y tumbas*, 174.

his life towards nationalism and fascism, presented the *gaucho*, in his 1916 *El payador*, as the foundation of Argentinian nationhood, and the poem as the national epic. In *Discusión*, Borges had argued that the work belonged more to the novel than to the epic.[7] Here he argues that to look to national themes for literature, and reject foreign ones, would have been inconceivable for Racine or Shakespeare, and concludes that local colour is in fact a foreign import: 'The Argentine cult of local color is a recent European cult that nationalists should reject as a foreign import' (TL 423).[8] He approvingly notes Gibbon's comments that there are no mentions of camels in the Koran. Enrique Banchs, writing sonnets about nightingales and pitched roofs in Buenos Aires, where neither exist, is in fact demonstrating the essential Argentine trait of reserve, *pudor*. He easily shows that another work often considered uniquely Argentinian, Ricardo Güiraldes's 1926 *Bildungsroman* of a young *gaucho*-become-landowner, derives much not only from symbolist French poetry, but also from Kipling's *Kim*, which in turn descends from *Huckleberry Finn*. To the argument that national literature should espouse Hispanic values, he counters that few Argentinians can actually cope with Spanish literature, and that 'Argentine history can confidently be described as an attempt to move away from Spain.'[9] To confront the essayists (Mallea, Scalabrini Ortiz, Martínez Estrada, Manuel Gálvez) who in the thirties and beyond argue about the Argentinian as alone, without history, and split away from Europe, Borges alludes to the passions aroused in Argentina by the Spanish Civil War and the Second World War. The Argentine tradition is the whole of Western culture, more so than in the case of individual European countries, immersed in their own particular national culture: 'I believe that our tradition is the whole of Western culture, and I also believe that we have a right to this tradition, a greater right than that which the inhabitants of one Western tradition or another may have' (TL 426).[10] Like the Irish whose difference, belonging and not belonging, allowed than to innovate in English literature, the South Americans can handle European culture in a new way: 'I believe that Argentines, and South Americans in general, are in an analogous

---

    [7] See 'La poesía gauchesca' (I 198).
    [8] 'El culto argentino del color local es un reciente culto europeo que los nacionalistas deberían rechazar por foráneo' (I 270).
    [9] 'la historia argentina puede definirse sin equivocación como un querer apartarse de España' (I 271).
    [10] 'Creo que nuestra tradición es toda la cultura occidental, y creo también que tenemos derecho a esa tradición, mayor que el que pueden tener los habitantes de una u otra nación occidental' (I 272).

situation; we can take on all the European subjects, take them on without superstition and with an irreverence that can have, and already has had, fortunate consequences' (TL 426).[11]

---

[11] 'Creo que los argentinos, los sudamericanos en general, estamos en una situación análoga; podemos manejar todos los temas europeos, manejarlos sin supersticiones, con una irreverencia que puede tener, y ya tiene, consecuencias afortunadas.' (I 273).

Family History, National History

Various critics and biographers, such as Piglia and Williamson, have focused on the way in which Borges tends to view national history in terms of his own family history, and an opposition between the paternal and maternal family lines. John King puts it succinctly:

> For Borges, as for Victoria Ocampo [the owner of *Sur*, literary maecenas, and member of a wealthy *criollo* landowning family], the history of Argentina was a family affair, a conflict between the civilisation of his father's side, equated with books and the English language, and the barbarism of his mother's lineage, synonymous with men of action and the Spanish language. Barbarism expresses both desire and shame. A desire for a simple world of hoodlums, knife fighters and military ancestors. (King 151)

King is simplifying a little, by immediately associating the military with barbarism and only one side of the family with the military, but nevertheless the opposition stands. Alan Pauls has recently given a snappy formulation of one of the major structures of Borges's world. Most oppositions in his work are subsumed into the category of the duel, seen as the very DNA of his prose: 'The duel – but also, in their way, battles, crime, chess and, especially *truco* [a River Plate card game] – is like the chip of Borges's fiction, its DNA, its finger print.'[1] Borges's first narrative, 'Hombres pelearon', 'Men Fought', published in *El idioma de los argentinos* (1928), was the story of a duel, and was rewritten, in different keys, over many years until 'The Story from Rosendo Juárez', in *Brodie's Report, El informe de Brodie* (1970). The theme covers many literal duels and rivalries between men, often rewriting literary texts such as *Martín Fierro*, and historical encounters, as between San Martín and Bolívar in 'Guayaquil'. The structure also articulates the tension between conceptual oppositions such as time and eternity, Platonism

---

1 'El duelo – pero también, a su modo, la batalla, el crimen, el ajedrez y, sobre todo, el *truco* – es como el chip de la ficción de Borges, su ADN, su huella digital' (Pauls, 42).

and Aristotelianism. The family theme is, in a way, one aspect of the general duel structure.

Borges's interest in his ancestors begins strictly with the independence struggle of Argentina from Spain, and he petulantly dismisses anything before as pre-history. In the 1967 interview with Jean de Milleret, he asserts:

> I am profoundly Argentinian and from Buenos Aires ... I am so Argentinian that I have no interest in my distant ancestors like the Iralas or the Garays or others who came before 1810 ... I have never given them any thought; I am even very ignorant about their lives. Anyway, they were pretty unintelligent characters, Spanish soldiers, and from the Spain of that time.[2]

Jorge Francisco Isidoro Luis Borges was born in Buenos Aires on 24 August 1899, though for some time he claimed to have been born in the first year of the twentieth century. The families of both his mother, Leonor Rita Acevedo, and his father, Jorge Guillermo Borges, but especially that of his mother, had been intimately involved in many of the key events in the history of Argentina. The city of Buenos Aires had been a remote outpost of the Viceroyalty of Peru until the late eighteenth century when it became an important trading centre, and was made the capital of the Viceroyalty of La Plata in 1776. In 1810 it revolted against Spanish rule, and in 1816 the independence of the Argentine Confederation was declared in Tucumán. Presiding over that Congress was Francisco Narciso de Laprida, the uncle of Borges's great-grandmother. In the years following the Congress there was a vicious and confused struggle between the conservative *federales*, who fought for the autonomy of the interior provinces from Buenos Aires, and the liberal *unitarios*, who advocated a centralized state. Laprida fell victim to that struggle when he was murdered in 1829 by the *montoneros* (*gaucho* cavalry) of the *caudillo* Félix Aldao. The most heroic god in the pantheon of Leonor Acevedo was her grandfather Colonel Isidoro Suárez, who led the cavalry charge at the battle of Junín in 1824 which defeated the Spanish forces in the Peruvian Andes, and was highly praised by Simón Bolívar. His fate was little better than that of Laprida, as he was forced into exile in Montevideo by Rosas, and died there in 1846. 'His lands were, of course, confiscated, and one of his brothers was executed' (Aut 208).

---

[2] 'Je suis foncièrement Argentin et de Buenos Aires ... Je suis même tellement Argentin que je ne m'intéresse pas à mes ancêtres lointains comme Irala ou Garay ou aux autres venus avant 1810. ... Jamais je n'y ai songé; je suis même très ignorant de leur vie. D'ailleurs c'étaient des personnes très peu intelligentes, des militaires espagnols, et de l'Espagne d'alors' (Milleret, 203).

Juan Manuel de Rosas was a clever and ruthless federalist leader, who became Governor of the Province of Buenos Aires in 1829 and leader of the United Provinces by 1835. Until he was defeated by Urquiza at Caseros in 1852, he ruled Buenos Aires tyrannically and brutally with the help of his notorious militia, the Mazorca, and the support of the mob, eliminating the *unitarios* or driving them into exile in Montevideo. Perhaps the most influential Argentinian book (with *Martín Fierro* and, now, *Ficciones*) was written, in serial form, from exile in Chile, in 1845, as a polemic against Rosas by the liberal Domingo Faustino Sarmiento, who was to become president in 1868. *Facundo* was given as subtitle an opposition which was to ring through Argentinian culture for decades: *Civilization and Barbarism, Civilización y barbarie*. Civilization was represented by the Buenos Aires-based European and North American ideals of liberal capitalism, progress, and enlightenment, while barbarism was associated with the uncouth customs of the *gauchos*, the political *caudillismo* which flourished among them, culminating in the regime of Rosas, and the retrograde Catholicism associated with the city of Córdoba. The *gaucho* is an ambiguous figure in the multi-genre *Facundo*, which combines political pamphlet, sociology, dramatic narration, and romantic anthropology. As a figure of nationalist and literary pride, he is the embodiment of the poetry, valour and vigour of the *pampas*, but politically he is the sign of everything that must be suppressed in the country by progress and mass European immigration. Both sides of Borges's family were of *unitario* tradition and detested Rosas: Leonor, who thrived on heroic stories from the family's past, referred to herself until old age, wearing the standard federalist insult with pride, as a 'salvaje unitaria', and looked nostalgically back to the family estates lost to the 'tyrant'. Judas Tadeo Acevedo, for example, her paternal grandfather, joined a revolt against Rosas, and lost the estates of San Nicolás, in the north of Buenos Aires Province. Her father, Isidoro de Acevedo Laprida, was traumatized as a boy by discovering a cartload of severed heads under a tarpaulin, and later fought against Rosas at the battles of Caseros and Cepeda, and against the federalist Urquiza in Pavón in 1861. For Leonor, the tyranny of Rosas was once again directed against her family in the populist regime of Juan Perón: she spent a month under house arrest in 1948 for publicly demonstrating against him.

The family of Jorge Guillermo Borges had some military history, but a more predominant line of intellectuals and writers. 'His great-uncle Juan Cristóstomo Lafinur was one of the first Argentine poets' (Aut 210), while his father Colonel Francisco Borges Lafinur, after a very successful military career, had been appointed Commander in Chief of the northern and western frontiers of the province of Buenos Aires, charged with containing the threat of Indian incursion. He lived in Junín, on the very edge of the *desierto*, as the untamed pampas were known, with his English wife Fanny Haslam, a native of Staffordshire, and of Northumbrian stock. His promising military and financial future was cut short when the Colonel was involved in a dispute between Sarmiento and Mitre over the presidential succession, and was killed at the Battle of La Verde in 1867 (W 24–5). His rather inglorious death was embellished by the family, and Borges followed their lead (Aut 204). Fanny Haslam's father, Dr Edward Young Haslam, had been a teacher and a respected journalist in the English-language newspapers of Buenos Aires, and his father 'a Methodist minister of some repute in the Midlands' (W 23–4). Fanny Haslam was herself a well-read lady, and of her son, Borges wrote: 'My father, Jorge Guillermo Borges, worked as a lawyer. He was a philosophical anarchist – a disciple of Spencer's – and also a teacher of psychology at the Normal School for Modern Languages' (Aut 204). Jorge Guillermo also wrote a novel, and it was through him that Borges met two writers who were to be significant influences in his work: the popular poet Evaristo Carriego, and the anarchist, metaphysician and avant-garde writer Macedonio Fernández. Whereas his father's family was characterized by intellectuals, Borges is scathing of the intellect of the Acevedos: 'Members of *criollo* or purely Spanish families are not generally intellectual. I can see that my mother's family, the Acevedos, is inconceivably ignorant.'[3] Borges admits that he has always yearned for heroic action, and as a child, felt shame at his bookish vocation:

> So, on both sides of my family, I have military forebears; this may account for my yearning after that epic destiny which the gods denied me, no doubt wisely. ... As most of my people had been soldiers – even my father's brother had been a naval officer – and I knew I would never be, I felt ashamed, quite early, to be a bookish kind of person and not a man of action. (Aut 208)

He clearly accepts, however, that he would be expected to do what his father was not able to do because of poor eyesight and other circumstances, an expectation which some critics see as a heavy burden: 'A tradition of literature ran through my father's family. ... I had to fulfill the literary destiny that circumstances had denied my father' (Aut 210–11). This family history and the tensions it creates in Borges emerge in different ways in different parts

---

[3] 'Quand on est de famille créole ou purement espagnole, alors on n'est en général pas intellectuel. Je vois, dans la famille de ma mère, les Acevedo sont d'une ignorance inconcevable' (Milleret, 39).

of his work. The specific and direct references to his forebears come mainly
in the poetry; the opposition between arms and letters structures some key
stories from the two main collections of stories, *Ficciones* and *El Aleph*;
barely disguised references to the effect that the hero worship had on his
family are explored in two stories from *Brodie's Report*.

The poem 'Isidoro Acevedo' from *Cuaderno San Martín* (1929) recreates
the final moments of Borges's maternal grandfather. Though he was actually
dying of 'pulmonary congestion', Borges makes his real death lie in a dream.
Interestingly, the dream is associated with literature, poetry: 'For just as other
men write poetry, / my grandfather made a dream'.[4] He conjures up a spot on
the pampa and the faces of comrades from Puente Alsina and Cepeda, and
chooses to die in a cavalry charge:

> He stormed into their lives
> for that visionary patriotic battle demanded by his faith, not
>   imposed by weakness;
> he gathered an army of Buenos Aires ghosts
> so that they would kill him.
> Thus, in the bedroom overlooking the garden,
> He died in a dream for the fatherland.[5]

The poem articulates the link between dreaming and literature which pervades
Borges's work, as in the wizard who dreams up a son in 'The Circular Ruins'.
It prefigures the story 'The Other Death', where a soldier who had acted as
a coward at the battle of Masoller and died later of pulmonary congestion
changes universal history by dreaming a heroic death in that same battle.
It also clearly has much in common with 'The South', where the Borges
character has parallel deaths in an anonymous Buenos Aires hospital and in
a knife fight out on the pampa. The sonnet 'Alusión a la muerte del Coronel
Francisco Borges (1833–1874)' from the collection *The Maker*, *El hacedor*
(1960) is interesting in the way it combines precise biographical dates with
a version of his death which Borges knew to be mythical: that of his grandmother and mother, and that of Euduardo Gutiérrez's *Siluetas militares* (Aut
210): 'There I leave him riding high in his epic universe / almost untouched
by my verse.'[6] There is a similar, but inverse, play in 'Biography of Tadeo

---

4   'Porque lo mismo que otros hombres escriben versos, / hizo mi abuelo un sueño'
('Isidoro Acevedo', in *Cuaderno San Martín*, I 86).

5   'Entró a saco en sus días / para esa visionaria patriada que necesitaba su fe, no que una
flaqueza le impuso; / juntó un ejército de sombras porteñas / para que lo mataran. / Así, en el
dormitorio que miraba al jardín, / murió en un sueño por la patria' (I 87).

6   'Alto lo dejo en su épico universo / y casi no tocado por el verso' (II 206).

Isidoro Cruz (1829–1874)' (note the dates of both deaths), where a precise biography is attributed to a literary character from *Martín Fierro*.

'Conjectural Poem', 'Poema conjetural', published in 1943 in *La Nación*, and included in *El otro, el mismo*, *The Self and the Other* (1964), evokes the violent death at the hands of *montoneros* of Francisco Laprida. Edwin Williamson (266) argues convincingly that, given the timing of the publication, shortly after the military coup of the nationalist and pro-fascist Generals Rawson and Ramírez, a parallel is drawn between the barbarism of Laprida's death, and the barbarism of Nazism and of the Generals who were to usher in the era of Perón. The statesman welcomes his violent death, his 'South American destiny', with a strange delight: 'I who dreamed of being another man, / well-read, a man of judgment and opinion, / will lie in a swamp under an open sky; / but a secret and inexplicable joy / makes my heart leap. At last I come face to face / with my destiny as a South American' (SP 159).[7] This is parallel to the case of Borges's grandmother, who in 'Story of the Warrior and the Captive Maiden', published in 1949, sees in the Yorkshire-woman captured by the savages, 'a monstrous mirror of her own fate' (A 38), 'un espejo monstruoso de su destino' (I 559). Borges's other famous ancestor, Colonel Suárez, is aligned very firmly with the struggle for freedom against the tyrant, in this case Perón, in 'A Page to Commemorate Colonel Suárez, Victor at Junín', dated 1953. Isidoro Suárez's career, like that of his namesake Tadeo Isidoro Cruz, is reduced to one essential moment, the battle of Junín: 'What is time's monotony to him, who knew / that fulfillment, that ecstasy, that afternoon?' (SP 169).[8] This instant is the same archetypal moment almost a hundred and twenty years later: 'Junín is two civilians cursing a tyrant / on a street corner, / or an unknown man somewhere, dying in prison' (SP 171).[9] Right up to the fifties and beyond, Borges's vision of national politics is clearly coloured by the family mythology he absorbed in his youth.

Almost more interesting is the manner in which Borges's family history is present in some important stories. In *'Deutsches Requiem'* the Nazi officer opens the account of his life with an evocation of military ancestors with clear parallels with those of Borges. An editor's footnote points out to the

[7] 'Yo que anhelé ser otro, ser un hombre / de sentencias, de libros, de dictámenes, / a cielo abierto yaceré entre ciénagas; / pero me endiosa el pecho inexplicable / un júbilo secreto. Al fin me encuentro / con mi destino sudamericano' (II 245).

[8] 'Qué importa el tiempo sucesivo si en él / hubo una plenitud, un éxtasis, una tarde' ('Página para recordar al coronel Suárez, vencedor en Junín', II 250)

[9] 'Junín son dos civiles que en una esquina maldicen a un tirano, / o un hombre oscuro que se muere en la cárcel' (II 251).

reader that Zur Linde omitted to mention his most illustrious forebear, a theologian and Hebrew scholar. In 'The South' Juan Dahlmann's dual death reflects his dual ancestry: a Hispanic military man and a German Protestant pastor. In 'Story of the Warrior and the Captive Maiden' the paradoxical relationship with barbarism of the two protagonists is reflected and projected into the present by the experience of Borges's grandmother Frances Haslam. In 'Tadeo Isidoro Cruz', Borges's family history is interwoven with the imaginary biography of Sergeant Cruz.

Two stories from the 1970 collection *Brodie's Report* read like an ironic farewell to the cult of the family hero. The satire is similar to that practised in the collaborative works of Borges and Bioy Casares. In 'The Elderly Lady', 'La señora mayor', which is at once cruelly satirical and poignantly tender, María Justina Rubio de Jáuregui is the centenarian daughter of a warrior of the Independence struggle. Many of the details of her life connect her to the Borgeses, and especially to his grandmother Leonor Suárez Haedo de Acevedo. Borges even repeats the terms with which he had described to Milleret the ignorance of the Acevedos. The family was, rather like Borges's family, 'of somewhat fallen fortune' (CF 376), 'venida a menos' (II 425), after losing estates over the years. The petit bourgeois mediocrity of their life is amusingly satirized: there are only two books in the house in addition to the dictionary of Montaner y Simón, which they had acquired on credit because it came with a little cabinet. Their snobbery is deliciously mocked. Their *criollo* disdain for Italian immigrants is evident in the comment that the old lady had married a certain Molinari, who *despite* his Italian extraction was 'a very well-educated man' (CF 376), 'una persona de lo más ilustrada' (II 425). (Carlos Argentino Daneri had been the victim of a similar focus in 'El Aleph'.) My favourite phrase is: 'In 1910 she refused to believe that the Infanta, who after all was a princess, spoke, against all one's expectations, like a common Galician and not like an Argentine lady' (CF 377).[10] (Argentinians call Spaniards *gallegos*, Galicians, who at the time would be associated with immigrant shopkeepers.) An official commission is sent to visit the old lady to celebrate her father, and in a nice oxymoronic touch, the mention of the case with the forebear's sword comes with the deflating offer from an ever-so-nice neighbour of the loan of a pot of geraniums for the reception.[11] A few days after the ceremony, the old lady died. Perhaps she thought the

---

[10] 'En 1910, no quería creer que la Infanta, que al fin y al cabo era una princesa, hablara, contra toda previsión, como una gallega cualquiera y no como una señora argentina' (II 426).
[11] 'Una vecina de lo más atenta les prestó para la ocasión una maceta de malvones' (II 427).

noise of the party had been the entry of Rosas's Mazorca. The other tale, 'Guayaquil', is a duel story. A patrician, *criollo* historian clearly identified with Borges, a descendant of Colonel Suárez of Junín fame, whose sword is displayed in his elegant salon, is treated with the same satirical distance as is 'Borges' in stories like 'El Aleph'. He comes across as snobbish, arrogant, and racist. He has been asked officially to travel to the Estado Occidental (a fictional area in Joseph Conrad's *Nostromo*!) to transcribe a letter by Simón Bolívar in relation to his famous and mysterious meeting with San Martín at Guayaquil at which the Argentine general ceded his place to Bolívar. His rival is an unprepossessing Jewish-German exile naturalized Argentinian. 'Borges' inexplicably repeats the gesture of his countryman San Martín, and gives way to the immigrant historian, who moreover uses the reasoning of Borges's favourite philosopher Schopenhauer.

Life and Literature

Childhood and adolescence, Spain

Borges was born in his maternal grandparents' house in central Buenos Aires, calle Tucumán, but moved in 1901 to calle Serrano in the neighbourhood of Palermo, a far less salubrious area with many southern Italian immigrants, and close to notorious establishments such as the Tierra del Fuego, where local toughs or *compadritos* fought knife-fights and danced tango. Though Borges writes that his mother's prim and snobbish household isolated the children from this world, he later became fascinated with it through the poems and accounts of a friend of his father's, Evaristo Carriego, a popular poet and bohemian who had befriended a notorious knife-fighter and local electoral boss Nicolás Paredes, who in turn became an important figure in Borges's mythology. It was in this year that his sister Norah Borges was born, a far more outgoing character than her gauche and timid brother, and a painter whose woodcuts illustrated many of his early reviews and collections of poetry. They were very close until Norah married the Spanish poet and literary historian Guillermo de Torre. While both grandmothers told him stories of heroic forebears and fortunes lost to Rosas and his Mazorca, with Fanny Haslam he was engulfed in English culture; indeed his upbringing in Serrano was bilingual in English and Spanish.

In the 'Autobiographical Essay' Borges writes: 'If I were asked to name the chief event in my life, I should say my father's library. In fact, I sometimes think I have never strayed outside that library' (Aut 209). In the same essay he confesses that, for him, reading had always preceded reality:

> My first real experience of the pampa came around 1909, on a trip we took to a place belonging to relatives near San Nicolás, to the northwest of Buenos Aires. I remember that the nearest house was a kind of blur on the horizon. This endless distance, I found out, was called the pampa, and when I learned that the farmhands were gauchos, like the characters in Eduardo Gutiérrez, that gave them a certain glamor. I have always come to things after coming to books. (212–13)

In his father's library he read countless books in English: Stevenson, Mark Twain, Poe, H. G. Wells, Dickens, *Don Quijote*, Burton's *A Thousand Nights and One Night*. He had to read *Martín Fierro* in secret because his mother forbad it, José Hernández having been 'an upholder of Rosas and therefore an enemy to our Unitarian ancestors' (Aut 210). When he came to write a book about the world of Evaristo Carriego in 1930 he wrote memorably in the Prologue:

> For years I believed that I had been brought up in a neighbourhood of Buenos Aires, a neighbourhood of perilous streets and striking sunsets. Actually, I was brought up in a garden, behind a wrought-iron fence, and in an endless library of English books. The Palermo of daggers and guitars was just round the corner (I am assured), but the characters that occupied my mornings and filled my nights with pleasurable horror were the blind buccaneer of Stevenson ... the traitor who abandoned his friend on the moon, the time-traveller.[1]

Guillermo Borges was a lawyer by trade but a literary man at heart. He was a friend of Macedonio Fernández, who was to be a crucial influence on Borges in later years (inspiring his thought on the inexistence of the individual personality, 'The Nothingness of Personality'), and had been on the point of joining him in an anarchist settlement in Paraguay (alluded to in Piglia's *La ciudad ausente*). His passions were books on metaphysics and psychology and literature about the East (Lane, Burton, and Payne). Borges picked up this later interest, which blossomed into the brilliant early essay 'The Translators of *The Thousand and One Nights*', published in *A History of Eternity* (1936). 'It was he who revealed the power of poetry to me—the fact that words are not only a means of communication but also magic symbols and music' (Aut 206–7). It is important to note that Borges's early and later work was predominantly poetry. It was also from his father that Georgie, as he was called familiarly, learned another two enduring passions: the idealism of Berkeley and the paradoxes of Zeno, which he illustrated with the help of a chess board: 'Achilles and the tortoise, the unmoving flight of the arrow, the impossibility of motion' (Aut 207). Zeno's paradoxes were for Borges an enduring chink in the carapace of reality and rationality. He ends 'The

---

[1] 'Yo creí, durante años, haberme criado en un suburbio de Buenos Aires, un suburbio de calles aventuradas y de ocasos visibles. Lo cierto es que me crié en un jardín, detrás de una verja con lanzas, y en una biblioteca de ilimitados libros ingleses. Palermo del cuchillo y de la guitarra andaba (me aseguran) por las esquinas, pero quienes poblaron mis mañanas y dieron agradable horror a mis noches fueron el bucanero ciego de Stevenson ... el traidor que abandonó a su amigo en la luna, y el viajero del tiempo' (I 101)

Perpetual Race of Achilles and the Tortoise' with the meditation: 'Would this bit of Greek obscurity affect our concept of the universe? – my reader will ask' (TL 47).[2] In a later essay on the Icelandic *kenningar* he gives a description of metaphysics which encapsulates eloquently the effect of much of his work, be it fiction or essay, 'lucid perplexity': 'The *kenningar* teach us that astonishment; they make the world seem a strange place. They can produce that lucid perplexity which is the unique honour of metaphysics, its reward and its source.'[3]

The literary production of the young Borges was no less precocious than it was prophetic, as he recalls having started to write at six or seven. He imitated the style of Cervantes in a romance called 'La visera fatal', an early experiment of a *porteño* Pierre Menard, and characteristically approaching writing through a reworking of previous texts. Another enterprise was a handbook of Greek mythology in 'quite bad English' cribbed from a French author: Borges was to write or co-write a whole series of handbooks, from *The Book of Imaginary Beings*, *El libro de los seres imaginarios*, with Margarita Guerrero, to *Medieval Germanic Literatures*, *Literaturas germánicas medievales*, with María Esther Vázquez, and in his later life was an enthusiastic and successful lecturer, a popularizer of culture in the best sense. His vast but eclectic culture came to a great extent from encyclopaedias. When he was 'nine or so' he translated Oscar Wilde's 'The Happy Prince' into Spanish. When it was published in the newspaper *El País*, signed 'Jorge Borges', people assumed it was his father's work. Borges was an assiduous and prolific translator; he wrote with great insight on translation ('The Homeric Versions', for example); and his works are populated with translators and commentators such as Averroes in 'Averroës' Search'. Translation for him was inseparable from cultural transmission, and indeed the elaboration of literary texts in general. Among others, Efraín Kristal writes convincingly about this in *Invisible Work. Borges and Translation*.

The family summered near Montevideo with the wealthy Haedos, the Uruguayan side of Leonor's family, and in Adrogué, a leafy town near Buenos Aires, in a house they owned and in the Hotel Las Delicias, evoked much later as Triste-le-Roy in 'Death and the Compass'. In 1914 the family left Argentina for Europe, to have Jorge Guillermo's eyes operated on, to provide a cosmopolitan education for the children, and to travel. They were surprised

---

[2]   '¿Tocar a nuestro concepto del universo, por ese pedacito de tiniebla griega?, interrogará mi lector' ('La perpetua carrera de Aquiles y la tortuga', I 248).

[3]   'Las *kenningar* nos dictan ese asombro, nos extrañan del mundo. Pueden motivar esa lúcida perplejidad que es el único honor de la metafísica, su remuneración y su fuente' (I 379).

by the outbreak of the Great War, and took refuge in Geneva, in neutral Switzerland. Georgie attended the Collège Calvin, where classes were in French; despite his own version of events, it would seem that he never in fact passed his *baccalauréat*. He did make vital literary discoveries: the poetry of Walt Whitman of whom he remained a lifelong admirer, and the philosophy of Schopenhauer. He also made a good friend, Maurice Abramovich, who introduced him to French symbolist poetry. In 1917, through the revolutionary events unfolding in Russia, Borges and his friends espoused revolutionary socialism; Borges was fiercely anti-militaristic, a position to which he would return very late in his life. He was much taken by German expressionist poetry, which was to condition his experiments in avant-garde poetry, with which he became involved over the following years.

It was also in Geneva that Jorge Luis underwent a traumatic experience, which, according to most commentators, stayed with him for the rest of his life. As he approached his eighteenth birthday, his father, on ascertaining that he was a virgin, proposed a very Hispanic solution, and arranged for him to visit a prostitute of his acquaintance. The young man was unable to consummate sex with a woman whom he suspected had also been the sexual partner of his father; he was deeply disturbed, and his family so preoccupied that they moved to Italy to strengthen his constitution. Estela Canto's memoirs of their relationship, *Borges a contraluz*, are most explicit: 'Borges's attitude towards sex was one of absolute panic, as if he feared the revelation he might find in it. Nevertheless, all his life was a struggle to achieve that revelation.'[4] On one of the only times when sex is seriously approached in his stories, in 'Emma Zunz', one senses a real personal involvement in Emma's preparation to face sex in a brothel: 'In April she would be nineteen, but men still inspired in her an almost pathological fear ...' (A 45).[5] Throughout his life, Borges was an 'eterno enamoradizo' falling in love with a string of attractive women, but failed to achieve a stable relationship until his final years with María Kodama. Between 1944 and 1946, he was involved with the attractive and sexually experienced Estela Canto. Estela offered to have sex with him before marriage, but Borges did not feel able. His sexual block, the spectre of impotence, had them visit the psychiatrist Kohen-Millar, who suggested that both his sexual inhibition, and his stammering and painful

---

[4] 'La actitud de Borges hacia el sexo era de terror pánico, como si temiera la revelación que en él podía hallar. Sin embargo, toda su vida fue una lucha por alcanzar esa revelación' (Canto, 17).

[5] 'En abril cumpliría diecinueve años, pero los hombres le inspiraban, aún, un temor casi patológico ...' (I 565).

timidity, connected to his relationship with his father, would be cured by a caring marriage. Estela, however, was not in love with Borges and left him for another man before the suggested remedy could be applied. Estela Canto (117) mischievously adds that it was the Peronists who aided the psychiatrist in curing Borges's fear of public speaking when they sacked him from his post at the Miguel Cané library and he was forced to lecture to earn enough money to subsist. Estela launches a fierce attack on Borges's mother Leonor, whom she accuses of 'castrating' her son with her tyrannical control (121). Canto and others such as Emir Rodríguez Monegal recount many anecdotes about her authoritarian ways.

The Borges family spent the years 1919 to 1921 in Spain, first in Mallorca, and then Seville and Madrid. In Spain, Borges was to espouse the avant-garde aesthetics of *ultraísmo*, supported by the Sevillian journal *Grecia* and coined by the Andalusian writer Rafael Cansinos-Asséns. In 1920 Borges published in *Grecia* an article entitled 'Al margen de la moderna estética' defining the spirit of *ultra*: youth, freshness of metaphor, rejection of the 'claridad y euritmia' (TR I 30), 'clarity and beautiful rhythms', presumably of the *modernistas*. Spain was at the time a hotbed of rival avant-garde movements, with the Chilean Vicente Huidobro in 1916 promoting his brand of literary cubism, *creacionismo*, the influence of Marinetti's futurism, Dada, and Apollinaire. In Madrid he began to publish more frequently, in *Ultra* and elsewhere, became a friend of the Spaniard Guillermo de Torre, and attended the *tertulia* in the Café Colonial of Cansinos-Asséns whom for many years he would consider his master.[6] A rival *tertulia* at the Café Pombo was presided over by Ramón Gómez de la Serna, who defined his pithy *greguerías* as 'humorismo + metáfora = greguería', 'humour + metaphor = greguería'. Looking back to this rivalry in 'La traducción de un incidente', where he decries the superficiality of European poetry, Borges constructs one of his first oppositions between writers and concepts, seen in terms of a duel or military conflict, which will become a defining dimension of his mind. Borges wrote two books in Spain, which he later destroyed: the literary and political essays of *Los naipes del tahur* (alluded to in 'El Aleph'), the aim of which was to be 'bitter and relentless, but they were, as a matter of fact, quite tame', and *Los salmos rojos* 'in praise of the Russian Revolution, the brotherhood of man, and pacifism' (Aut 223).

---

6   See Irma Zangara, 'Primera década de Borges escritor', in *Textos recobrados 1919– 1929*.

Return to Argentina, the Nineteen Twenties

Back in Buenos Aires, and missing Europe, Borges took to attending the Saturday *tertulias* of Macedonio Fernández at the Café la Perla in the Plaza del Once. 'As in Madrid Cansinos had stood for all learning,' he comments, 'Macedonio now stood for pure thinking' (Aut 227). An eccentric genius, who would leave behind his manuscripts every time he changed lodging house, Macedonio was a Socratic master for Borges, and discoursed on subjects which were to become staple Borges conceits: the unreality or dream reality of existence, the insubstantiality or inexistence of personal identity, the incommunicability of truth. Borges soon began to throw himself into a fury of literary and editorial activity. He was determined to introduce *ultraísmo* into Argentina, devoid of its futurist trappings and fixation with the modern, and in 1921 founded *Prisma*, a mural magazine which lasted for two editions, and which was pasted around the city by Borges and his collaborators at night. It prompted the publication in the established, all-inclusive and catholic journal *Nosotros* of an anthology of ultraist poetry.[7] His next enterprise was the first period of *Proa*, 1922–23, a lively avant-garde magazine involving an *ultraísta* grouping which included his cousin Guillermo Juan, Eduardo González Lanuza, and Norah Lange. It ran for three editions, the first of which contained a key essay by Borges: 'The Nothingness of Personality', 'La nadería de la personalidad', reproduced in *Inquisiciones*.

In 1923, Borges's first book, *Fervor de Buenos Aires*, appeared, and a good percentage of the three hundred copies were distributed by stuffing them into the pockets of coats hanging in the cloakroom of *Nosotros*. He was to publish another two collections of poetry during the twenties, *Moon Across the Way*, *Luna de enfrente*, and *San Martín Copybook*, *Cuaderno San Martín*. The first of these Borges described as being a 'riot of sham local color', and he radically revised, suppressed, and toned down the avant-garde excesses of all of these collections when they appeared in his collected works (Aut 232). Borges also published three collections of essays during this decade of extraordinary creativity: *Inquisiciones* (1925), *The Size of my Hope*, *El tamaño de mi esperanza* (1926), and *The Language of the Argentines*, *El idioma de los argentinos* (1928). Borges refused any new printings of these works during his life, and even claims to have burnt any copies that he could afford to buy. Luckily for us, María Kodama authorized their publication by Alianza in 1995. The prose is often contorted and precious, but the collections contain fascinating and revealing pieces.

---

[7] See King, 14–15.

On his return from a second, one-year trip to Europe in 1923–24, Borges found the literary scene somewhat changed. The wealthy, cosmopolitan and extrovert Oliverio Girondo had published his landmark avant-garde poetry of *Veinte poemas para ser leídos en el tranvía* in 1922, and moved to take a central position in the recently founded journal *Martín Fierro* (1924–27), edited by Evar Méndez. Girondo's manifesto and the attitude of the journal, which was very successful, were stridently avant-garde, rebellious and internationalist. Borges did publish in it, but felt more at home in the second *Proa*, which he re-launched with Ricardo Güiraldes and Rojas Paz, who had fallen out with Méndez. Borges later wrote of *Martín Fierro*: 'I disliked what *Martín Fierro* stood for, which was the French idea that literature is being continually renewed – that Adam is reborn every morning, and also for the idea that, since Paris had literary cliques that wallowed in publicity and bickering, we should be up to date and do the same' (Aut 236). Such pieces reflect Borges's interest in a specifically Argentine and *criollo* aesthetic and identity at the time. His 'Complaint of every *Criollo*', 'Queja de todo criollo', laments the effects of progress and immigration, which shared 'la culpa ... de que nuestra ciudad se llame Babel', 'the blame for our country being called Babel', adding: 'Ya la república se nos extranjeriza, se pierde', 'Our republic is going foreign; we are losing it' (Inq 149). In his title essay in *El tamaño de mi esperanza* (1926), however, his *criollismo* is far more outgoing and inclusive: 'Let us have *criollismo*, then, but a *criollismo* which dialogues with the world and self, with God and death.'[8]

In talking of artificially created cliques, Borges is referring to the famous opposition between the Florida and Boedo groups, which he always insisted was a farce (though he uses the term 'Boedo' pejoratively at least twice in *Evaristo Carriego*). Many commentators disagree. Roberto Mariani attacked *Martín Fierro* for usurping the title of a national text when its contributors vaunted their European culture, complex literary language, and French elegance (King 21). Méndez replied by pouring scorn on the left-wing magazine *Extrema Izquierda*. Mariani himself, in a piece reproduced in an anthology of manifestos edited by Nelson Osorio, offers a usefully schematic account of the differences between the two groups which pitched *Martín Fierro* and *Proa* against *Extrema Izqierda*, *Los Pensadores*, and *Claridad*. While the first group stands for the avant-garde, *ultraísmo*, *greguería*, metaphor, and Gómez de la Serna, the second stands for the left wing, realism,

---

8 'Criollismo, pues, pero un criollismo que sea conversador del mundo y del yo, de Dios y de la muerte' (TE 17).

short story and novel, content, and Dostoyevsky. John King illustrated the split very clearly:

> It is interesting in this context that in 1926 Ricardo Güiraldes published *Don Segundo Sombra* and Roberto Arlt published *El juguete rabioso*. These two writers, with their divergent views as to the social function of literature, can be taken as symbols of the split that existed in Argentina even in the 1920s and continued after the appearance of *Sur* in 1931: whereas Güiraldes is a constant memory in *Sur* – the first edition bears his photograph – Arlt never would be published in its pages. (King 22)

The Nineteen Thirties

Faced with an upturn in right-wing nationalism, and revisionist history writing which would reclaim Rosas as a defender of the *criollo* against the foreigner, Borges together with a varied group of important intellectuals which included Marechal, Macedonio Fernández, Roberto Arlt, Xul Solar (Marechal and Francisco Luis Bernárdez would later move to the right and quarrel with Borges) founded the Committee of Young Intellectuals for Irigoyen (W 161). Borges, following family tradition, had always been fiercely loyal to Irigoyen (1916–22, 1938–40), the charismatic and populist leader of the Radical Party, and put pressure on the editor of *Martín Fierro* to support the campaign. Méndez's refusal and the resignation of Borges, Marechal, and Bernárdez from the editorial board prompted the closure of the magazine in January 1928. In 1930, in the first of a series of coups which bedevilled Argentina for many decades of the twentieth century, General Aramburu overthrew the shambolic regime of Irigoyen, which had been undermined by the economic crisis of 1929. Edwin Williamson quotes a letter from Borges to his friend the Mexican poet and scholar Alfonso Reyes in which he laments the passing of a Myth, 'the whole bizarre myth of the Doctor', and the espousal of a new sober realism:

> Now Buenos Aires has had to repudiate its homegrown mythology, and make do with a few scraps of enthusiasm, mixed with a few so-called acts of heroism in which no one believes, and the standard opinion that at least these soldiers aren't thieves. We have sacrificed Myth for the sake of realism, what do you think of that? (cit. W 173)

Williamson links this moment to the demise of Borges's *criollismo*, his attempt to write the mythology of the *arrabal* and the *orillas*.

From this point of view, the publication in 1930 of his *Evaristo Carriego* was something of an anachronism, and, moreover, largely ignored. Like many of Borges's prose works of the period, this is a curiously oblique exercise in marginality. Loosely structured, and disparate in material, it nevertheless contains some fine displays of style, in its atmospheric descriptions of Palermo, in the memorable evocation of Nicolás Paredes, and intense metaphysical insights in the most unlikely of material. In studying the life and poetry of Carriego, his friendship with Paredes, and his discovery of the aesthetics of the Buenos Aires *orillas*, Borges is talking vicariously of his own experience. He becomes a sort of double or ghost of Carriego: his version of Palermo is parallel to that of Carriego, it is a rewriting in a different mode, poetry turned into poetic prose, what Lafon, after Genette, calls transvocalization. This prompts seminal musings on the relationship between reader and writer and the dissolving of the notion of personality. Eternity is glimpsed in such repeated identities across time, a notion developed also in the chapter on *el truco*:

> I know that these habits of Carriego's that I have listed bring him close to us. They repeat him infinitely in us, as if Carriego survived instilled in our destinies, as if each of us were Carriego for a few instants. I believe that this is literally the case, and that those momentary identities (not repetitions!), which annihilate the supposed flow of time, are proofs of eternity.[9]

In his Prologue to Carriego's complete works, Borges seems to reconstitute the aim of his own *criollismo*, the forging of a myth of Buenos Aires, in Carriego's discovery of a full meaning in South America, which he had believed was ontologically elsewhere: in France, in the pages of Dumas:

> He felt exiled from life. Life was in France, he thought, in the bright clash of steel, or when the armies of the Emperor flooded the land, but my lot is the twentieth century, the belated twentieth century in a mediocre South American neighbourhood ... Carriego was engrossed in these musings when something happened. The strumming of a laborious guitar, the uneven row of low houses seen through the window, Juan Muraña [a famous knife-fighter] touching his *chambergo* hat in response to a greeting ... the moon in the square of the *patio*, an old man with a fighting cock, something, anything. Something we will be unable to recover, something the meaning but not the form of which we know, something everyday and trivial and

---

[9] 'Esas frecuencias que enuncié de Carriego, yo sé que nos lo acercan. Lo repiten infinitamente en nosotros, como si Carriego perdurara disperso en nuestros destinos, como si cada uno de nosotros fuera por unos segundos Carriego. Creo que literalmente así es, y que esas momentáneas identidades (¡no repeticiones!) que aniquilan el supuesto correr del tiempo, prueban la eternidad' (I 119).

previously unnoticed, which revealed to Carriego that the universe (which is entirely in being in each moment, in any place, and not only in the works of Dumas) was also there, in the mere present, in Palermo, in 1904. *Come in, for the gods are here too*, said Heraclitus of Ephesus to the people who found him warming himself in the kitchen.

I have occasionally suspected that any human life, however intricate and peopled it may be, actually consists of one moment: the moment when a man knows for ever who he is.[10]

Argentinian life is not exile; Palermo is the centre of the world. The Emersonian pantheism seen here underlies much of Borges's world; the moment that defines a life is explored in stories like 'A Biography of Tadeo Isidoro Cruz'.

From the publication of *Cuaderno San Martín* in 1929, until the compilation *The Maker* in 1960, Borges published no collections of poetry. His works of the thirties give the impression of a man casting round in a somewhat forlorn way for a voice. In *Evaristo Carriego* his own voice is mediated by that of another; in *Discusión*, and *A History of Eternity* (1936) he wrote erudite, obscure and bookish essays. In *A Universal History of Iniquity*, *Historia universal de la infamia* (1935), he rewrites and reformulates existing stories. The Prologue to *Discusión* encapsulates his gloom: 'Life and death have been missing from my life. From that impoverishment comes my laborious love for these trifles.'[11] Williamson contrasts Borges's solipsism with the exuberant showmanship of the individual he sees as his lifetime rival, Oliverio Girondo, who in 1932 publicized his surrealist collection *Espantapájaros* with the staged funeral of a scarecrow academician which could be linked to the figure of Borges. Borges was not fortunate or adept

---

[10] 'se creía desterrado de la vida. La vida estaba en Francia, pensó, en el claro contacto de los aceros, o cuando los ejércitos del Emperador anegaban la tierra, pero a mí me ha tocado el siglo XX, el tardío siglo XX, y un mediocre arrabal sudamericano ... En esa cavilación estaba Carriego cuando algo sucedió. Un rasguido de laboriosa guitarra, la despareja hilera de casas bajas vistas por la ventana, Juan Muraña tocándose el chambergo para contestar un saludo ... la luna en el cuadrado del patio, un hombre viejo con un gallo de riña, algo, cualquier cosa. Algo que no podremos recuperar, algo cuyo sentido sabemos pero no cuya forma, algo cotidiano y trivial y no percibido hasta entonces, que reveló a Carriego que el universo (que se da entero en cada instante, en cualquier lugar, y no sólo en las obras de Dumas) también estaba ahí, en el mero presente, en Palermo, en 1904. *Entrad, que también aquí están los dioses*, dijo Heráclito de Éfeso a las personas que lo hallaron calentándose en la cocina.

Yo he sospechado alguna vez que cualquier vida humana, por intricada y populosa que sea, consta en realidad de un momento: el momento en que el hombre sabe para siempre quién es' (I 157–8).

[11] '*Vida y muerte le han faltado a mi vida. De esa indigencia, mi laborioso amor por estas minucias*' (I 177).

in matters of love; his eyesight grew steadily worse, culminating in blindness in the fifties after a series of operations beginning in 1928. The long
night-time treks round the outskirts of Buenos Aires with literary friends
and girlfriends which he had so enjoyed in the twenties were becoming less
of an option. His increasing classicism alienated him from the avant-garde,
while he intensely disliked the nationalism, Anglophobia, and racism which
developed throughout the decade. María Esther Vázquez (146–7) recounts a
suicide attempt in February 1934. Borges bought a gun in a neighbourhood
where nobody knew him, a detective novel and a bottle of gin. He took the
train to Adrogué and booked in at the Hotel Las Delicias, but was finally
unable to pull the trigger. Vázquez claims that he was haunted by the idea
of suicide for years, and credibly evokes the murder–suicide of Lönnrot in
'Death and the Compass', who goes to Triste-le-Roy knowing tacitly that
Scharlach was waiting to kill him. Borges has clearly identified Triste-le-Roy
with the Hotel Las Delicias.

Discusión has essays of great interest in the development of Borges's
literary and intellectual outlook. Apart from an essay on gauchesque poetry, he
moves right away from the local to questions of poetics, language and reality,
Kabbalistc and Gnostic thought, translation and philosophy. One rather quirky,
short essay, dated 1930, 'The Superstitious Ethics of the Reader', seems to
foreshadow the radical practice of Borges's fiction. He argues against the
fixation on pathos, and on literary style and perfection, arguing that it is the
theme of Don Quixote, its human interest, which survives its mere language,
or translation into German or Hindi: 'the *Quixote* wins posthumous battles
against its translators and survives every negligent translation'.[12] If the literary
is the least essential part of literature, if silent reading ignores the musicality
of poetry, might it not be that literature is purposefully moving towards its
own dissolution: 'Might literature foretell a time when it falls silent, and
savage its own merits, become enamoured of its own dissolution, court its
own end?'[13] Is this what he is practising in *A Universal History of Iniquity*?
Significantly, this essay is closely followed by another where the absolutely
contrary conception of language is expounded, that of the Scriptures dictated
by the Holy Spirit: 'A Defense of the Kabbalah'. Here chance in the choice of
words is excluded, divine language is infinitely significant: 'This premise …
turns the Scriptures into an absolute text, where the collaboration of chance

---

[12] 'el *Quijote* gana póstumas batallas contra sus traductores y sobrevive a toda descuidada
versión' ('La supersticiosa ética del lector', I 204).
[13] 'la literatura es un arte que sabe profetizar aquel tiempo en que habrá enmudecido, y
encarnizarse con su propia virtud y enamorarse de la propia disolución y cortejar su fin' (I 205).

is calculated at zero' (TL 86).[14] The tension between the concept of a divine language set against the noise and babble of everyday discourse is, I believe, at the heart of many of Borges's best stories. 'The Homeric Versions' offers key insights into literature seen as a process of translation and rewriting. Borges applies Russell's definition of any external object to a literary text: 'a circular system radiating possible impressions' (TL 69). Translations of the *Iliad* are 'merely different perspectives on a mutable fact', and in the case of a text like Homer's *Odyssey* our ignorance of the linguistic conventions of the period implies the categorical difficulty of 'knowing what pertains to the poet and what pertains to the language' (TL 70).[15] No translation is thus more faithful than another. This 'essential game of attention', however, is also possible within the same literature: rewriting is a change of emphasis. The importance of the unique individual author is undermined in this scheme; every text is a draft to be rewritten in the collective text of a culture, or across cultures: 'there can only be drafts. The concept of the "definitive text" corresponds only to religion or to exhaustion' (TL 70).[16] It is in this vein that Borges offers his famous *boutade*: 'All the foregoing books I read in English. When later I read *Don Quixote* in the original it sounded like a bad translation to me' (Aut 209). Needless to say, all the English translations that Borges discusses are given in Spanish.

'Una nota sobre Walt Whitman' explores an aspect of literary personality which is developed in different ways in two pieces from *The Maker*, 'Everything and Nothing*', and 'Borges and I': the split between the literary persona and the writer as private individual. Whitman dramatizes himself as a 'semi-divine hero' in *The Leaves of Grass*, but Borges points out that the 'mero vagabundo feliz', the 'simple, happy wanderer' presented in the poems could not have written them. Walt Whitman the writer derived his literature from other writers, while his character extracted them from lived experience:

> Walt Whitman the man, was the director of the *Brooklyn Eagle*, and read his fundamental ideas in the pages of Emerson, Hegel, and Volney; Walt Whitman the poetic persona, extracted them from his contact with America, illustrated with imaginary experiences in New Orleans bedrooms and Georgian battle fields.[17]

---

[14] 'Esa premisa ... hace de la Escritura un texto absoluto, donde la colaboración del azar es calculable en cero' ('Una vindicación de la Cábala', I 211).

[15] 'la dificultad categórica de saber lo que pertenece al poeta y lo que pertenece al lenguaje' ('Las versiones homéricas', I 240).

[16] 'no puede haber sino borradores. El concepto de *texto definitivo* no corresponde sino a la religión o al cansancio' (I 239).

[17] 'Walt Whitman, hombre, fue director del *Brooklyn Eagle*, y leyó sus ideas fundamen-

Whitman in his poetry was everything and everybody, a mere mirror to his
reader. This is what most clearly links him to the Shakespeare of '*Everything
and Nothing*'. Shakespeare is intimately aware that behind his face there is
no one, no core of personal identity: 'There was no one inside him; behind
his face ... and his words (which were multitudinous, and of a fantastical and
agitated turn) there was no more than a slight chill, a dream someone had
failed to dream' (CF 319).[18] When acting and writing, 'nobody was as many
men as that man' (CF 320);[19] beyond the representation, was only 'the hated
taste of unreality' (CF 319).[20] Being is play acting and dreaming: 'The fundamental identity of living, dreaming, and performing inspired him to famous
passages' (CF 320).[21] 'Borges and I' is a less dramatic piece, an ironic and
quizzical version of the disparity between the 'Borges' created by the media
and popular myth, and the individual who looks on him with alarm and mild
distaste.

A Universal History of Iniquity was published in 1935, and consists of
three sections. The main seven narrations are Borges's wilfully divergent
versions of existing, pointedly international stories or romances, of villains
and pirates, the sources of which are listed in a bibliography. Lafon calls this
'réécriture dans la déviance' (97). In the 1954 prologue, Borges puts down
the exercise to timidity: 'They are the irresponsible sport of a shy sort of man
who could not bring himself to write short stories, and so amused himself by
changing and distorting (sometimes without aesthetic justification) the stories
of other men' (CF 4).[22] They were published in *Crítica* between 1933 and
1934, 'for popular consumption', according to Borges, and were not intended
for publication in a book. 'El hombre de la esquina rosada', on the other hand,
published under the title 'Hombres de las orillas' in *Crítica* in 1933, is a stylized, archetypically Argentinian story of knife-fighting, which I will discuss
in detail later. The third element, 'Etcétera', consists of very brief translations and elaborations of purportedly real sources. While 'El hombre de la
esquina rosada' derived from an earlier 1927 sketch, 'Hombres pelearon', is

tales en las páginas de Emerson, de Hegel y de Volney; Walt Whitman, personaje poético, las
edujo del contacto de América, ilustrado por experiencias imaginarias en las alcobas de New
Orleans y en los campos de batalla de Georgia' (I 252).
   18 'Nadie hubo en él; detrás de su rostro ... y de sus palabras, que eran copiosas, fantásticas
y agitadas, no había más que un poco de frío, un sueño no soñado por alguien' (II 181).
   19 'nadie fue tantos hombres como aquel hombre' (II 181).
   20 'el odiado sabor de la irrealidad' (II 181).
   21 'La identidad fundamental de existir, soñar y representar le inspiró pasajes famosos' (II
181).
   22 '*Son el irresponsable ejercicio de un tímido que no se animó a escribir cuentos y que se
distrajo en falsear y tergiversar (sin justificación estética alguna vez) ajenas historias*' (I 291).

already a real story, and constitutes an important strand in Borges's thematic world; it is *A Universal History* that he considers to have been the origin of his fiction, an origin more impure and hybrid than the straight narration:

> The real beginning of my career as a story writer begins with the series of sketches entitled *Historia universal de la infamia* ... The irony of this is that 'Streetcorner Man' really was a story but that these sketches and several of the fictional pieces which followed them, and which very slowly led me to legitimate stories, were in the nature of hoaxes and pseudo-essays. In my *Universal History*, I did not want to repeat what Marcel Schwob had done in his *Imaginary Lives*. He had invented biographies of real men about whom little or nothing is recorded. I, instead, read up on the lives of known persons and then deliberately varied and distorted them according to my own whims. For example, after reading Herbert Asbury's *The Gangs of New York*, I set down my free version of Monk Eastman, the Jewish gunman, in flagrant contradiction of my chosen authority.
>
> (Aut 238–9)

Ronald Christ points out the importance of Borges's here opening out to universal themes through English sources. Not only are the direct listed sources of his stories written in English or translated into it, but the literary filters through which he transforms his sources refer back to the favourite adventure stories of his childhood: his re-reading of Stevenson and Chesterton. The focus here is not only on the exoticism and horror of the stories, but on the self-conscious amalgam of the childhood readings with all the recent readings and intellectual apparatus, footnotes, bibliography, etc. of his maturity. Borges in 1954 describes the stories as baroque, and adds that *this time* he had opted not to change or suppress them: *'quod scripsi, scripsi'*. Lafon (98) comments that what distinguishes these works from the baroque works of the twenties which were suppressed is their parody: 'baroque excess, which he later found difficult to recognize as his own in his direct writings (poems, essays), is, however, inseparable from the parody which forms the very basis of *A Universal History of Iniquity*'. Borges claimed that behind the stories there was nothing, that they were pure surface: 'Gallows and pirates fill its pages, and that word *iniquity* strikes awe in its title, but under all the storm and lightning, there is nothing. It is all just appearance, a surface of images (CF 5).[23] What is meaningful about the exercise is its status as writing, its generic instability, the precariousness of any notion of authorship in the parodic rewriting, its preparation for the breakthrough of *Ficciones*.

---

[23] '*Patíbulos y piratas lo pueblan y la palabra infamia aturde en el título, pero bajo los tumultos no hay nada. No es otra cosa que apariencia, que una superficie de imágenes*' (I 291).

The Prologue insists on the unhappiness of Borges in this period: 'The man who made it was a pitiable sort of creature, but he found amusement in writing it' (CF 5).[24] He could not have been encouraged by the reception of his next book: a miscellaneous collection of essays and two 'notes', *A History of Eternity*, *Historia de la eternidad*, published in 1936, and which sold thirty-seven copies. As far as the public was concerned, Borges had written himself into a corner. Tucked away at the back of the collection, however, is a gem, a spoof book review which is also a story, the history of the story, its critical reception, possible sources, etc. 'The Approach to Al-Mu'tasim', 'El acercamiento a Almotásim', is the kernel of Borges's mature fictional output from the late thirties to the early fifties. It demands separate and detailed consideration together with the stories of *Ficciones* and *El Aleph*. So well disguised as a review is the story that no less a discerning reader than Adolfo Bioy Casares ordered a copy of the non-existent reviewed book from England. The main focus of the collection is, unsurprisingly, time, which Borges claims is one of his most central concerns: 'For us, time is a jarring, urgent problem, perhaps the most vital problem of metaphysics, while eternity is a game or a spent hope' (TL 123).[25] The title essay of the selection has two parts, an erudite review of the theological discussion of the notion of eternity, and the reproduction of a very personal experience of timelessness originally published in *The Language of the Argentines* as 'Feeling in Death', 'Sentirse en muerte'. It is complemented by an essay on Nietzsche, 'The Doctrine of Cycles'. The 1943 essay 'Circular Time' was added later. I will consider Borges's preoccupation with time, which was expanded in his 'A New Refutation of Time', 'Nueva refutación del tiempo', from *Otras inquisiciones*, separately.

Also included in the collection is a fascinating study of the English, French and German translators of *The Arabian Nights*, which complements his study of the translations of Homer. The essay is not only erudite and incredibly detailed but wickedly witty and replete with paradox. The translators are presented as rivals, as writing not so much to achieve perfection as to surpass and obliterate their predecessor. Though the Frenchman Galland introduces texts, such as the story of Aladin, which were not in the original, even his enemies dare not change the canon. Borges, as ever, is keenly aware of anachronism. Galland's translation produced amazement and happiness in his readers, whereas 'we, their mere anachronistic readers of the twentieth century, perceive only the cloying flavor of the eighteenth century in

---

[24] '*El hombre que lo ejecutó era asaz desdichado, pero se entretuvo escribiéndolo*' (I 291).

[25] 'El tiempo es un problema para nosotros, un tembloroso y exigente problema, acaso el más vital de la metafísica; la eternidad, un juego o una fatigada esperanza' (I 353).

them' (TL 93).[26] French, he quips, not quite impartially, is less timeless than English. Borges constantly brings us back to the question of emphasis developed in early essays. To stress the erotic in the original, to create a new *Decameron*, is a mere commercial decision. To stress the magic, to write an oriental *Ancient Mariner* or *Bateau ivre* deserves another sort of heaven. Our Western minds conceive this fact as universal, a universality constructed by a Frenchman, and which the unhappy Arabs do not recognize as the text reveals nothing particularly new to them: 'The universal imposition of this assumption on every Western mind is Galland's work; let there be no doubt on that score. Less fortunate than we, the Arabs claim to think little of the original; they are already acquainted with the men, mores, talismans, deserts, and demons that the tales reveal to us' (TL 96).[27] Borges's lucid exploration of Orientalism pre-dates that of Said and post-colonialism by various decades. The world created by the translation is so much a product of its culture, and so much a function of its readership that a translation back into Arabic would be absurd: 'I suspect that the Arabic language is incapable of a "literal and complete" version of Mardrus' paragraph, and neither is Latin or the Spanish of Miguel de Cervantes' (TL 105).[28] This last comment anticipates the marvels of 'Pierre Menard, Author of the *Quixote*': how vastly divergent is Menard's literal version from its seventeenth-century Spanish equivalent! Burton and Mardrus's prose (like the thought processes of Menard) are inhabited by centuries of intervening texts, which give them extraordinary resonance.[29] In Mardrus we see the Orient through the exoticism of Flaubert, in Burton through the hard obscenity of John Donne:

> My reason is this: the versions by Burton and Mardrus, and even by Galland, can only be conceived of *in the wake of a literature*. Whatever their blemishes or merits, these characteristic works presuppose a rich (prior) process. In some way, the almost inexhaustible process of English is adumbrated in Burton – John Donne's hard obscenity, the gigantic vocabularies of Shakespeare and Cyril Tourneur, Swinburne's affinity for the archaic, the crass erudition of the authors of 17th-century chapbooks,

---

[26] 'Nosotros, meros lectores anacrónicos del sigo veinte, percibimos en ellos el sabor dulzarrón del siglo dieciocho' ('Los traductores de *Las 1001 Noches*', I 398).

[27] 'La imposición occidental de ese parecer en todas las mentes universales, es obra de Galland. Que ello no quede en duda. Menos felices que nosotros, los árabes dicen tener en poco el original: ya conocen los hombres, las costumbres, los talismanes, los desiertos y los demonios que esas historias nos revelan' (I 401).

[28] 'Yo sospecho que el árabe no es capaz de una versión "literal y completa" del párrafo de Mardrus, así como tampoco lo es el latín, o el castellano de Miguel de Cervantes' (I 408).

[29] See Emerson: 'The translation of Plutarch gets its excellence by being translation on translation. There never was a time when there was none' (716).

the energy and imprecision, the love of tempests and magic. In Mardrus's laughing paragraphs, *Salammbô* and La Fontaine, the *Mannequin d'osier* and the *ballets russes* all coexist. (TL 108)[30]

What, he wonders, would Kafka's deformation of the text through the lens of German *Unheimlichkeit* have made of it? A final comment: before discussing the richness of Burton and Mardrus, he begs to disagree with the authority of the Encyclopaedia Britannica and the community of Arabists. Is he suggesting that it is his very Argentinianness, perhaps his part in the struggles to invent or record a *criollo* identity, which allows him to appreciate the constructed-ness and layering of the versions of the Orient: 'it matters not at all that a mere man of letters – and he of the merely Argentine Republic – prefers to dissent' (TL 108).[31]

Borges was to find life in Buenos Aires less pleasurable than the pages of *The Arabian Nights*. His dear English grandmother Fanny Haslam died in 1935 and his father in 1938. His father's suffering a stroke in 1937 reminded Borges of the precariousness of his economic position, working part time on the literary supplement of *Crítica* and contributing pieces on foreign books to *El Hogar*. Through contacts, he was given the post of First Assistant at the Miguel Cané branch of the Municipal Library in the working-class area of Almagro Sur, far across the city from his house. He was paid a pittance, and his description of the internal hierarchy is clearly evocative of Kafka: 'While there were Second and Third Assistants below me, there was also a Director and First, Second, and Third Officials above me' (Aut 240). His colleagues were antipathetic to him, being interested only in 'horse racing, soccer matches and smutty stories' (Aut 241). They were also lazy and keen to justify their employment. They advised him to reduce the rate at which he catalogued books to such an extent that he had much of the day free to read and write. The humiliation he felt is evident in his picking out a particular detail:

---

[30] 'Mi razón es ésta: las versiones de Burton y de Mardrus, y aun la de Galland, sólo se dejan concebir *después de una literatura*. Cualesquiera sus lacras o sus méritos, estas obras características presuponen un rico proceso anterior. En algún modo, el casi inagotable proceso inglés está adumbrado en Burton —la dura obscenidad de John Donne, el gigantesco vocabu-lario de Shakespeare y de Cyril Tourneur, la ficción arcaica de Swinburne, la crasa erudición de los tratadistas de mil seiscientos, la energía y la vaguedad, el amor de las tempestades y de la magia. En los risueños párrafos de Mardrus conviven *Salammbô* y La Fontaine, el *Manequí de Mimbre* y el *ballet ruso*' (I 411–12).

[31] 'nada importa que un mero literato – y ése, de la República meramente Argentina – prefiera disentir.' (I 411).

Now and then during these years, we municipal workers were rewarded
with gifts of a two-pound package of maté to take home. Sometimes in the
evening, as I walked the ten blocks to the tramline, my eyes would be filled
with tears. These small gifts from above always underlined my menial and
dismal existence. (Aut 242)

He worked at the library for nine years until 1946 when Perón came to power:
'They were nine years of solid unhappiness.' Borges recalls a fellow worker
wondering about the coincidence between his name and the identical one he
had come across in an encyclopaedia. Nonetheless, on the tram journey to
work and back, Borges was able to read the *Divine Comedy*, the six volumes
of Gibbon's *Decline and Fall*, and an immense number of other texts. In the
cellar or on the flat roof when it was warm, he was able to work in relative
tranquillity. The Miguel Cané Library was transposed onto one of his best
known stories: 'My Kafkian story "The Library of Babel" was meant as
a nightmare version or magnification of that municipal library, and certain
details in the text have no particular meaning. The numbers of books and
shelves that I recorded in the story were literally what I had at my elbow.
Clever critics have worried over those ciphers, and generously endowed them
with mystic significance' (Aut 243–4). Indeed many of the books which were
to form part of *Ficciones* were written, in whole or in part, while he 'played
truant'.

On the hot evening of Christmas Eve 1938, Borges suffered an accident
which is often seen as a turning point in his life. Borges was rushing up a
stairway to bring the beautiful Emita Risso Platero home for dinner, when
he felt something brush his head. When he arrived upstairs Emita nearly
fainted as he was covered with blood from a head wound caused by running
into an open and freshly painted window. Though the wound was stitched
up, septicemia set in and he was close to death for several days. His mother
did not leave his side as he suffered nightmares and insomnia. Fearing for
his mind and reason, he was moved to tears when he was able to understand
a text read to him by his mother. To test his faculties, he undertook a piece
of writing which was different from what he had previously excelled at: the
fictionalized account of a French writer who recreates pages of *Don Quijote*:
'Pierre Menard, author of the *Quixote*'. José Bianco (352), effectively the
editor of *Sur*, remembers receiving it from Borges, and exclaiming 'Nunca he
leído nada semejante'; 'I've never read anything like it.' He rushed to publish
it, giving it pride of place in number 56 of *Sur*. María Esther Vázquez gives
a dramatic version of Borges's metamorphosis: 'It was obvious that after the
accident at Christmas 1938 Borges had changed. It was as if an avid appetite

[gusto desmesurado] for fantastic literature, which had always interested him, had taken over all the available space in his creative mind and turned him into another person who continued to live together with the obscure employee of the Miguel Cané Library' (V 167). There may be much truth in her version, but one must not forget 'The Approach to Al-Mu'tasim', published in 1936, which belongs just as much to the cycle of *Fictions* and *The Aleph*, as does 'Pierre Menard'. One of Borges's most emblematic stories, 'The South', published in *La Nación* in 1953, and later added to *Fictions*, is clearly an elaboration on the Christmas Eve accident.

Maturity, success, Peronism

In 1932 the 33-year-old Borges had met a young writer aged eighteen called Adolfo Bioy Casares at the grand house of Victoria Ocampo. Vázquez (134) writes that 'the friendship of Bioy was one of the things that gave Borges most happiness and joy in his life'. Bioy came from a wealthy landed family; he was strikingly handsome and a notorious womanizer, quite a contrast with the awkward Borges (Wilson, 96), but quickly became engaged in literary collaboration and an endless dialogue about literature which would last virtually to Borges's death. Their conversations from 1947 are collected in the sixteen hundred pages of Bioy's *Borges*: what a shame that Bioy had not started the diary in the mid-thirties! Apparently, towards the end, they were separated to an extent by María Kodama. Borges would spend most nights at the houses of Bioy and his wife Silvina Ocampo, the youngest sister of Victoria, the two men retiring after dinner to write together, their uncontainable guffaws resounding through the house. According to Vázquez, Silvina felt excluded by this private and exclusive world they created, and was exasperated by their 'cacareo en conjunto', 'joint cackling'. The same biographer remarks that 'a respectful reticence prevented familiarity'; 'un respetuoso pudor les impedía la confianza' (V 134). Their collaboration began in 1935 or 1936 when they spent a week together in an *estancia* of the Bioy family, El Rincón Viejo, in Pardo, to write a publicity leaflet for *leche cuajada* La Martona, and moved on to notions of more literary collaboration. Bioy remarks that 'any collaboration with Borges was equivalent to years' worth of work'.[32]

Borges himself recounts how the composite writer Bustos Domecq was born:

---

[32] 'Toda colaboración con Borges equivalía a años de trabajo' (Bioy, 28).

I had invented what we thought was a quite good plot for a detective story. One rainy morning, he told me we ought to give it a try. I reluctantly agreed, and a little later that same morning the thing happened. A third man, Honorio Bustos Domecq, emerged and took over. In the long run he ruled us with a rod of iron and to our amusement, and later to our dismay, he became utterly unlike ourselves, with his own whims, his own puns, and his own very elaborate style of writing. Domecq was the name of a great-grandfather of Bioy's and Bustos of a great-grandfather of mine from Córdoba. Bustos Domecq's first book was *Six Problems for don Isidro Parodi* (1942), and during the writing of that volume he never got out of hand. (Aut 246)

Parodi is a blind detective who solves criminal mysteries from his prison cell, and is visited by a grotesque selection of Argentinian characters whose pretentiousness, snobbery, racism and ignorance is hyperbolically satirized (see King, 113–16, Avellaneda 57–92). The unspeakable Gervasio Monte-negro emerges, rather like Unamuno's Víctor Goti, from being a character in the stories to write the prologue to the collection.[33] Among many other joint projects, *Crónica de Bustos Domecq*, published under their real names in 1967, stands out. These are hilarious articles written on 'imaginary, extrava-gantly modern artists'. 'Both the author and his subjects are fools', comments Borges, 'and it is hard to know who is taking in whom' (Aut 247). In 'Home-naje a César Paladión', for example, Paladión goes well beyond Pierre Menard in publishing under his own name a whole string of works from *Los parques abandonados* (Banchs) to *The Hound of the Baskervilles* and *Uncle Tom's Cabin*. As important as these joint works, are the anthologies they compiled: of Argentinian poetry, detective writing, fantastic literature, etc. In 1936 they founded a journal, *Destiempo*, which went very much against the grain of the literary modes and tics prevalent at the time.

From its inception in 1931 until the 1960s, Borges was involved in the journal *Sur*. *Sur* was one of the most important journals in Latin America, and funded by the considerably wealthy Victoria Ocampo, who was the friend of many members of the elite of European and North American intellectuals: from Ortega y Gasset to Virginia Woolf, and who insisted on a decidedly internationalist content to the journal. Borges was always somewhat uneasy with the social pretensions of Victoria Ocampo, and from the beginning was wary of the presence of Girondo, Guillermo de Torre and Gómez de la Serna

---

[33] Typical of his style is the following: '*Rasgo que augura el más sombrío de los diag-nósticos sociológicos: en este fresco de lo que vacilo en llamar la Argentina contemporánea, falta la ecuestre silueta del gaucho y en su lugar campea el judío, el israelita, para denunciar el fenómeno en toda su repugnante crudeza ...*' (OC 18).

on the editorial committee. He was, however, close to José Bianco, and of course, to Bioy Casares and Silvina Ocampo. Borges published many of the stories that he wrote in the late thirties and early forties in *Sur*, which were brought together and published by *Sur* in 1941 as *The Garden of Forking Paths*, *El jardín de senderos que se bifurcan*. The book was received as a revelation by the group, and glowingly reviewed by Bioy, who claimed that Borges 'had invented a new genre by discovering "the literary possibilities of metaphysics" and combining these with the pursuit of the "ideal" inherent in detective fiction, namely, "inventiveness," "rigor" and "elegance" in the structuring of a narrative' (W 259–60). The collection was entered for the Premio Nacional de Literatura, in 1942, but did not win any of the three prizes (W 260; Ortega 78–9). It was criticized for being 'an exotic and decadent work', which clearly points to the insistence on the local increasingly demanded by the nationalists. The first prize was given to Arturo Acevedo Díaz for a gaucho novel. Borges was later to allude to this humiliation in his story 'The Aleph', where his rival in literature and love, the mediocre Daneri, wins the second prize, while the submission of 'Borges', *Los naipes del tahur* (which Borges had written and destroyed in Spain), won nothing. As a protest at the injustice, José Bianco published a 'Desagravio a Borges' in *Sur* with laudatory contributions from twenty-one writers, and organized an important dinner for him in the same year. A couple of years later SADE (Sociedad Argentina de Escritores) awarded him a prize which had been specially created to honour him.

In February 1946 the right-wing nationalist and populist Juan Domingo Perón was elected to the Presidency, and in July it was announced that Borges, a well know anti-nationalist and a staunch defender of the Allies, was to be moved from his job at the Miguel Cané Library. Borges described the event in the following way:

> One day soon after, I was honored with the news that I had been 'promoted' out of the library to the inspectorship of poultry and rabbits in the public markets. I went to the City Hall to find out what it was all about. … 'Well,' the clerk answered, 'you were on the side of the Allies – what do you expect?' (Aut 244)

Borges quickly resigned, but there is some confusion about the exact details of the move. Vázquez reports that Salinas, secretary of state for culture, secretario de Cultura de la Municipalidad, claimed that in order to avoid having to dismiss Borges outright, at the request of Borges's friend Francisco Luis Bernárdez and others, he transferred him to the 'Escuela de Apicultura', the School of Beekeeping (V 191). The possible change by Borges and his friends in the Unión Democrática from *apicultura* to *avicultura*, beekeeping to the poultry industry, with Borges's adding 'and rabbits' for good measure, became the accepted story. SADE organized a banquet for Borges for which he penned a vigorous attack on the Peronist regime: 'dictatorships foster oppression, servilism, cruelty; more abominably, they foster idiocy ... mere discipline takes the place of lucidity. Fighting those sad monotonies is one of the many duties of the writer.'[34] Borges was quickly becoming the figurehead of the intellectual opposition to Perón. *Sur* of course was also fiercely anti-Peronist and pro-Ally.

Leonor Acevedo de Borges and most people of her class were horrified by the vulgarity of Perón, his wife Eva, and the vociferous *descamisados*. In September 1948, Borges's mother and his sister were demonstrating against the legalization of the re-election of Perón when they were arrested and taken to the police station. His Mother was put under house arrest because of her age, but Norah spent a month in prison. Borges himself was shadowed by a policeman, and non-uniformed officers would attend his lectures, yawning and trying to take notes on his obscure philosophical and literary discourses. In 1950 he was elected president of SADE, a post he occupied until the Society was banned in 1953. In 1946 Borges had become director of *Los Anales de Buenos Aires*, where he discovered and published two important writers: the Argentinian Julio Cortázar, one of the greatest story-writers and novelists of the continent, and the Uruguayan Felisberto Hernández. The loss of his position at the library left Borges with few means of support. Two influential friends, Victoria Ocampo and Esther Zemborain de Torres Duggan (whose name sounds like a Borgesian invention), intervened to secure him posts lecturing in English and North American literature at the Asociación Argentina de Cultura Inglesa and the Colegio Libre de Estudios Superiores. Borges almost miraculously overcame his legendary timidity and discovered that not only was he an excellent, if eccentric lecturer, but he also enjoyed it immensely.

A brief consideration of a small number of texts may serve to illustrate Borges's attitudes towards anti-Semitism, the Second World War and Peronism. 'Mythology' and 'unreality', which had been amiable aesthetic or metaphysical categories, become here bitter terms of denunciation. 'Yo judío', 'I, a Jew' (TL 110–11), published in *Megáfono* in 1934, is an ironic

---

[34] 'las dictaduras fomentan la opresión, el servilismo, la crueldad; más abominable es el hecho de que fomentan la idiotez. ... la mera disciplina usurp[a] el lugar de la lucidez. Combatir esas tristes monotonías es uno de los muchos deberes del escritor' (cit. V 193).

putdown of an article in *Crisol* accusing Borges of 'maliciously hiding his Jewish ancestry'. Ignorance, he writes, is adept at changing the facts of the past into a mythology of its own liking:

> Like the Druzes, like the moon, like next week, the distant past is one of those things that can enrich ignorance [*sic*, that ignorance can enrich]. It is infinitely malleable and agreeable, far more obliging than the future and far less demanding of our efforts. It is the famous scene favored by all mythologies. (TL 110)[35]

He confesses to having often fantasized about his ancestry, and having been not unpleased to think of himself as a Jew. One book had declared almost all the families of Buenos Aires at the time of Rosas, including the Acevedos, to be Jewish, but it had been proved that his Acevedo family was 'irreparably Spanish'. He thanks the article for encouraging his hope, but declares that he is despairing of finding evidence that he is linked to Heine, the ten Sephiroth, Ecclesiastes and Chaplin. The Jews are a small race, he quips, so what would we think of someone in the year 4000 who found descendants of the province of San Juan populating much of the Earth?

'A Comment on August 23, 1944', 'Anotación al 23 de agosto de 1944', was published in *Otras inquisiciones* in 1952. He compares hearing the news of the liberation of Paris with the announcement of the earlier fall of the same city. He is struck by the 'puzzling and flagrant enthusiasm of many who were supporters of Hitler' (TL 210) at the liberation of the French capital. He could not ask them for an explanation of the phenomenon as their incoherence was so systematic: they adored the Germanic race, but hated 'Saxon' America; they condemn the Versailles settlement but applaud the marvels of the *Blitzkrieg*; they apply the canon of Jesus to the actions of England, but that of Zarathustra to those of Germany, etc. He then remembered the day when a Germanophile announced that the Germans had occupied Paris. Despite the latter's victorious announcement, Borges had realized from his insolent bluster and strained voice that he too was terrified. For the Europeans and Americans, he concludes, the only possible order is that of Rome and the West: 'To be a Nazi (to play the energetic barbarian, Viking, Tartar, sixteenth-century conquistador, gaucho, or Indian) is, after all, mentally and

---

[35] 'Como los drusos, como la luna, como la muerte, como la semana que viene, el pasado remoto es de aquellas cosas que puede enriquecer la ignorancia ... Es infinitamente plástico y agradable, mucho más servicial que el porvenir y mucho menos exigente de esfuerzos. Es la estación famosa y predilecta de las mitologías' (TR II 89).

morally impossible' (TL 211).[36] Nazism is unreal, like the hells of Erigena, and nobody 'en la soledad central de su yo' can hope for its triumph. Hitler, he conjectures, '*wants to be defeated*. Hitler is blindly collaborating with the inevitable armies that will annihilate him, as the metal vultures and the dragon (which must have known that they were monsters) collaborated, mysteriously, with Hercules' (TL 211).[37] The tragic paradoxes of Nazism are hauntingly explored in the 1947 story '*Deutsches Requiem*', where a German Nazi, whose intellectual profile is not dissimilar to that of Borges, explains his life while awaiting execution. In the Afterword to *El Aleph*, Borges again tilts against the Argentine Germanophiles and their ignorance: 'During the last war, no one could have wished more earnestly than I for Germany's defeat; no one could have felt more strongly than I the tragedy of Germany's fate; "*Deutsches Requiem*" is an attempt to understand that fate, which our own "Germanophiles" (who know nothing of Germany) neither wept over nor even suspected' (A 134).[38]

Two pieces on Peronism though very different in style, share an acutely sinister and grotesque atmosphere. 'The Monster's Feast', 'La fiesta del monstruo', was written in 1947 by Borges and Bioy Casares, circulated in typescript at the time, and finally published in *Nuevos cuentos de Bustos Domecq* in 1977. It is a chilling and disturbing story: 'Biorges' writes more cruelly and graphically than Borges ever did on his own. It is written in the first person as a pastiche of the urban *lunfardo* of a Peronist thug bussed into central Buenos Aires to attend a rally and speech by Perón, el Monstruo. The language is a witty and stylized piece in which the reader is partly charmed and partly sickened by the banter of an obese yob, until the party comes across a slight, red-haired and bespectacled Jewish student who refuses to salute their flag and the photo of Perón, and proceeds to stone him to death. As the bloody description develops, the imperturbable witty banter becomes

---

[36] 'Ser nazi (jugar a la barbarie enérgica, jugar a ser un viking, un tártaro, un conquistador del siglo XVI, un gaucho, un piel roja) es, a la larga, una imposibilidad mental y moral' (II 106).

[37] 'Hitler, de un modo ciego, colabora con los inevitables ejércitos que lo aniquilarán, como los buitres de metal y el dragón (que no debieron de ignorar que eran monstruos) colaboraban, misteriosamente, con Hércules' (II 106).

[38] 'En la última guerra nadie pudo anhelar más que yo que fuera derrotada Alemania; nadie pudo sentir más que yo lo trágico del destino alemán; "*Deutsches Requiem*" quiere entender ese destino, que no supieron llorar, ni siquiera sospechar, nuestros "germanófilos", que nada saben de Alemania' (I 629).

intolerable. Finally, 'Morpurgo, to get the lads laughing, made me stick my penknife into what was left of his face.'[39]

'The Mountebank', 'El simulacro', short piece of two paragraphs published in *The Maker*, is a bizarre *mise-en-abyme* which denounces the performed nature, the *unreality* of the regime of Perón and Eva Duarte, as 'A Comment' had denounced that of Nazism. The anecdote is set in 1952, the year of the death and multitudinous funeral of Evita, which was followed by an almost unbelievable series of dramas surrounding the embalmed body of the heroine of the Argentine dispossessed. A tall indigenous looking man came into a remote Chaco village and set up a trestle on which he set out a cardboard box with a blonde-haired doll. The local population visited it to pay their homage, and paid two pesos per visit. The ceremony was a play within a play, as in *Hamlet*. The man in mourning was not Perón, but Perón was not Perón either, but a 'crass mythology':

> In it, one can see the perfect symbol of an unreal time, and it is like the reflection of a dream or like that play within a play in *Hamlet*. The man in mourning was not Perón and the blond-haired mannequin was not the woman Eva Duarte, but then Perón was not Perón, either, nor was Eva, Eva—they were unknown or anonymous persons (whose secret name and true face we shall never know) who acted out, for the credulous love of the working class, a crass and ignoble mythology. (A 152)[40]

On a more serene and cerebral level, Borges published the essays of *Other Inquisitions*, *Otras inquisiciones*, in 1952. This is the third of his three major works. After his blindness, Borges did eventually come to publish two collections of short stories after a long hiatus: *Brodie's Report* in 1970, and *The Book of Sand*, *El libro de arena*, in 1975. There are some good stories in both collections, but they show signs of tiredness and repetition. They were dictated, and show little of the intellectual and stylistic tension of his great works. The bulk of his later production was poetry, often in conventional forms and meters which allowed him more easily to compose them in his head. Some argue that in his poetry lies the real, authentic Borges. This may be true, but it is not the important Borges who wrote the best Spanish prose

---

[39] 'Luego Morpurgo, para que los muchachos se rieran, me hizo clavar la cortaplumita en lo que le hacía las veces de cara' (OC 401).

[40] 'En ella está la cifra perfecta de una época irreal y es como el reflejo de un sueño o como aquel drama en el drama, que se ve en *Hamlet*. El enlutado no era Perón y la muñeca rubia no era la mujer Eva Duarte, pero tampoco Perón era Perón ni Eva era Eva sino desconcidos o anónimos ... que figuraron, para el crédulo amor de los arrabales, una crasa mitología' (II 167).

works since the Golden Age, and revolutionized the practice of writing in Latin America and elsewhere.

Consecration

In 1955 Perón was overthrown by a military coup known as the Revolución Libertadora. Power was soon taken by General Aramburu, who embarked on a campaign to eradicate the influence of Peronism. Borges was ecstatic at the regime change and supported this 'democratic regeneration' enthusiastically, which eventually ended in the cessation of his relationship with Estela Canto, a member of the Communist Party, which favoured a rapprochement with the Peronists, and to bitter quarrels with previous friends such as Martínez Estrada, and Ernesto Sábato. The new situation also allowed his name to be put forward for the Directorship of the National Library. Borges mentions the names of the same ladies who had secured him teaching posts at two institutions, together with support from those schools, *Sur*, and the newly reopened SADE, though Williamson also suspects the hand of his ambitious and protective mother. His taking up the Directorship coincided pretty much with the final onset of blindness. Remarkably, he shared the paradoxical honour of blind librarian with two illustrious predecessors in the post: José Mármol, author of the Romantic novel about Rosas, *Amalia*, and Paul Groussac. In 1958 Borges expressed the paradox with wit and serene melancholy in 'Poem of the Gifts': 'No one should read self-pity or reproach / into this statement of the majesty / of God, who with such splendid irony / granted me books and blindness at one touch' (SP 95).[41] His prestige within Argentina was confirmed when he was elected to the Chair of English and American Literature at the University of Buenos Aires, despite the fact that he had not finished his secondary education. As Williamson explains, there was a political dimension to the appointment. Betina Edelberg had been approached by doña Leonor to intervene on Borges's behalf and approached 'the historian Alberto Salas, who as "Decano Interventor" had been charged by the Aramburu government with the task of getting rid of Peronist appointees and naming new professors' (W 336). In the light of this, Borges's own account in the 'Autobiographical Essay' is rather disingenuous.

Borges's reputation abroad was launched in France. Roger Caillois, who had been trapped in Buenos Aires by the war, returned to Paris in 1945 and

---

[41] 'Nadie rebaje a lágrima o reproche / esta declaración de la maestría / de Dios, que con magnífica ironía / me dio a la vez los libros y la noche' ('Poema de los dones', II 187).

worked at Gallimard, where in 1951 he published a translation of *Ficciones* by Borges's friend the bilingual Néstor Ibarra and Paul Verdevoye. Caillois in 1953 brought out his own translations of a selection of Borges texts, which he called *Labyrinthes*, a title later to be taken up by translations into English. In 1955 (W 346) a translated anthology came out in Italy to enormous acclaim; two of Borges's most notable followers in fiction are the Italians Italo Calvino and Umberto Eco. In 1961 Borges's life was changed when he was awarded the Formentor Prize for his work, which he shared with Samuel Beckett. The prize was awarded by six publishing houses in France, Italy, Spain, Germany, New York and London. The prize was ten thousand dollars and the translation and publication of a book in each of the countries represented. As Borges puts it: 'As a consequence of that prize, my books mushroomed overnight throughout the western world' (Aut 254).

It was also at this time that Borges's globe-trotting began, which would continue until his death in Geneva in 1986. At first he would be accompanied by his youthful and energetic mother, later by María Esther Vázquez, Norman Thomas di Giovanni, and until his death by María Kodama, who would become his wife near his end. Accompanied by Leonor Acevedo, he left Argentina for the first time since 1924 for the University of Texas at Austin as Visiting Professor, and developed a real liking for the United States. The Methodism of the Haslams emerged in his reaction to the country: 'We South Americans tend to see things in terms of convenience, whereas people in the United States approach things ethically. This—amateur protestant that I am—I admired above all. It even helped me overlook skyscrapers, paper bags, television, plastics, and the unholy jungle of gadgets' (Aut 255). In 1967 he held the Charles Eliot Norton Chair of Poetry at Harvard, and after that he received an endless string of prizes, such as the Cervantes in 1980, and a succession of honorary degrees from the University of Cuyo in Mendoza in 1956, through Oxford, Columbia, Harvard, la Sorbonne, to Cambridge in 1984.

Politically, the older, blind Borges, was often ill-informed, misguided, and stridently conservative. In his final years, he explicitly stated that he had returned to the anarchism and pacifism of his youth, instilled in him by his father and Macedonio Fernández, but in the intervening years, Borges railed against the Cuban Revolution and especially Ernesto Guevara; he campaigned hard against the return of Perón, who died in 1974 after only a few months in power; he rejoiced at the overthrow of Isabelita Perón by the infamous Videla, whom he thanked for saving the country from chaos. His greatest misjudgement came in 1976 when he accepted the Grand Cross of the Order of Merit from the Chilean junta, and visited Chile where he received an honorary doctorate and accepted an invitation to a private dinner with General Augusto Pinochet, whose brutal regime had overthrown the democratically elected socialist Salvador Allende in 1973. It is generally agreed that this visit and his extreme declarations to the press prevented him from receiving the Nobel Prize which *Ficciones*, *El Aleph*, and *Otras inquisiciones* amply merited. Borges, however, became more aware of the atrocities committed by the junta during the so-called Dirty War after the 1976 revolution. After receiving a visit from an old friend whose daughter had become a *desaparecida* and hearing other similar stories, he signed a petition demanding a government enquiry, and by 1981 was a public enemy of the regime. The 1983 war between Britain and Argentina when General Galtieri, as a nationalist and populist gesture, invaded the Malvinas/Falkland Islands, and the needless deaths involved distressed him greatly, as is evident in the short prose poem which is the penultimate piece in Borges's *Complete Works*. Juan López was an Argentinian soldier who loved Conrad; John Ward had learned Spanish to read the *Quixote*.

> They would have been friends, but they saw each other's face but once, on some too notorious islands, and each of them was Cain, and each Abel. / They were buried together. Snow and corruption know them. / The events I recount happened in a time that we cannot understand.[42]

Borges famously said to Richard Burgin: 'I don't think a writer should be judged by his opinions, by his political opinions' (Burgin 122), and cites the case of that apologist of British Empire, Kipling, in whose work warm sympathy for the Indians and their plight shines through almost in spite of the writer (Christ, 266). I believe that Borges's best politics lie in his stories and essays: in their lucid awareness of the functioning of language, of the dangerous seduction of plots and arguments, of the constructedness of what is presented as natural and inevitable, their playful dismantling of authority. Borges died on 14 June 1986 in Geneva, his hand in that of María Kodama.

---

[42] 'Hubieran sido amigos, pero se vieron una sola vez cara a cara, en unas islas demasiado famosas, y cada uno de ellos fue Caín, y cada uno, Abel. / Los enterraron juntos. La nieve y la corrupción los conocen. / El hecho que refiero pasó en un tiempo que no podemos entender' (III 500).

Metaphysics, the Cult of Courage

Three short texts published in the 1928 collection *The Language of the Argentines*, *El idioma de los argentinos*, point both to founding preoccupations within Borges's corpus: metaphysics and time, the cult of courage and the duel, and to a key textual practice: rewriting, and reusing similar or identical pieces in different contexts. Michel Lafon, in *Borges ou la réécriture*, studies and theorizes the textual manoeuvres in great detail. These texts are 'El truco'; 'Men Fought', 'Hombres pelearon'; and 'Feeling in Death', 'Sentirse en muerte'. In the three cases the process is different. The short and schematic text of 'Men Fought' is published first with two different titles; it is radically rewritten with abundant use of local colour and dialect, again with two different titles, best known as 'El hombre de la esquina rosada'; much later, in a more metafictional mode, a character from the second version becomes the narrator who corrects Borges's story in 'The Story from Rosendo Juárez', 'Historia de Rosendo Juárez'. The very personal experience recounted in 'Feeling in Death' is reproduced twice with virtually no textual modifications, but inserted into two larger, highly philosophical, essays: 'History of Eternity' and 'A New Refutation of Time'. 'El truco' is first published as verse in the 1923 *Fervor de Buenos Aires*; it is translated into prose and expanded in *The Language of the Argentines*; two years later this prose piece is reproduced as a 'complementary page' in *Evaristo Carriego*; the poem is rewritten in the 1969 edition of his poetry. Lafon points to the fact that the later version of the poem incorporates elements of the prose version.

Metaphysics: eternity and the refutation of time

At the beginning of his essay 'A New Refutation of Time', dated 1946 and included in *Otras inquisiciones*, in the very title of which the temporal adjective 'new' knowingly torpedoes the refutation, Borges muses on his lifelong preoccupation with the refutation of time, in which he does not believe, 'de la que yo mismo descreo', but which visits him 'with the illusory force of a truism' (TL 318), 'con ilusoria fuerza de axioma' (II 137). Paradox and oxymoron are at the heart of the matter. He goes on to point to the centrality of the process in all his work, and points out the texts where it is 'prefigured':

> This refutation is to be found, in one form or another, in all of my books. It is prefigured in the poems 'Inscription on Any Tomb' and 'Truco' in my *Fervor de Buenos Aires* (1923); it is openly stated on a certain page of *Evaristo Carriego*; and in the story 'Feeling in Death', which I transcribe below. (TL 318)[1]

The page from *Evaristo Carriego* is probably one of the moments I discussed earlier. The first poem mentioned develops a key notion in Borges, 'The Nothingness of Personality', 'La nadería de la personalidad': the self is an illusion. On a tombstone, name, fame, deeds and fatherland are so many baubles to be consigned to oblivion. The most intimate and defining moments of a man's life are common to all men; one man is thus all men, immortality is assured through their repetition through time; 'others' lives', 'vidas ajenas' are thus one's own life; each man is a reflection and replica of all others:

> The essentials of the dead man's life / – the trembling hope, / the implacable miracle of pain, the wonder of sensual delight – / will abide forever. / Blindly the uncertain soul asks to continue / when it is the lives of others that will make that happen, / as you yourself are the mirror and image / of those who did not live as long as you / and others will be (and are) your immortality on earth.' (SP 21)[2]

'Truco' is an Argentinian card game. The second version of the poem (B) eliminates some of the *criollista* traits of the first (A). The phrase 'los brillantes embelecos de una mitología criolla y tiránica',[3] 'the brilliant trickeries of a tyrannical and *criollo* mythology', becomes 'las floridas travesuras de una mitología casera', 'the flowery flourishes of a home-made mythology'. 'Una lentitud cimarrona / va refrenando las palabras / que por declives patrios

---

[1] 'Esa refutación está de algún modo en todos mis libros: La prefiguran los poemas 'Inscripción en cualquier sepulcro' y 'El truco' de mi *Fervor de Buenos Aires* (1923); la declaran cierta página de *Evaristo Carriego* (1930) y el relato 'Sentirse en muerte', que más adelante transcribo' (II 137).

[2] 'Lo esencial de la vida fenecida / – la trémula esperanza, / el milagro implacable del dolor y el asombro del goce – / siempre perdurará. / Ciegamente reclama duración el alma arbitraria / cuando la tiene asegurada en vidas ajenas, / cuando tú mismo eres el reflejo y la réplica / de quienes no alcanzaron tu tiempo / y otros serán (y son) tu inmortalidad en la tierra' (I 35).

[3] I quote the earlier version (A) from *Obra poética 1923–1967* (Buenos Aires: Emecé, 1969), 27–8; the later (B) version from I 22. The translation of A is my own; the translation of B is in SP 13.

resbalan', 'a sly slowness / reins in their words / which glide down the slopes of the fatherland', becomes 'una lentitud cimarrona / va demorando las palabras', 'a furtive slowing-down / keeps all words in check'. In both, the complex language and traditions of the card game create a world divorced from the everyday. I prefer the first version of this process:

> Cuarenta naipes han desplazado la vida. / Amuletos de cartón pintado / conjuran en placentero exorcismo / la maciza realidad primordial / de goce y sufrimiento carnales. (A)

> Forty cards have displaced life. / Amulets of coloured card / avert by an agreeable exorcism / the solid primordial reality / of bodily pleasure and suffering.

The game, which is a human system, a specialized and stylized language in which the words are 'amulets of painted card', replaces the complexity of real life. Players in the present necessarily repeat the hands of players of generations past: 'los jugadores de esta noche / copian remotas bazas'; 'the players of that evening / re-enact ancient tricks'. The effect is similar to the shared moments in the previous poem: they bring back to life or immortalize, 'a little', those earlier players:

> hecho que inmortaliza un poco, / apenas, / a los compañeros muertos que callan

> an act which immortalizes a little, /slightly, / the dead partners who are silent. (A)

> hecho que resucita un poco, muy poco / a las generaciones de los mayores / que legaron al tiempo de Buenos Aires / los mismos versos y las mismas diabluras

> an act that brings to life, but very faintly, / the generations of our forefathers / who bequeathed to the leisure time of Buenos Aires / truco, with all its bids and deceptions. (B)

The prose version from *Evaristo Carriego* is, like the 1923 poem, highly *criollista*; it celebrates the *arrabal*, the world of electioneering thugs, the recondite poetic density of the language of the game, but also stresses the presence of the metaphysical in the local: 'It's a narrow world, I admit: the ghostly presence of local politics and its mischief, a world ultimately invented by back-yard wizards and neighbourhood sorcerers, but, all the same, no less able to replace this real world, no less inventive and diabolical in its ambition.'[4] The metaphysical is made more explicit in the prose, yet is still inseparable from the local: 'the players suddenly become old-time *criollos* and shed their habitual selves'.[5] From the repetition of hands, 'time is shown to be a fiction'.[6]

It does not take much of a leap of imagination to move from the repetition of the game of long-dead *criollos* to the rewriting of previous texts by individual writers. The effect on the individual is similar: he becomes a ghost. In 'The Library of Babel', 'the certainty that everything has already been written annuls us, or renders us phantasmal' (F 73).[7] In 'The Circular Ruins', the wizard is a spectre dreamed up by an earlier wizard.

'Feeling in Death' is the account of a densely personal experience.[8] Its importance for Borges is suggested by the occasion, fifty-five years after its publication, reported by Williamson, when the writer consults a Japanese monk about the significance of the revelation. He describes the experience by elimination as neither adventure nor thought: 'a triviality too evanescent and ecstatic to be called an adventure, too irrational and sentimental for thought'.[9] It happened on one of the long evening walks through the backstreets of the city which were so significant for Borges. His practice and state of mind recall those of both the surrealists (and Julio Cortázar) and the mystics: chance and receptivity. 'I accomplished, to the unsatisfactory degree to which it is possible, what is called strolling at random. ... I took in the night, in perfect, serene respite from thought.'[10] The scene was of low houses, a fig tree, a mud street which bizarrely suddenly evokes pre-Columbian America: 'a street of elemental dirt, a dirt of a still unconquered America'.[11] A pink wall, which seemed to emit its own light, generated a feeling of intense tenderness: 'a low, rose-colored wall seemed not to harbor the moonlight but to shimmer with a gleam all its own. Tenderness could

---

4 'Es un mundo angosto, lo sé: fantasma de política de parroquia y de picardías, un mundo inventado al fin por hechiceros de corralón y brujos de barrio, pero no por eso menos reemplazador de este mundo real y menos inventivo y diabólico en su ambición' (I 146).

5 'los jugadores, acriollados de golpe, se aligeran del yo habitual' (I 145).

6 'se trasluce que el tiempo es una ficción' (I 147).

7 'La certidumbre de que todo está escrito nos anula o nos afantasma' (I 470).

8 I am quoting from the text of 'Feeling in Death' in 'History of Eternity', TL 137–9 and I 365–6.

9 'fruslería demasiado evanescente y extática para que la llame aventura; demasiado irrazonable y sentimental para pensamiento'.

10 'Realicé en la mala medida de lo posible, eso que llaman caminar al azar. ... Aspiré noche, en asueto serenísimo de pensar.'

11 'la calle era de barro elemental, barro de América no conquistado aún'.

have no better name than that rose color.'[12] He suddenly thought aloud: 'This is the same as it was thirty years ago ... *I am in the year eighteen hundred and something* [1898, a year before his birth].'[13] He felt as if he were dead, viewing the scene from somewhere other than his personal self: 'I felt as the dead feel, I felt myself to be an abstract observer of the world.'[14] The amalgam of fear and knowledge defined the experience as metaphysical: 'an indefinite fear imbued with knowledge that is the greatest clarity of metaphysics'.[15] He felt that he suddenly possessed the 'reticent or absent meaning of the inconceivable word *eternity*'. The moment and the moment thirty years before were not simply identical, they were the *same* moment: 'When we can feel this oneness, time is a delusion which the indifference and inseparability of a moment from its apparent yesterday and its apparent today suffice to disintegrate.'[16] As in 'Inscription' and 'Truco', elemental feelings are limited in number, common and eternal: 'The elemental experiences – physical suffering and physical pleasure, falling asleep, listening to a piece of music, feeling great intensity or great apathy – are even more impersonal. I derive, in advance, this conclusion: life is too impoverished not to be immortal.'[17]

A reference to a bird in the piece suggests that Keats was not far from his mind when writing up his experience: 'Perhaps a bird was singing and I felt for it a small, bird-sized fondness, but there was probably no other sound in the dizzying silence except for the equally timeless noise of crickets.'[18] Keats's nightingale, evoked in 'History of Eternity' (I 356), is similarly timeless: 'The voice I heard this passing night was heard / In ancient days by emperor and clown: / Perhaps the self-same song that found a path / Through

---

[12] 'una tapia rosada parecía no hospedar luz de luna, sino efundir luz íntima. No había manera de nombrar la ternura mejor que ese rosado.'

[13] 'Esto es lo mismo de hace treinta años ... *Estoy en mil ochocientos y tantos.*'

[14] 'Me sentí muerto, me sentí percibidor abstracto del mundo.' The experience is certainly a personal one, but note the strong parallel with Emerson's essay *Nature*: 'I become a transparent eye-ball; I am nothing; I see all' (Emerson, 10). The paradoxical overlap between the personal or the anecdotic and an intertextual reference or source is common in the stories.

[15] 'indefinido temor imbuido de ciencia que es la mejor claridad de la metafísica'.

[16] 'El tiempo, si podemos intuir esa identidad, es una delusión: la indiferencia e inseparabilidad ['indisolubilidad' in *El idioma*] de un momento de su aparente ayer y otro de su aparente hoy, bastan para desintegrarlo ['desordenarlo' in *El idioma*].'

[17] 'Los [momentos humanos] elementales – los de sufrimiento físico y goce físico, los de acercamiento del sueño, los de la audición de una música, los de mucha intensidad o mucho desgano – son más impersonales aún. Derivo de antemano esta conclusión: la vida es demasiado pobre para no ser también inmortal.'

[18] 'Tal vez cantaba un pájaro y sentí por él un cariño chico, y de tamaño de pájaro; pero lo más seguro es que en ese ya vertiginoso silencio no hubo más ruido que el también intemporal de los grillos.'

the sad heart of Ruth' (Keats, 287). In 'Keats's Nightingale', 'El ruiseñor de Keats', Borges argues that English critics have found it hard to come to terms with the meaning of the nightingale because, being from an 'Aristotelian' culture, where the individual rules over the general, they fail to see in the bird the Platonic archetype. It is significant that both in the essay from *Otras inquisiciones* and in *History of Eternity* Borges quotes a passage from Schopenhauer on the timelessness of cats:

> Whoever hears me assert that the grey cat playing just now in the yard is the same one that did jumps and kicks there five hundred years ago will think whatever he likes of me, but it is a stranger form of madness to imagine that the present-day cat is fundamentally an entirely different one. (TL 127)[19]

(Timeless cats appear at particularly archetypal moments in the stories, e.g. in 'The South' and in 'The End'.)

Of the two philosophical essays in which 'Feeling in Death' is embedded, 'A History of Eternity' considers eternity from the Platonist, neo-Platonist, and Christian theological perspectives, while 'A New Refutation of Time' takes idealism as the starting point of its argument. In the Prologue to *A History of Eternity*, Borges makes it clear that eternity is a mental construct designed to release man from the tyranny of chronological time: 'eternity, lovingly yearned for by so many poets, is a splendid artifice which frees us, albeit in a fleeting manner, from the unbearable oppression of the successive'.[20] The ideas in both essays are complex and illustrated with a rather overwhelming proliferation of quotes. I will extract just a few key points. He quotes the neo-Platonist Plotinus on the intelligible heaven, where the eternal forms of Reality, of which everything is a copy, can be contemplated. Irenaeus provides a Christian vision of eternity in which the successive is cancelled in the Divine Mind, which sees everything simultaneously: 'Nothing comes to pass in this world, but all things endure forever, steadfast in the happiness of their condition' (TL 124).[21] Borges has the Christian idea of eternity derive from the polemic around the nature of the Trinity, a notion which he repeatedly described as monstrous: 'a case of intellectual teratology, a distor-

---

[19] 'Quien me oiga asegurar que ese gato que está jugando ahí es el mismo que brincaba y que traveseaba en ese lugar hace trescientos años pensará de mí lo que quiera, pero locura más extraña es imaginar que fundamentalmente es otro' (II 96; see also I 356).

[20] 'la eternidad, anhelada con amor por tantos poetas, es un artificio espléndido que nos libra, siquiera de manera fugaz, de la intolerable opresión de lo sucesivo' (I 351).

[21] 'Nada transcurre en ese mundo en el que persisten todas las cosas, quietas en la felicidad de su condición' (I 354).

tion only the horror of a nightmare could engender' (TL 130).[22] Misguided Gnostic notions of the Trinity were resolved by declaring that 'the double process – the Son engendered by the Father, the Holy Spirit issuing from the two – did not occur in time, but consumes past, present, and future once and for all' (TL 130).[23] Elsewhere in the essay, Borges holds nostalgia to be the model for eternity, which he repeatedly evokes in the Latin of Hans Lassen Martensen: 'Aeternitas es merum hodie, est inmediata et lucida fruition rerum infinitarum' [Eternity is merely today; it is the immediate and lucid enjoyment of the things of eternity] (TL 130). He links this enjoyment to that provided by the enumerations which he himself practises so memorably. The phrase is also a decent description of the Aleph which features in a much later story. In that story, as when he introduces his personal experience of eternity in 'New Refutation', he stresses the successive nature of language: 'All language is of a successive nature; it does not lend itself to reasoning on eternal, intemporal matters' (TL 324).[24]

The structure of 'A New Refutation of Time' is curious in that it gives two versions of the same essay, rather than providing a synthesis. As elsewhere, work is always work in progress, just another draft. In the second essay Borges is schematic about the conclusions of idealism. Berkeley denied the existence of objects outside our perceptions, the impressions of our senses. Hume denies that there is a subject behind the perception of changes: 'Berkeley denied matter; Hume denied the spirit. Berkeley did not wish us to add the metaphysical notion of matter to the succession of impressions; Hume did not wish us to add the metaphysical notion of a self to the succession of mental states' (TL 328).[25] Borges takes the argument a step further. Given the abolition of matter and of self outside perception, why should time exist outside each present moment? Thought becomes a process independent of individuals, which renders the Cartesian cogito invalid. He reports Lichtenberg's proposal that rather than the first-person ' "I think", we should say impersonally "It thinks," as we say "It thunders" or "There is lightning" ' (TL

---

[22] 'un caso de teratología intelectual, una deformación que solo el horror de una pesadilla pudo parir' (I 359).

[23] 'el doble proceso – generación del Hijo por el Padre, emisión del Espíritu por los dos – no aconteció en el tiempo, sino que agota de una vez el pasado, el presente y el porvenir' (I 359).

[24] 'Todo lenguaje es de índole sucesiva; no es hábil para razonar lo eterno, lo intemporal' (II 142).

[25] 'Aquél había negado la materia, éste negó el espíritu; aquél no había querido que agregáramos a la sucesión de impresiones la noción metafísica de materia, éste no quiso que agregáramos a la sucesión de estados mentales la noción metafísica de un yo' (II 145).

321).[26] (Rimbaud has a similar point in his 1871 letter to Paul Demeny, one of the so-called 'Lettres du Voyant', which leads to the notable conclusion, not alien to Borges, that 'Je est un autre' (Rimbaud, 250).) With the notion of the absence of the individual self, if a thought is repeated identically in two moments, those moments are the same moment, and time, again, is abolished. This leads to the famous phrase on the readers of Shakespeare, which we have already seen echoed in a similar one on Carriego: 'Is not one single repeated terminal point enough to disrupt and confound the series in time? Are the enthusiasts who devote themselves to a line of Shakespeare not literally Shakespeare?' (TL 323).[27] I suppose one could say on such occasions that 'it Shakespeares'.

Memorably and melancholically at the end of the essay, Borges reminds us that the whole essay was little more than 'verbal games'. Time, the world, and the individual are only too real:

> *And yet, and yet* ... To deny temporal succession, to deny the self, to deny the astronomical universe, appear to be acts of desperation and are secret consolations. Our destiny (unlike the hell of Swedenborg and the hell of Tibetan mythology) is not terrifying because it is unreal; it is terrifying because it is irreversible and iron-bound. Time is the substance of which I am made. Time is the river that sweeps me along, but I am the river; it is a tiger that mangles me, but I am the tiger; it is a fire that consumes me, but I am the fire. The world, unfortunately, is real; I, unfortunately, am Borges. (TL 332)[28]

The tension between time and its denial, through plot, dream, literature, or identification with the other, is one of the major structural constants of the stories. 'The Secret Miracle', 'El milagro secreto', is a clear example. Hladík is granted by God a year outside time in which to weave the time-denying symmetries of his play, but at the end of the story, time imposes itself as the

---

[26] 'Lichtenberg, en el siglo XVIII, propuso que en lugar de *pienso*, dijéramos impersonalmente *piensa*, como quien dice *truena* o *relampeaguea*' (II 139).

[27] '¿No basta *un solo término repetido* para desbaratar y confundir la serie del tiempo? ¿Los fervorosos que se entregan a una línea de Shakespeare no son, literalmente, Shakespeare?' (II 141).

[28] *And yet, and yet* ... Negar la sucesión temporal, negar el yo, negar el universo astronómico, son desesperaciones aparentes y consuelos secretos. Nuestro destino (a diferencia del infierno de Swedenborg y del infierno de la mitología tibetana) no es espantoso por irreal; es espantoso porque es irreversible y de hierro. El tiempo es la sustancia de que estoy hecho. El tiempo es un río que me arrebata, pero yo soy el río; es un tigre que me destroza, pero yo soy el tigre; es un fuego que me consume, pero yo soy el fuego. El mundo, desgraciadamente, es real; yo, desgraciadamente, soy Borges' (II 148–9).

Nazi bullet hits his chest. In 'The South', the chronological time of the city and the individual is mirrored in the archetypal time of literature and myth. In one, Borges unfortunately is Borges; in the other he is a *gaucho*, a knife-fighter, his romantic ancestors. In 'The Theologians' the struggle between linear time and circular time is embodied in the intellectual duel, the life and death struggle between the two theologians.

The cult of courage, duels

If 'Truco' and 'Feeling in Death' prefigure Borges's later refutations of time, Borges's first narrative work, 'Men Fought', 'Hombres pelearon', inaugurates a long and complex network (*réseau* in Lafon) of pieces on a challenge between knife-fighters. Borges recognized it as archetypal within his work: 'The story is one I have been retelling, with small variations, ever since. It is the tale of the motiveless, or disinterested, duel—of courage for its own sake' (Aut 232). At the centre of the web is 'Man on Pink Corner', 'El hombre de la esquina rosada', which has been described as the 'favourite text of those who have understood nothing about Borges's work' (Lafon 99). There are four main moments in the series: 'Police Legend', 'Leyenda policial', was published in *Martín Fierro* in 1927, and in *El idioma de los argentinos* as 'Hombres pelearon' in 1928. 'Men of the Neighbourhoods', 'Hombres de las orillas', was published in *Crítica* in 1933, under the pseudonym Francisco Bustos, and as 'Hombre de la esquina rosada' in *A Universal History of Iniquity*, in 1935. The 1952 text 'The Challenge', 'El desafío', included in *Evaristo Carriego*, gives new versions of the story told in 'Hombres pelearon'. 'The Story from Rosendo Suárez', 'Historia de Rosendo Suárez', from the 1970 *Brodie's Report*, is explicitly a revisiting of the text of 'Hombre de la esquina rosada'. (There is also a 1950 film script by Bioy Casares and Borges, *Los orilleros*, which clearly reworks many of the *topoi* previously established, but perhaps we can do without this further complication.) The process of rewriting these narratives is one of inversion, expansion, and speculation, modulation of narrative voice and perspective. We witness the complexity and reflexivity of the mature Borges narrative emerging in the process.

'Men Fought' is a short, two-page narration recounting how El Chileno, a fighter from South Buenos Aires, travels north to challenge Pedro el Mentao, and is killed by him in a knife-fight. It is an impersonal third-person narration, though, as Lafon points out, it has many characteristics of the poetry of the period. Take the stylized counterpoint between physical description of the *arrabal* (neighbourhood) and the personified knives which do the fighting:

'Hablo de cuando el arrabal, rosado de tapias, era también relampagueado de acero'; 'I speak of when the *arrabal*, rose-coloured with fences, was also lightning with steel' (IA 133). In 'El desafío' after telling two similar stories, Borges makes explicit what Lafon sees as the primitive model here: 'En ambas el provocador resulta derrotado'; 'The challenger is defeated in both' (I 167). In the story of Welceslao Suárez, who tears off his own hand in the fight against his younger challenger, Borges sees all the qualities of the epic or even chivalresque tale, which are absent from what he provocatively calls the 'peleas de borracho', 'drunken fights' (I 167) of the national masterpiece *Martín Fierro*.

Borges recounts how it took him six years of elaboration to go from the earlier piece to 'Man on Pink Corner', which he presents almost as a homage to an individual who had been important in *Evaristo Carriego*: 'A friend of mine, don Nicolás Paredes, a former political boss and professional gambler of the Northside, had died, and I wanted to record something of his voice, his anecdotes and his particular way of telling them. I slaved over every page, sounding out each sentence and striving to phrase it in his exact tones' (Aut 238). He had to hide his labours from his mother, who disapproved of such low-life themes. Indeed the story is replete with virtually untranslatable local language, e.g. 'La milonga déle loquiar, y déle bochinchar en las casas, y traía olor a madreselvas el viento. Linda al ñudo la noche' (I 334; CF 49). The geographical poles of the first story are reversed, and courage is replaced by cowardice. The simple dualism of the first story is decentred when a third actor is introduced, who takes over the role of the hero, with considerable theatricality. The narrative ploy is one which Borges would use again to great effect: the identity of the narrator is only fully revealed at the end, and turns out to have been one of the protagonists. He addresses his account to an 'ustedes', to listeners who he assumes know little of the world described, and his main addressee is revealed in the last lines to be 'Borges'.

Rosendo Juárez, el Pegador, 'hombre de Paredes', 'one of Paredes's men', is challenged in a *boliche* by Francisco Real, el Corralero. Rosendo inexplicably refuses to fight, though the narrator could not hear what was said, and when his much coveted girlfriend hands him his knife, suggesting he might need it, he throws it into the Maldonado River, which conveniently flowed outside the window. For the narrator, Rosendo had been a model: 'we boys in the neighborhood would imitate him right down to the way he spat' (CF 45),[29] and witnessing his cowardice, blushed with shame. The Corralero,

---

[29] 'los mozos de la Villa le copiábamos hasta el modo de escupir' (I 331).

is 'confuso', disconcerted, by such breaking of the rules, and claims to feel such 'asco', digust, at the cowardice that he refrains from butchering his rival, and walks into the night with his booty: la Lujanera. The narrator also goes out and returns to the dance; shortly afterwards la Lujanera returns with el Corralero, who is dying from a knife wound received from an unknown person who had challenged him in the dark. The narrator intervenes to defend la Lujanera against the accusation that she was the murderer, adopting the stylized arrogant drawl of the local tough guy: 'medio desganado de guapo' (I 336). He concludes by telling how he returned to his house, where la Lujanera was waiting for him, her third attachment of the night, and slyly reveals that he had been the killer of el Corralero. The narrator takes the place of the original pair in the contest as a sort of supplement which disturbs the original binary structure, which had already been reversed; he introduces a fake theatricality, mimicry, and additional literariness, which is augmented by the fact that he is both protagonist and decidedly cunning narrator.

'The Story from Rosendo Juárez' retells the story from yet another perspective, that of the apparent coward Rosendo, and expands the mirrorings of the previous story into more complex internal mirrorings between characters, which seem in turn to reflect the self-conscious specularity of its intertextual mirroring and rewriting. The *lunfardo* slang and stylized *criollismo* have vanished in the later story. The story is told by an ageing Rosendo, who is pleased that the mythical Maldonado had been channelled underground and made part of the Buenos Aires sewer system, and seeks respectability by living in San Telmo, a 'barrio de orden', 'respectable area' (II 414). His love of progress seems to mirror that of the reformed *gaucho* outlaw Martín Fierro at the end of the second part of the narrative poem, the *Vuelta*, who has veered towards the political views of Sarmiento, the enemy of the *gauchos*. The narration is not simply the first-person narration of the previous story, addressed to Borges, but is framed by Borges's account of his meeting with Rosendo, who wished to set the story right, and give the true version of events, in the process denouncing Paredes who would tell lies, not so much to deceive people, as to make a better story. Rosendo had read Borges's 'novel' about him in much the same way that don Quixote, in the second part of Cervantes's novel, has read not only the first part of the account of his life, but also the apocryphal version of Avellaneda.

Rosendo recounts his first knife-fight as a youth. He had been challenged by Garmendia, an older and more experienced man, but manages to kill him. He thus conforms to the original paradigm of 'Men Fought' and 'The Challenge'. That is, however, except for the fact that he had taken advantage of his opponent's stumbling as they made their way to the fighting place to attack him by surprise. He is caught by the police because of the ring he had stolen from Garmendia, echoing the ring finger severed from el Corralero, but released in exchange for becoming a 'guapo electoral', a thug used to fix elections, of Paredes. (He also hated the Radicals, he adds, the long-standing political party of the Borges's, and their founder Alem, a friend of Borges's grandfather Isidoro Suárez.) He is approached by a dear and ageing friend Luis Irala, who talks of challenging the younger man who had stolen his wife. Rosendo argues that it is folly to challenge a highly proficient fighter, whom he could not defeat, for the sake of a woman who no longer loved him. Irala is killed in a futile contest which mirrors the model of Rosendo's fight with Garmendia. The mirroring destroys any prestige the model might have for Rosendo, who later feels *asco*, disgust, at the bloody spectacle of a cock fight, inverting the logic of El Corralero's feeling disgust at Rosendo's refusal of violence in 'Man on Pink Corner'. On the fateful night recounted first in this latter story, Rosendo, on seeing El Corralero, realizes that 'we were dead ringers for each other', and in the strutting arrogance of the other sees himself reflected in an embarrassing mirror: 'I looked at that swaggering drunk just spoiling for a fight, and it was as if I was looking at myself in a mirror, and all of a sudden I was ashamed of myself' (CF 363).[30] The shame he feels inverts that felt by the narrator of the previous story at the refusal to fight.

The intertextual reflection and inversion of the previous story (and its antecedents) is thus echoed in the three internal mirrorings: between the Garmendia–Juárez fight and that between Irala and Aguilera; between both and the cock fight; between Rosendo and his challenger El Corralero. In Rosendo's awareness of being a character in a novel, the simple knife-fight veers towards the metaphysical, as outlined in the essay 'Magias parciales del *Quijote*': 'Why does it worry us that don Quixote should be a reader of the *Quixote*, and Hamlet a spectator of *Hamlet*? I think I have found the cause: inversions of this sort suggest that if characters in a fiction may be its readers and spectators, we, its readers and spectators, may be fictitious.'[31] The youths of 'Man on Pink Corner' had modelled themselves on Rosendo, a real individual for them; Rosendo is aware of having modelled himself on a literary character by Eduardo Gutiérrez, Juan Moreira, setting off an endless

---

[30] 'éramos de una misma estampa ... En ese botarate provocador me vi como en un espejo y me dio vergüenza' (II 413).

[31] ¿Por qué nos inquieta que don Quijote sea lector del *Quijote*, y Hamlet, espectador de *Hamlet*? Creo haber dado con la causa: tales inversions sugieren que si los caracteres de una ficción pueden ser lectores o espectadores, nosotros, sus lectores o espectadores, podemos ser ficticios' (II 47).

regression of derivation: 'For years I pretended to be some kind of Moreira
– who in his day was probably imitating some other stage show gaucho' (CF
361).[32] (The line between life and literature is further blurred by a lovely
guest appearance in the story. The young man in black who wrote verses on
'slums and filth, subjects which were of no interest to decent folk', and who
wrote Rosendo's letter of reference from Paredes, is clearly both a friend of
Borges and a character in one of his works: *Evaristo Carriego*.)

The duel sequence outlined here leads to intertextuality and metaphysics.
As Rosendo repeats the gestures of past fighters like Moreira, the *truco*
players repeat the hands of remote generations. The metaphysical sequence
inaugurated by 'Feeling in Death' and 'Truco' ends up in the duel between
warring concepts of time, and of the individual. Such rivalries can be traced
through Borges's work as a key structural principle.

Texts at war

Many if not most of Borges's texts are based on the duel, opposition, the
struggle between rivals. It is important to stress from the beginning that the
opponents depend one on the other to the extent that they become doubles, or
two essential aspects of one function. Literal duels are common enough: the
knife-fight on the pampa in 'The South'; the rewriting of the end of *Martín
Fierro* whereby Fierro dies in a duel with the brother of the negro he had
killed; the fights between policemen and outlaws in 'A Biography of Tadeo
Isidoro Cruz'. Perhaps the most outrageously brutal is 'The Other Duel', 'El
otro duelo', where two men who hated each other so obsessively that they
each became the slave to the other are to be executed after a battle between
Colorados and Blancos in Uruguay. Their throats are cut and bets are placed
on which can run further before dying.

Real literary rivalries are a variation on the theme. The one alluded to
most frequently at the beginning of Borges's career is that between Góngora
and Quevedo, but the one he felt most personally was that between Gómez
de la Serna and Cansinos Asséns, the second of which he had considered his
master in Spain. Their relationship is described as a military battle:

> Friendship binds people together; hatred joins them too. Gómez de la Serna
> and Rafael Cansinos Asséns are two names who have become brothers

---

[32] 'Durante años me hice el Moreira, que a lo mejor se habrá hecho en su tiempo algún
otro gaucho de circo' (II 412).

through a war-like fraternity, like swords crossed in the heat of battle. The eternal discord within art has become embodied in those tacitly, but viscerally opposed adversaries: in the thick-set, sturdy and corporeal writer from Madrid ... and the Andalusian, as tall as the flames from a raging fire.[33]

Borges is tempted to deconstruct the opposition between them: the practitioner of fantasy is tragic in his fight against his Castilian seriousness, while there is an element of game in the tragic writer's search for metaphors. He finally prefers to leave the opposition as a banner to be flourished by the young followers of one or the other.

Literary and philosophical schools follow the same pattern. The 'expression of personal truth in pre-established forms' of classicism faces the 'spiritual vehemence' of the baroque.[34] *Culteranismo* with its focus on language faces *conceptismo* with its stress on ideas. The contest between Aristotelianism and Platonism is perhaps the most important for in it the status of language and its categories as truth or approximation to reality through arbitrary signs is played out:

> Coleridge observes that all men are born Aristotelians or Platonists. The latter feel that classes, orders and genera are realities; the former feel that they are generalizations; for the latter, language is no more than an approximate game of symbols; for the former it is the map of the universe. The Platonist knows that the world is in some way a cosmos, an order; for the Aristotelian, that order may be an error or a fiction woven by our incomplete knowledge.[35]

In the later stories, the intellectual rivalries are largely invented. In 'The Theologians', John of Pannonia and Aureliano spend their lives in polemics which range structured time, e.g. circular time against time as flow, time ordered by patterns against time characterized by change and difference.

---

[33] 'La amistad une; también el odio sabe juntar. Dos nombres hermanados por una fraternidad belicosa como de espadas que en ardimiento de contienda se cruzan son los de Gómez de la Serna y Rafael Cansinos Asséns. La discordia eterna del arte se ha incorporado en esos adversarios tácitos y entrañalmente opuestos; en el madrileño tupido, espeso y carnal ... y en el andaluz, alto como una llamada de amotinada hoguera' ('La traducción de un incidente', Inq 17).

[34] 'dicción de la verdad personal en formas prefijadas' (Inq 20).

[35] 'Observa Coleridge que todos los hombres nacen aristotélicos o platónicos. Los últimos sienten que las clases, los órdenes y los géneros son realidades; los primeros, que son generalizaciones; para éstos, el lenguaje no es otra cosa que un aproximativo juego de símbolos; para aquéllos es el mapa del universo. El platónico sabe que el universo es de algún modo un cosmos, un orden; ese orden, para el aristotélico, puede ser un error o una ficción de nuestro conocimiento parcial' (II 96).

When they die God considers that they are one and the same person. One concept of time necessarily implies the other. In 'The Duel' two close friends, both artists, Clara Glencairn and Marta Pizarro, fight out a secret battle around the split between abstract and representational art. When one dies the other's career becomes meaningless, and she ceases to paint. In many of the central stories, the hostile doubling is between interdependent roles: detective and criminal, detective and plodding policeman in 'Death and the Compass'; traitor and hero, coward and brave man in 'The Shape of the Sword' and 'The Other Death'; intellectual and soldier in 'The South' and elsewhere; poet and mathematician in 'Ibn-Hakam al-Bokhari'. In other stories the struggle is between warring concepts and those who embody them, such as Sarmiento's binary of civilization and barbarism in 'Story of the Warrior and the Captive Maiden'.

Taking this structure to its most abstract, archetypal almost, many of his stories depend on the play between sameness or analogy and difference. As in so many places, Emerson defines Borges's thought. In his essay on Plato, he stresses how thought must embrace both unity and variety simultaneously, like the two sides of the medal of Jove:

> Philosophy is the account which the human mind gives to itself of the constitution of the world. Two cardinal facts lie forever at the base; the one, and the two. – 1. Unity, or Identity; and, 2. Variety. We unite all things, by perceiving the law which pervades them; by perceiving the superficial differences, and the profound resemblances. But every mental act, – this very perception of identity or oneness, recognizes the difference of things. Oneness and otherness. It is impossible to speak, or to think, without embracing both. (Emerson, 637)

The play is often between a world where no human structuring is involved, and one ordered by analogy, plot, and language. Clear examples are the difference between the desert and the garden in 'Averroës' Search', between the divine labyrinth of the desert and the human labyrinth in 'The Two Kings and the Two Labyrinths'. In 'The Lottery in Babylon' the human symbolic scheme of the initial lottery is opposed to its final expansion where it becomes indistinguishable from the infinitely complex functioning of the world. In 'The Library of Babel', the virtually infinite world of all the possible combinations of letters, where phrases only coincide with human languages by chance, is tacitly opposed to human libraries, which are written in codified, human languages. The mind of Funes, in 'Funes, His Memory', is based almost entirely on difference: he cannot forget details and thus grasp analogy, which is one of the two dimensions of language. His mental world is contrasted with the forgetful, but infinitely readable, version of 'Borges' in the story. On the other extreme from undifferentiated chaos, we have the magical or divine reduction of plurality to a minute symbol: the fourteen-word phrase in 'The Writing of the God', the coin in 'The Zahir', which is the whole universe. 'The Aleph' is the mirror construct, where no reduction takes place, and every aspect of the world is simultaneously visible. Literature seems to lie between the dangerous extremes of the Zahir and the Aleph. Literary plots, like theology or *el truco*, are codified, often magical structures set against the chance, randomness, and oppression of everyday life. In 'Death and the Compass' the murder of Yarmolinsky was chance, a meaningless bungled burglary. The detective, the criminal and Borges conspire to give it meaning by writing it into a plot of Jewish mysticism. Literary plotting and political plotting are often teasingly linked. The most obvious example is 'Theme of the Traitor and the Hero', where the political history of Ireland is staged and rewritten according to the plots of Shakespeare's *Macbeth* and *Julius Caesar*.

Borges theorizes the link between literary plots and analogical magic in 'Narrative Art and Magic'. The 'overwhelming disorder of the real world' is set against the work of art 'which should be a rigorous scheme of attentions, echoes, and affinities'. 'Every episode', he continues, 'in a careful narration is a premonition' (TL 81).[36] Rather than trying to reproduce the endless complexity of the real, art should espouse the precise logic of magic:

> I have described two causal procedures: the natural or incessant result of endless, uncontrollable causes and effects; and magic, in which every lucid and determined detail is a prophecy. In the novel, I think that the only possible integrity lies in the latter. Let the former be left to psychological simulations. (TL 81–2)[37]

[36] 'Ese recelo ... es impertinente o inútil en el asiático desorden del mundo real, no así en una novela, que debe ser un juego preciso de vigilancias, ecos y afinidades' ('El arte narrativo y la magia', I 231).

[37] 'He distinguido dos procesos causales: el natural, que es el resultado incesante de incontrolables e infinitas operaciones; el mágico, donde profetizan los pormenores, lúcido y limitado. En la novela, pienso que la única posible honradez está con el segundo. Quede el primero para la simulación psicológica' (I 232).

II
KEY WORKS

From book review to fiction: 'The Approach to Al-Mu'tasim'

'The Approach to Al-Mu'tasim' ('El acercamiento a Almotásim'), written in 1935, is the starting point of Borges's mature fictions. Borges saw it in this light:

> [It] is both a hoax *and* a pseudo-essay. It purports to be a review of a book published originally in Bombay three years earlier. I endowed its fake second edition with a real publisher, Victor Gollancz, and a preface by a real writer, Dorothy L. Sayers. But the author and the book are entirely my own invention. I gave the plot and details of some chapters – borrowing from Kipling and working in the twelfth-century Persian mystic Faridud-Din Attar – and then carefully pointed out its shortcomings. The story appeared the next year in a volume of my essays, *Historia de la eternidad* (*A History of Eternity*), buried at the back of the book together with an article on the 'Art of Insult'. Those who read 'The Approach to Al-Mu'tasim' took it at face value, and one of my friends [Bioy Casares] even ordered a copy from London. It was not until 1942 that I openly published it as a short story in my first story collection, *El jardín de senderos que se bifurcan* ... it now seems to me to foreshadow and even to set the pattern for those tales that were somehow awaiting me, and upon which my reputation as a storyteller was to be based. (Aut 239–40)

The piece presents itself then as a book review, though its title is not accompanied by the name of the author, as was his normal practice in reviews. It is the review of a novel which Borges is simultaneously writing and summarizing in the story. The title is both that of Borges's story and the invented text reviewed. It inaugurates Borges's fruitful conceit of the conflation of reading and writing. In the Foreword to *The Garden of Forking Paths*, he writes:

> It is a laborious madness and an impoverishing one, the madness of composing vast books – setting out in five hundred pages an idea that can be perfectly related orally in five minutes. The better way to go about it is

to pretend that those books already exist, and offer a summary, a commentary on them. (F 5)[1]

He reminds us of this practice in Carlyle's *Sartor Resartus* and Butler's *The Fair Haven*, but comments that these two did in fact end up writing their full books, whereas, 'a more reasonable, more inept, and more lazy man, I have chosen to write notes on *imaginary* books'.[2] Gérard Genette points out that this practice is the mirror of what happens in 'Pierre Menard', where the author writes an existing text:

> Writing from his own resources a rigorously literal *Quixote*, Menard allegorizes reading considered as, or disguised as, writing. By attributing his stories to others, Borges, on the contrary, presents his writing as an act of reading, disguises his writing as reading. These two practices ... are complementary, and the very soul of hypertextual activity.[3]

Following on from Genette, Eduardo Ramos-Izquierdo has written the most rigorous analysis of the story's 'hypertextuality' in his splendid 230-page study of a story of ten paragraphs.

Borges's story is generically hybrid: story and review. The supposed novel he is reviewing is in the first paragraph accused of 'hybridity', 'hibridación' (F 26; I 414), in that it is a combination of the detective novel and an allegorical poem. Various texts by Kipling are mentioned by Borges and his critics, but in this context it is *Kim* which springs most readily to mind as a general source. In that novel, in the interminable trekking of Kim and his Buddhist lama master through the wide geography of Northern India, the political intrigue and spying of the colonial 'Great Game' are inextricably intertwined with the search for the mystical River. Both novel and story are quests; the story tells of the search by a Bombay law student, through wild and diverse adventures across India, for an ultimately superior being through his reflections in lesser individuals. As he approaches the inconceivable Al-Muta'sim,

---

[1] 'Desvarío laborioso y empobrecedor el de componer vastos libros; el de explayar en quinientas páginas una idea cuya perfecta exposición oral cabe en pocos minutos. Mejor procedimiento es simular que esos libros ya existen y ofrecer un resumen, un comentario' (I 429).

[2] 'Más razonable, más inepto, más haragán, he preferido la escritura de notas sobre libros imaginarios' (I 429).

[3] 'Ecrivant de son propre fonds un Quichotte rigoureusement littérale, Ménard [*sic*] allégorise la lecture considérée comme, ou déguisée en écriture. Attribuant à d'autres l'invention de ses contes, Borges présente au contraire son écriture comme une lecture, déguise en lecture son écriture. Ces deux conduites ... sont complémentaires [et] l'âme même de l'activité hypertextuelle' (Genette 296).

there is a suggestion that he may come face to face with himself. The notion prefigures the end of 'Death and the Compass' where Lönnrot faces his double Red Scharlach, and the haunting Afterword of *The Maker*:

> A man sets out to draw the world. As the years go by, he peoples a space with images of provinces, kingdoms, mountains, bays, ships, islands, fishes, rooms, instruments, stars, horses, and individuals. A short time before he dies, he discovers that that patient labyrinth of lines traces the lineaments of his own face. (CF 327)[4]

For the Idealist in Borges, it is doubtful that one can go beyond the confines of one's own mind and perceptions.

The story alternates between the summarizing of the plot of the reviewed novel and the metatextual commentaries on its construction, publishing history, sources, and existing reviews on it. The two dimensions of the story are not, of course, as separate as this might suggest. The structure of the first two paragraphs, for example, on the history of criticism of the novel and its publication, reflects the retrogressive search for Al-Muta'sim. In the first paragraph three individual reviewers are reported to have made more or less identical points about the novel. The first two are real English writers, Philip Guedalla and Mr Cecil Roberts, while the third is the reviewer–author–narrator of Borges's story. The first two, comments the reviewer, write in different dialects. Guedalla writes sarcastically and dismissively that the novel is 'a rather uncomfortable combination' (the original English is provided here together with the Spanish 'translation' to convince us further of the authenticity of the source) 'of one of those Islamic allegorical poems that seldom fail to interest their translator and one of these detective novels that inevitably surpass John H. Watson's' (F 26).[5] Roberts is more measured, scholarly and precise in his analysis: he detects 'the dual, and implausible, influence of Wilkie Collins and the illustrious twelfth-century Persian poet Farīd al-dīn Attār' (F 26).[6] Significantly Borges puts the second critic first: he had repeated the first's ideas 'pero en un dialecto colérico', 'in choleric

---

[4] 'Un hombre se propone la tarea de dibujar el mundo. A lo largo de los años puebla un espacio con imágenes de provincias, de reinos, de montañas, de bahías, de naves, de islas, de peces, de habitaciones, de instrumentos, de astros, de caballos y de personas. Poco antes de morir, descubre que ese paciente laberinto de líneas traza la imagen de su cara' (II 232).

[5] 'una combinación algo incómoda (*a rather uncomfortable combination*) de esos poemas alegóricos del Islam que raras veces dejan de interesar a su traductor y de aquellas novelas policiales que inevitablemente superan a John H. Watson' (I 414).

[6] 'la doble, inverosímil tutela de Wilkie Collins y del ilustre persa del siglo doce, Ferid Eddin Attar' (I 414).

accents'. The inversion reflects the student's search through reflections. The change from one 'dialect' to another prefigures the difference between the two editions of the novel: the first has more of the characteristics of a novel, the second of allegory. The third voice, that of the reviewer-Borges, comes last, though of course he is the first (and only) writer of the story. He offers a possible source for the hybridity: Chesterton, one of Borges's favourite writers, only to dismiss the idea.

The second paragraph examines the various editions of the novel of the lawyer Mir Bahadur Alí. (Ramos-Izquierdo persuasively points out the echoes of the similarly sonorous Cide Hamete Benengeli, Cervantes's apocryphal first author of *Don Quijote*.) The cover declares it to be the first detective novel published by a native of Bombay City. (The much earlier Kipling was also a native of Bombay.) The many Indian journals where the fake book was reviewed are all real publications. A second, illustrated, edition, entitled *The Conversation with the Man Called Al-Mu'tasim*, is the one that the reviewer has, 'with the (perhaps merciful) omission of the illustrations' [!].[7] He has not been able to find the first edition, 'which I suspect is greatly superior', 'que presiento muy superior'. The missing *editio princeps* is clearly equivalent to the missing first man Al-Mu'tasim, source of all light. The history of the publication mirrors the plot.

The next three paragraphs tell/summarize the plot of the novel. A student, who has lost the Muslim faith of his family, becomes involved in a riot on the tenth night of Muharram, and kills, or believes he has killed, a Hindu. The riot is seen as being between 'God the indivisible against the gods', unity against plurality, a fundamental tension in Borges, and also a prefiguration of the search of the student for the one source within the vast disorder of India. This first part clearly follows, and cites, Kipling's story 'On the City Wall'. Later in the story an 'inquisitor', which sounds rather like the author of *Inquisiciones*, is reported to have suggested this source, but the author dismisses the similarity as inevitable in any description of Muharram. The student takes refuge in a circular tower, a *dakhma* where the Pharsis left their deceased to be devoured by vultures, in a garden. On the tower, he meets a vile character, urinating vigorously as he squats in the moonlight, whose profession is to steal the gold teeth from the corpses. The thief rails against a *malka-sansi* woman, from the caste of thieves. The student 'reasons that the wrath and hatred of a man so thoroughly despicable is the equivalent of a hymn of praise' and so 'resolves … to find this woman' (F 28); 'resuelve

---

[7] 'con omisión – quizá misericordiosa – de las ilustraciones' (I 414).

... buscarla'.[8] Ramos Izquierdo shows that this passage derives directly from another text by Kipling, 'The Vengeance of Lal Beg'. Given Borges's liking for offering his own development of others' plots, Ramos has the corpse thief as the abandoned husband of the *malka-sansi* out for revenge. He also resolves, faced with the threat posed by his possible murder, to 'lose himself in India'.

There follows a dizzying enumeration of the peripeteia of his journeys in eight dramatic and exotic phrases, each introduced by a first-person verb in the present tense, which purport to summarize the next nineteen chapters, before he ends up back in Bombay a few yards from the garden. The circularity suggests the student's possible vision of himself at the end of the novel. The reviewer Borges sums up the plot, and recounts an encounter which seems to be a curious repetition of his encounter with the thief on the tower. In a detestable and vile man he suddenly sees 'some mitigation of the evil' (F 29), 'alguna mitigación de infamia' (I 416), just as Robinson Crusoe sees the footprint in the sand.[9] He muses that the mitigation must be the reflection of a certain goodness in a better person, and concludes that *'somewhere in the world there is a man from whom this clarity, this brightness, emanates'* (F 29).[10] He resolves to search out that man, as he had resolved to search out the woman from the thief caste.

(In the light of the strange repetition of the two vile men and the repeated resolution to search, I wonder whether another echo, lost in the translation, is significant. After talking to the man on the tower of death, the student is 'aniquilado' (annihilated, i.e. exhausted) and falls asleep. The last stage of the journey towards enlightenment in the Persian poem is later revealed to be 'Aniquilación'. Might he not die on the tower and dream the rest of the story? This would make it equivalent in structure to 'The South'. The circularity of the tower has long been commented on; the ascent of the tower would prefigure the 'ascenso místico' described later. The student takes refuge in the tower, 'busca amparo' (I 415); the name Al-Mu'tasim is later revealed etymologically to signify 'El buscador de amparo' (I 417), which might back the hypothesis of his death and dream, or might just point to the oneness of searcher and sought.)

---

8 'Arguye que el rencor de un hombre tan minuciosamente vil importa un elogio. Resuelve – sin mayor esperanza – buscarla.' (I 415).

9 The 'miraculous shock', 'milagroso espanto' he feels seems to echo the speculation that Valéry's M. Teste will have a similar moment of enlightenment: 'quelle heureuse et sainte terreur, quelle épouvante salutaire' (Valéry, 34).

10 'En algún punto de la tierra hay un hombre de quien procede esa claridad' (I 416).

Ramos-Izquierdo notes the clear echo of Borges's interest in gnosticism in the ascent of the student towards the ultimate source of light. Borges had written about the ideas handled here in his 'A Defense of Basilides the False', 'Una vindicación del falso Basílides', in *Discusión*. The ultimate Divinity inhabits timeless Plenitude, *pleroma*. From him, by emanation and degradation, a series of three hundred and sixty-five heavens, with progressively less powerful powers or *aeons*, culminates in the creation by a demiurge of the fallen earth of men. The student's ascent would be a reversal of the fall, a return through the reflections of reflections to Unity. The student gradually follows the trace of brilliance through countless men, until one day he stands before a bead curtain, and hears the unbelievable voice of Al-Mu'tasim, at which point the novel ends.

The reviewer goes on to discuss what he knows of the difference between the two editions of the novel, and takes up a theme which had occupied him in various previous and later essays: that of the novel and allegory ('H. G. Wells and Parables', 'Nathaniel Hawthorne', 'From Allegories to Novels'). In this last essay, he writes that 'Allegory is a fable of abstractions, as the novel is a fable of individuals' (TL 339).[11] The second edition falls into the category of allegory, suggesting an uninteresting 'single, unitary God who molds Himself to the dissimilarities of mankind' (F 30).[12] In the first edition, Al-Mu'tasim is a pilgrim, and in the second this leads to an 'extravagant theology': the idea that 'the Almighty is also in search of Someone, and that Someone, in search of a yet superior … Someone, and so on, to the End – or better yet, the Endlessness of time. Or perhaps cyclically' (F 30–1).[13] Here Bahadur Ali falls for the 'basest of art's temptations: the temptation to be a genius'.[14] The idea of infinite regression is one to which Borges returns, in 'The Circular Ruins' for example. The idea on genius seems to come from M. Teste: 'le génie *est facile*' (Valéry, 22).

The final paragraph before the long footnote turns to the sources of the novel. The importance of Farīd al-dīn Attār's *Conference of the Birds* is underplayed as the reviewer compares it to the parallels between Homer's *Odyssey* and Joyce's *Ulysses*. He had never understood why the critics had been so fixated on the insignificant points of contact. The importance of 'On the City Wall' is underplayed with similar duplicity. T. S. Eliot is roped in to

---

[11] 'La alegoría es fábula de abstracciones, como la novela lo es de individuos' ('De las alegorías a las novelas', II 124).

[12] 'un Dios unitario que se acomoda a las desigualdades humanas' (I 417).

[13] 'el Todopoderoso está en busca de Alguien, y ese Alguien de Alguien superior … y así hasta el Fin – o mejor el Sinfín – del Tiempo, o en forma cíclica' (I 417).

[14] 'la más burda de las tentaciones del arte: la de ser un genio' (I 417).

criticize the inexistent novel, comparing it to Spenser's *The Faërie Queen*, in which the heroine never appears: like Al-Mu'tasim, of course. Invented interventions are combined with real ones with the mention of R. W. Church's, who actually did make this point on Spenser. The real and invented opinions of British critics, critics in India, an 'inquisitor', T. S. Eliot, and Church are followed by an 'I' who humbly suggests another precursor: the Kabbalist Isaac Luria, and his notion of transmigration called *Ibbûr*. The significance is clear. Souls which have not fulfilled the commandments are banished into strange forms of existence, but can be helped by souls with which they form a sort of family group to return to a higher form of existence in preparation for their reintegration into the soul of Adam, the father of mankind.[15]

A long, erudite footnote gives the plot of *Conference of the Birds*, which offers a clear interpretation of the end of the novel. The King of Birds, the Sīmurg, whose name means 'thirty birds', drops one of its feathers in China. To escape from the state of anarchy, other birds set off on a pilgrimage to find the palace of their king on the circular mountain which surrounds the Earth. As the last thirty birds approach the mountain, 'they see that they are the Sīmurg and that the Sīmurg is each, and all, of them'. Borges has the information from Richard Burton's translation and the study of Margaret Smith. In parentheses after this explanation comes a brief but important passage from the *Enneads* of the third-century neo-Platonist Plotinus. Fishburn sums up his philosophy: 'According to Plotinus all forms of existence derive from the One and all strive ultimately to return to their ultimate source and remain there' (FH 190). Borges talks of Plotinus's 'paradisal extension of the principle of identity'. The passage is actually a radically shortened version of the passage he had originally reproduced in 'History of Eternity': 'Everything in the intelligible heavens is everywhere. Any thing is all things. The sun is all stars and each star is all stars and the sun' (F 32). These two works cited are clearly related, and the Identity they articulate, glimpsed also in the Kabbalistic notion of restitution to the body of Adam, is encapsulated in Al-Mu'tasim. This cluster of ideas and sources is of great importance for Borges, and related in his mind to the Schopenhauerian notion of the Will, the Platonic archetype, the ecstatic dissolution of self in Whitman and Emerson. In the latter's essay 'Nature', after describing how he becomes nothing, a 'transparent eye-ball', he goes on to declare: 'the currents of the universal being circulate through me; I am part or particle of God' (Emerson, 10).

---

[15] See Alazraki, *Kabbalah*, 25.

Genette talks of 'The Approach' as writing disguised as reading. As we go through the process of its composition carefully, however, the process is again reversed, or rather we see the absolute inseparability of reading and writing. Writing is rewriting, quotation and translation. Again Emerson is pertinent: 'When we are praising Plato, it seems we are praising quotations from Solon, and Sophron, and Philolaus. Be it so. Every book is a quotation; and every house is a quotation out of all forests, and mines, and stone quarries; and every man is a quotation from all his ancestors' (Emerson, 634). The link between ancestors and literary sources is a particularly revealing one for Borges. The romantic notion of originality is thoroughly dismantled in the story. Shakespeare, for Borges and for Emerson, is close to the centre of such debates:

> Shakespeare knew that tradition supplies a better fable than any invention can. If he lost any credit of design, he augmented his resources; and, at that day, our petulant demand for originality was not so much pressed. ... He knows the sparkle of the true stone, and puts it in high place, wherever he finds it. Such is the happy position of Homer, perhaps; of Chaucer, of Saadi. They felt that all wit was their wit. And they are librarians and historiographers, as well as poets. (Emerson, 713–14)

Emerson could easily have been writing about Borges here, poet and librarian. The 'I' of the reviewer–writer which timidly emerges from time to time, is finally absorbed into the literary continuum, just as the nameless student from Bombay is absorbed into the oneness of Al-Mu'tasim.

Fictions Part I: *The Garden of Forking Paths* (1941)

'Pierre Menard, Author of the *Quixote*', 'Pierre Menard, autor del *Quijote*'

'Pierre Menard' was written in 1939 as Borges was recovering from the head wound and subsequent septicaemia resulting from his accedent on Christmas Eve. Borges himself contributed to the mythology behind the story in his 'Autobiographical Essay'. Fearing for his intellectual powers, and not daring to try to write a book review, he decided to write 'something I had never really done before' (Aut 243): a story. Thus the Borges-story writer was born, reborn from the near death experience. Of course, Borges had already written stories, and a rather similar exercise four years previously in 'Al-Mu'tasim'. It is also seen by critics as the inspiration for a whole new critical understanding of intertextuality. Lafon shows how it inspired Genette, his 'Utopies Littéraires' and *Palimpsestes*, the *Nouvelle Critique*, and his own *Borges ou la réécriture*. It is (rightly) seen as a predecessor of Barthes's notion of the 'death of the author', and North American equivalents. In 'The Approach', Borges pretends to write a review and summary of a novel which he is in fact simultaneously inventing and writing himself. In 'Pierre Menard' an internal French narrator tells of his friend Pierre Menard who had somehow rewritten verbatim, not copied, two chapters and part of a chapter of a real novel written some three hundred and twenty years previously: Cervantes's *Don Quijote*.

It may be useful to start with the final paragraph of the story, which clearly explains the mechanism behind its writing: deliberate anachronisms and erroneous attributions. Borges attributes the *Quijote* to an early twentieth-century Frenchman, and imagines what it might mean coming from his pen and mind.

> Menard has (perhaps unwittingly) enriched the slow and rudimentary act of reading by means of a new technique – the technique of deliberate anachronism and fallacious attribution. That technique, requiring infinite patience and concentration, encourages us to read the *Odyssey* as though it came

after the *Aeneid*, to read Mme Henri Bachelier's *Le jardin du Centaure* as
though it were written by Mme Henri Bachelier [I assume this means that
someone else had written it for her]. This technique fills the calmest books
with adventure. Attributing the *Imitatio Christi* to Louis Ferdinand Céline
or James Joyce – is that not sufficient renovation of those faint spiritual
admonitions? (F 42–3)[1]

Translation, as we saw with the translators of the *Arabian Nights*, has
a similar effect in swerving away from the original text by applying new
literary conventions and world views. Borges has already commented in an
early essay, 'Literary Pleasure', that our anachronistic reading of the *Quijote*
can improve it by turning what was originally a trite commonplace into a
colourful and original exclamation: 'Time – Cervantes' friend – has sagely
revised his drafts' (TL 30).[2] Our understanding of older texts is inevitably
done through the lens of intervening literature. Thus, Cervantes contrasts
chivalresque romances with the poor provincial reality of his time, while
for Menard, this reality has become something altogether more literary and
exotic, out of Bizet and Mérimée: 'the land of Carmen during the century
that saw the Battle of Lepanto and the plays of Lope de Vega' (F 39). Menard
had thus been pretty heroic in avoiding talk of gypsies and conquistadors and
Philip IIs; he puts the exoticism of Flaubert's historical novel *Salammbô* to
shame. Remember that there are no camels in the *Koran*. From the time of
the *Universal History*, Borges had considered reading to be a later, and more
sophisticated, act than writing: 'I sometimes think that good readers are poets
as singular, and as awesome, as great authors themselves. ... Reading, mean-
while, is an activity subsequent to writing—more resigned, more civil, more
intellectual' (CF 3).[3] The invisible work of Menard was the writing of chapters 9 and 38 of the *Quijote*, and a fragment of 22. Chapter 38 contains the

---

[1]   Menard (acaso sin quererlo) ha enriquecido mediante una técnica nueva el arte dete-
nido y rudimentario de la lectura: la técnica del anacronismo deliberado y de las atribuciones
erróneas. Esa técnica de aplicación infinita nos insta a recorrer la *Odisea* como si fuera posterior a la *Eneida* y el libro *Le jardin du Centaure* de Madame Henri Bachelier como si fuera de
Madame Henri Bachelier. Esta técnica puebla de aventura los libros más calmosos. Atribuir a
Louis Ferdinand Céline o a James Joyce la *Imitación de Cristo* ¿no es una suficiente renovación
de esos tenues avisos espirituales? (I 450).

[2]   'El tiempo – amigo de Cervantes – ha sabido corregirle las pruebas' ('La fruición literaria', IA 97). For a similar meditation, dated 1955, on our now inevitable reading of the
Mancha as no less poetical than Simbad the Sailor or the geography of Ariosto, see 'Parable of
Cervantes and the *Quijote*', 'Parábola de Cervantes y de Quijote', in *El hacedor* (CF 315; II
177).

[3]   'A veces creo que los buenos lectores son cisnes aun más tenebrosos y singulares que
los buenos autores. ... Leer, por lo pronto, es una actividad posterior a la de escribir: más
resignada, más civil, más intelectual' (I 289).

last part of the famous 'Discourse on Arms and Letters', which is commented on in the story extensively, but the others are not described. When we look at them, however, we see that they are not just any bits of the novel rewritten, but an inspiration for the conception of the story. Chapter 22 contains the story of Ginés de Pasamonte, the galley slave who tells Don Quijote that he has written the story of his life, which he presents as destined to overshadow *Lazarillo de Tormes* and all others like it. An invented character explains his writing of an autobiography to an invented character who has gone mad by reading too many novels, and who will later discuss his own status as the hero of a chronicle by Cide Hamete Benengeli (which for the reader might stand for the novel by Cervantes).[4] The doubling and *mise-en-abyme* is already there in the original text.[5] Chapter 9 is even more significant as it deals with the authorship of *El Quijote*. Chapter 8 ends abruptly with Don Quijote and the *vizcaíno* about to bring down their swords on the other's head, and an explanation that the author had not found any more written records of his hero's action. The first author had been rewriting documents about a supposedly real knight. The writer identifying himself as the 'second author' vows to find more documents, and finds them by chance in the street in the Arab manuscript of Cide Hamete Benengeli, which he orders to be translated, and which becomes, presumably, the text of the rest of the novel. The second author, who will soon become the transcriber of the translation of the Moor, casts doubt on his impartiality, because he believes that the people of the Arab nation are prone to lie. He complains that 'historians' should not twist truth, 'cuya madre es la historia' (Cervantes, *Don Quijote*, 110), 'whose mother is history', simply asserting that they should say exactly what happened. Translating, transcribing, the relaying of authors, and unreliability, are already at the base of the *Quijote*. Its practice is echoed and amplified in Borges's text.

'Pierre Menard' is not narrated by Borges, but by a snobbish and pretentious provincial writer who, nevertheless, seems gradually to morph into him. His earlier interventions are thoroughly satirized in a manner similar to that adopted later by Borges and Bioy in their collaborations, or by 'Biorges' in Rodríguez Monegal's coinage. The final paragraph, however, which we have examined, is Borges at his best. The same sort of slippage is seen in Menard's evaluation of the importance of the *Quijote* in one paragraph. He starts by

<hr/>

4   Anthony Close saved me here from an undeliberately anachronistic reading of *Don Quijote* through Unamuno's *Niebla*, and worse.

5   The chapter also contains Don Quijote's condemnation of the right of individuals to imprison others, which Borges claimed, in 'Our Poor Individualism', reconciled him with the Spanish novel as it chimed with a similar moment in *Martín Fierro* and echoes Argentinian anarchistic individualism.

saying that it was a 'contingent work' and 'not necessary' (F 38–9), as might be the case for a Frenchman, but goes on to refer to it as 'the immortal book', and ends by contradicting his first evaluation: its writing in the seventeenth century was a 'reasonable, necessary, perhaps even inevitable undertaking' (F 39).[6] (Lafon mentions these contradictions.) It is finally Borges who is re-reading and rewriting Cervantes's text. Menard's dates echo those of Borges. He published his first poems in 1899, the year of Borges's birth, and presumably died in the same year as his friend dated his account of his work: Nîmes, 1939, the year that Borges actually penned it in Buenos Aires.

The story begins with an introduction to the petty literary atmosphere in Nîmes, continues with an annotated list of the nineteen 'visible' works by Menard, discusses two works which had inspired the rewriting enterprise, and, alternating between the voice of the narrator(–Borges) and a letter from Menard, goes on to describe the process of composition, and offers a comparative reading of two identical passages, by Cervantes and Menard, before concluding. It opens with the internal author, in terms reminiscent of the Dreyfus period, berating a certain Madame Henri Bachelier for publishing, in a Protestant newspaper whose readers were 'few and Calvinist (if not Masonic and circumcised)' (F 33), a deceitful catalogue of Menard's work, with omissions and spurious additions. There is a lovely irony here in the context of a writer one of whose major contributions was the technique of 'fallacious attribution'. He rectifies the catalogue with a definitive one of his own, and lauds the society ladies who protected and promoted Menard and himself. The countess of Bagnoregio broke her 'noble reserve' to endorse his catalogue in the magazine *Luxe*, though he goes on to say that she publishes an annual volume to rectify the press criticism of her, 'inevitably' incited by her own activity.

The catalogue is a curious and daunting amalgam, which according to Borges in the Foreword to *Fictions* is a 'diagram of his mental history'. Fishburn and Hugh's dictionary comes in very handy here. His first publication was a symbolist sonnet published twice, with variations. The important point is the variations: the timid beginning of the virtually infinite variations he would have to essay to coincide with another writer's text. This focus is furthered in his monograph on Lull, who devised an *ars combinatoria* which would combine the basic principles of life to produce answers to important questions. His monograph on the construction of a poetic language largely unrelated to the concepts of ordinary language is presumably again a timid

---

6 'una empresa razonable, necesaria, acaso fatal' (I 448).

start on thinking beyond his own habitual terms of reference. Three pieces are on various attempts to construct a universal language, an enterprise which fascinated Borges as can be seen in his brilliant 'John Wilkins' Analytical Language', which was a declared inspiration for Foucault's *Les Mots et les choses*. Menard writes on Descartes, Leibnitz, Wilkins, and George Boole. In his essay Borges famously illustrates the delirious arbitrariness of such schemes by the (invented) Chinese encyclopaedia which includes the categories 'those drawn with a very fine camel's-hair brush' and 'etcetera' (TL 231).[7] The implications for Menard's own linguistic odyssey are clear enough. Two pieces are on chess; in one he argues for and then against the notion of eliminating one of the rook's pawns. The parallel, apart from the futility of the exercise, would be between the vast number of logical alternatives involved in chess and in choosing from many thousands of words the next one, which would coincide with Cervantes's text. He translates Quevedo's *Aguja de navegar cultos*, the point of which only becomes clear in the light of the second part of the title, which is *con la receta para hacer Soledades en un día*, a recipe for rewriting the works of his rival Góngora in a day. Menard coincides with another longstanding interest of Borges: the paradox of Zeno whereby Achilles can never catch the tortoise, and motion is proved impossible. Leibnitz's refutation of the paradox, and his phrase 'ne craigner point, monsieur, la tortue', 'fear not the tortoise, sir', perhaps plays with the chance of overcoming the abyss of infinity opened up by Zeno, and faced by Menard. Rewriting on a minor, tinkering scale is involved in his transposing Valéry's 'Le Cimetière marin' from decasyllables into Alexandrines. His invective against Valéry was the exact opposite of his own real opinion: a good practice for justifying to himself the writing of the views of a seventeenth-century Spaniard which he might have found abhorrent: this is one reason given later in the story for his surprising decision in favour of arms against letters in the famous discourse. The author excludes from the list, but reproduces in a footnote, Bachelier's listing of a literal translation into French of Quevedo's literal translation into Spanish of St Francis of Sales's *Introduction à la vie dévote*. Borges's suggestion is that the literal translation back into the French would be wildly different from the original. Or is he suggesting that the reason why no copies of the translation can be found is that it was identical and thus invisible? In any case, translation is, as ever, at the centre of Borges's view of literary creation and transmission.

Two texts are cited which illustrate the two opposite methods that Menard

---

[7] 'dibujados con un pincel finísimo de pelo de camello' and 'etcétera' (II 86).

must choose between on embarking on his task. Novalis talks of the reader
or critic's *total identification* with any author. Another work has Christ on
a boulevard, Hamlet on la Cannebière Street in Marseille, Don Quijote on
Wall Street. The author claims that Menard hated such 'useless carnivals'
as the latter, which merely caused 'the plebeian delight in anachronism or
(worse yet) captivating us with the elementary notion that all times and
places are the same, or are different' (F 36).[8] We will see, however, that it is
rather the second option that Menard takes, and should note that in the final
paragraph, 'deliberate anachronism' is one of Menard's greatest legacies.
The two corresponding possible methods for Menard are, after Novalis, to
become Miguel de Cervantes, or to write the *Quijote* as Pierre Menard. All
he would have to do was to know Spanish perfectly, fight against the Moors,
and forget European history between 1602 and 1918! In a gesture worthy of
M. Teste, he rejects his impossible task as too easy, or rather less interesting
than arriving at the text of *Don Quijote* from the experiences and world view
of a twentieth-century Frenchman. The two possibilities, of course, repre-
sent polar opposite notions of reading. One is something like the intentional
fallacy, where a critic might discover the exact, univocal meaning intended
by the author. The other is, anachronistically, an extreme form of death of
the author, deconstruction, and dissemination, where latent meanings of the
text can be liberated from the tyranny of the author; or a radically subjective
and anachronistic reading where meaning depends on the circumstances and
whims of each reader. The author sometimes reads the whole of the *Quijote*
as if written by his friend, a move from the fantastic rewriting to a relatively
simple 'fallacious attribution'.

One of the most amusing parts of the story comes when identical passages
of the two writers are compared. They may be identical, but Menard's text
is 'almost infinitely richer' (F 40), 'casi infinitamente más rico' (I 449). It
is considered paradoxical that Menard should come down in favour of arms
against letters, despite being a contemporary of Julien Benda, who argued
against the involvement of writers in politics, and the pacifist Bertrand Russell.
Bachelier suggested the subordination of the author to the psychology of
his character; others, quickly dismissed, a transcription of the *Quijote*; the
baroness of Bacourt sees the influence of Nietzsche, an argument judged
irrefutable, while the author suggests that Menard is indulging his taste for
saying the opposite of what he means. What seems absurd in the case of

---

8   'carnavales inútiles, sólo aptos … para ocasionar el plebeyo placer del anacronismo o
(lo que es peor) para embelesarnos con la idea primaria de que todas las épocas son iguales, o
de que son distintas' (I 446).

the writer is perfectly logical in a reader. The culture of a twentieth-century reader is clearly affected by the influence of Nietzsche, and all the other texts which have intervened, including the *Quijote* and all its re-readings over the centuries. Anthony Close's *The Romantic Approach to Don Quijote* maps some of those reinterpretations. The phrase 'truth, whose mother is history' comes in for similar treatment. Whereas Cervantes merely advises telling the truth of what happened in the past, for Menard historiography, the act of interpreting and writing history creates its own object, according to ideology, etc.: 'Historical truth, for Menard, is not "what happened"; it is what we *believe* happened' (F 41).[9] Cervantes's style is the natural Spanish of his time, whereas that of Menard is contrivedly archaic and affected.

Menard is inspired to his own laboriously futile task by a meditation (clearly by Borges, and much quoted) on the fate of intellectual exercises over time. Initial fresh relevance pales into scholarly note or nationalistic pomp:

> There is no intellectual exercise that is not ultimately pointless. A philo-sophical doctrine is, at first, a plausible description of the universe; the years go by, and it is a mere chapter – if not a paragraph or proper noun – in the history of philosophy. In literature, that 'falling by the wayside,' that loss of 'relevance,' is even better known. The Quixote, Menard remarked, was first and foremost a pleasant book; it is now an occasion for patriotic toasts, grammatical arrogance, obscene *de luxe* editions. Fame is a form – perhaps the worst form – of incomprehension. (F 41)[10]

It should be pointed out that the opposite view is *also* held by Borges: classic texts are 'all for all men'; 'A classic is that book which a nation or a group of nations or a long lapse of time have decided to read as if everything in its pages were deliberate, fatal, as deep as the cosmos and capable of generating an endless number of interpretations.'[11]

---

[9] 'La verdad histórica, para él, no es lo que sucedió; es lo que juzgamos que sucedió' (I 449).

[10] 'No hay ejercicio intelectual que no sea finalmente inútil. Una doctrina filosófica es al principio una descripción verosímil del universo; giran los años y es un mero capítulo – cuando no un párrafo o un nombre – de la historia de la filosofía. En la literatura, esa caducidad final es aun más notoria. "El Quijote – me dijo Menard – fue ante todo un libro agradable; ahora es una ocasión de brindis patrióticos, de soberbia gramatical, de obscenas ediciones de lujo. La gloria es una incomprensión y quizá la peor' (I 449–50).

[11] 'Clásico es aquel libro que una nación o un grupo de naciones o el largo tiempo han decidido leer como si en sus páginas todo fuera deliberado, fatal, profundo como el cosmos y capaz de interpretaciones sin término' ('Sobre los clásicos', II 151).

'Tlön, Uqbar, Orbis Tertius'

'Tlön' was published in May 1940 in *Sur*, and has been given pride of place
at the head of all editions of *Ficciones* despite the fact that 'Pierre Menard'
was written the previous year. At thirteen pages, it is one of Borges's longest.
It describes the process of the invention of a world based on the principles of philosophical idealism, and the take-over of the real world of the
1940s by the invented world. A few lines before the end, in a Postscript
dated 1947, but written together with the rest of the story in 1940, there is
the suggestion that the story can be read as an allegory of totalitarianism.
Like 'The Approach' and 'Pierre Menard' it consists of the research and study
by 'Borges' of a series of fake texts, adorned with complex bibliographical
details, where real authors write invented books, or invented authors such
as Silas Haslam, one of Borges's family surnames, write equally invented
books. The reviewers of 'The Approach' and apologists of 'Pierre Menard'
are replaced by a host of Borges's friends, who investigate the mysterious
texts: Néstor Ibarra, Drieu la Rochelle, Martínez Estrada, and many more.
In 'The Approach', the reviewed text provided philosophical content and an
adventure plot. Here the invented texts, especially the eleventh volume of *The
First Encyclopaedia of Tlön*, provide the philosophical content of idealism
which defines the invented world. The plot of the invasion is not given in
the summarized invented text, though it is prefigured by it, but in a direct
narration by Borges.

The account of the emergence of the texts which bring Tlön into existence
is labyrinthine in the extreme. The famous opening line is 'I owe the discovery
of Uqbar to the conjunction of a mirror and an encyclopedia' (F 7).[12] Encyclopaedias are a sort of cultural mirror put up to the universe, but we will
see that when the encyclopaedia, in turn, is reflected in a mirror, we do not
see our own universe, but a strangely unreal and finally nightmarish place.
Bioy Casares had been dining with Borges in a rented house in Ramos Mejía,
and late that night they discovered that mirrors had something monstrous
about them. (Borges as a child had been terrified by mirrors (Jurado, 25).)
The mirror prompts Bioy, again memorably, to remember a 'saying by one
of the heresiarchs of Uqbar: *Mirrors and copulation are abominable, for they
multiply the number of mankind.*'[13] He recalls the phrase from the *Anglo-
American Cyclopedia*, probably invented by Borges as a replica of the *Britan-*

---

[12] 'Debo a la conjunción de un espejo y de una enciclopedia el descubrimiento de Uqbar'
(I 431).

[13] 'uno de los heresiarcas de Uqbar había declarado que los espejos y la cópula son abomi-
nables porque multiplican el número de los hombres' (I 431).

nica, but when they check in a copy in the house, the article is not there. The next day, however, Bioy finds it in his own copy. Four pages had been added, which contained the history of a region nebulously located in Asia Minor, Uqbar, one of whose legendary regions is Tlön. The belief was attributed to the Gnostics of the area, for whom '*the visible universe was an illusion or, more precisely a sophism*'. We are back in the world of neo-Platonism and Gnosticism, where the primal Unity is refracted into a dispersed plurality of phenomenal reality. (Borges liked to repeat Occam's ' "*Entia non sunt multiplicanda praeter necessitatem*" [what can be done with fewer is done in vain with more]' (TL 67, I 214).

The bibliography of the interloping article offers a sort of *mise-en-abyme* which suggests the nature of the invention of Uqbar and its invention Tlön. The real theologian Johannes Valentinus Andreä, who was reported to have written a book on Tlön, had in reality invented the mystical community of the Rosicrucians, claiming that the texts he wrote were two centuries old. His apocryphal texts and invented community were later realized when the Rosy Cross was actually founded. This model is reflected twice in the story, the first time by the Mexican polymath Alfonso Reyes, who, frustrated in the search for the other volumes of the encyclopaedia, had suggested that the group of friends involved in the search should rewrite it themselves over a generation.

The next interruption of Tlön into the world comes at the beginning of the second part, in the emblematic hotel in Adrogué. The character Herbert Ashe had supposedly been a friend of Borges's father, indeed critics have tended to see him as a projection of the father: both die of a ruptured aneurysm, Ashe in 1937, and Jorge Guillermo in 1938, after suffering a stroke in late 1937. Borges first learned of idealism from his father, and he may be speaking of him when he writes: 'In life, Ashe was affected with unreality, as so many Englishmen are' (F 10).[14] His name suggests the extinguishing of some original fire, as does 'his weary rectangular beard [which] had once been red'.[15] He remembers Ashe 'in the illusory depths of the mirrors', an echo of the house in Ramos Mejía, 'holding a book of mathematics, looking up sometimes at the irrecoverable colors of the sky'.[16] The infinite complexity of the hues of the sunset is juxtaposed to an abstract system of the intellect, prefiguring the final replacement of reality with a world derived from

---

14 'En vida padeció de irrealidad, como tantos ingleses' (I 433).
15 'Su cansada barba rectangular había sido roja' (I 433).
16 'con un libro de matemáticas en la mano, mirando a veces los colores irrecuperables del cielo' (I 433).

philosophical texts. After Ashe died, Borges found a package with the eleventh volume of the encyclopaedia of Tlön. Its history is as variegated as the India covered by the pilgrim in 'The Approach', and a similar occasion for a splendid enumeration:

> I now held in my hands a vast and systematic fragment of the entire history of an unknown planet, with its architectures and its playing cards, the horror of its mythologies and the murmur of its tongues, its emperors and its seas, its minerals and its birds and fishes, its algebra and its fire, its theological and metaphysical controversies. (F 11–12)[17]

The more sensational aspects of the planet were broadcast by the popular press, but Borges now begins the long exposition of the thought system of Tlön.

I will come back to that thought system, but it is important at this stage to mention a moment in the history of Tlön which is important structurally in the wider story, and becomes a *mise-en-abyme*. Borges had always been fascinated by idealism, while recognizing that to think exclusively in its terms was impossible. In 'A New Refutation of Time' he writes: 'To understand it is easy; the difficulty lies in thinking within its limitations' (TL 320).[18] Indeed at the end of that essay he famously conceded that time, the world, and the self are very real: 'The world, unfortunately, is real; I, unfortunately, am Borges' (TL 332). Borges enjoys the speculation, sees the world on occasions through it, but is aware of the materiality of the real world. This duality, the split and difference between the philosophical system and reality, is important. It crucially does not exist in Tlön, where language, religion and literature are dictated by its terms:

> Hume declared for all time that while Berkeley's arguments admit not the slightest refutation, they inspire not the slightest conviction. That pronouncement is entirely true with respect to the earth, entirely false with respect to Tlön. The nations of that planet are, congenitally, idealistic. Their language and those things derived from their language – religion, literature, metaphysics – presuppose idealism. (F 13)[19]

---

[17] 'Ahora tenía en las manos un vasto fragmento metódico de la historia total de un planeta desconocido, con sus arquitecturas y sus barajas, con el pavor de sus mitologías y el rumor de sus lenguas, con sus emperadores y sus mares, con sus minerales y sus pájaros y sus peces, con su álgebra y su fuego, con su controversia teológica y metafísica' (I 434).

[18] 'Comprenderla es fácil: lo difícil es pensar dentro de su límite' (II 138).

[19] 'Hume notó para siempre que los argumentos de Berkeley no admiten la menor réplica y no causan la menor convicción. Ese dictamen es del todo verídico en su aplicación a la tierra; del todo falso en Tlön. Las naciones de ese planeta son – congénitamente – idealistas. Su

The most bizarre musings by Borges on literature and reality are, in Tlön, everyday common sense. Reality seemed, for most of their history, to be impervious to the thought of the inhabitants, but towards the end of Borges's account of the encyclopaedia volume, reality itself starts to be affected by thought:

> Century upon century of idealism could hardly have failed to influence reality. In the most ancient regions of Tlön one may, not infrequently, observe the duplication of lost objects: Two persons are looking for a pencil; the first person finds it, but says nothing; the second person finds a second pencil, no less real, but more in keeping with his expectations. These secondary objects are called *hrönir*. (F 19)[20]

For the previous hundred years, however, the creation of objects by thought had been systematized in prisons and schools, and applied to archaeology. A sinister note enters an account which had been amusing cultural satire: 'The systematic production of *hrönir* ... has been of invaluable aid to archaeologists, making it possible not only to interrogate but even to modify the past, which is now no less plastic, no less malleable than the future.'[21] History can be rewritten. This was clearly significant in a period of totalitarian regimes like that ruling Germany where, as Borges lamented in a 1938 article, literary history was realigned according to the tastes of Nazi ideology,[22] and in Argentina where the revisionist historians were coming to rethink Rosas as a nationalist hero. There is another significant detail here: a school principal 'happened to die' (F 19), 'murió casualmente' (I 439), during an excavation, prompting the realization that 'no witnesses who were aware of the experimental nature of the search could be allowed near the site'.[23] Other examples of the relation between the mind and reality revert to simple humour. Such is the case where Berkeley's precept that 'to be is to be perceived' is demon-

---

lenguaje y las derivaciones de su lenguaje – la religión, las letras, la metafísica – presuponen el idealismo' (I 435).

[20] 'Siglos y siglos de idealismo no han dejado de influir en la realidad. No es infrecuente, en las regiones más antiguas de Tlön, la duplicación de objetos perdidos. Dos personas buscan un lápiz; la primera lo encuentra y no dice nada; la segunda encuentra un segundo lápiz no menos real, pero más ajustado a su expectativa. Esos objetos secundarios se llaman *hrönir*' (I 439).

[21] 'La metódica elaboración de *hrönir* (dice el onceno tomo) ha prestado servicios prodigiosos a los arqueólogos. Ha permitido interrogar y hasta modificar el pasado, que ahora no es menos plástico y menos dócil que el porvenir' (I 439–40).

[22] See 'A Disturbing Exposition' (TL 200–1).

[23] 'la improcedencia de testigos que conocieran la naturaleza experimental de la busca ...' (I 439).

strated by the disappearance of a doorway when the beggar who used to sleep under it died and was no longer able to perceive it.

Here the main text dated 1940 seems to end, and at the beginning of the '1947 Postscript' we are told that the preceding story had been published in Borges, Bioy and Silvina Ocampo's influential *Antología de la literatura fantástica*, which is not true, but serves to augment the contrast between fantasy and what we read in the 'Postscript'. The 'Postscript' takes up again the penetration of the Western world by Tlön. Herbert Ashe was again at the centre of the plot. A letter was found in a book which had belonged to him from a certain Gunnar Erfjord, whose surname was shared by Borges's family and by one of the loves of his life, Norah Lange. In it the genesis of Tlön is recounted. A secret benevolent society had been founded at the beginning of the seventeenth century, including George Berkeley, one of the founders of idealism, and Dalgarno, a Scottish philologist who devised a universal language (FH). Their aim was to invent a country; each expert would designate a successor. The movement was re-born two centuries later in Memphis, Tennessee, with clear echoes of the foundation of the Rosicrucians. The fabulously rich Ezra Buckley (which reads like a *hrön* of Berkeley) decided that to invent a country was a paltry affair and that only a planet would suffice. By 1914 the forty volumes of the secret First Encyclopaedia of Tlön were completed, with instructions that the enterprise be kept secret. An expansion of these volumes in a Tlön language would follow, and constitute 'Orbis Tertius'.

As at the beginning of the story, 'Borges' is personally involved in the discovery of objects from Tlön. He is worried that 'an unsettling coincidence made me witness to the second intrusion as well' (F 22).[24] The paranoia surely reflects the fate of the witness to the production of *hrönir*, but also suggests that the events in the 'real' world are a mirror of those in the eleventh volume of the Encyclopaedia. He witnesses the finding of two alien objects in curiously diverse places. The first is a compass with writing in a Tlön language in the salon of (Borges's real friend) Princess de Faucigny Lucinge as she is unpacking her silverware sent from Poitiers. Together with his friend Enrique Amorim, the novelist husband of Borges's cousin Esther Haedo, he comes across a small metal cone of extraordinary weight in the affairs of a man who has died delirious in a *pulpería* in Uruguay where they are detained by the flooded river. In 1944 the volumes of the Encyclopaedia were discovered and the world was inundated with copies and summaries. So

---

[24] 'Un azar que me inquieta hizo que yo también fuera testigo de la segunda [intrusión]' (I 441).

far, apart from the unearthly weight of the cone, Tlön seems to have consisted of texts, but now a radical change is dramatically announced by 'Borges': 'Almost immediately reality "caved in" at more than one point' (F 24).[25] This coincides with the move in Tlön when thought actually changes reality, another prefiguration.

It is immediately made clear that the nature of that 'giving way' has to do with totalitarian systems: 'The truth is, it wanted to cave in. Ten years ago, any symmetry, any system with an appearance of order—dialectical materialism, anti-Semitism, Nazism—could spellbind and hypnotize mankind' (F24).[26] What totalitarianism and Tlön seem to have in common is that the natural order of the world and reality, which is ordered by divine laws, i.e. unknowable and inhuman (with the meaning of non-human) laws, and by the angels, is replaced by a world ordered by human thought and its political equivalent in dogma and ideology, by chessmen:

> It would be futile to reply that reality is also orderly. Perhaps it is, but orderly in accordance with divine laws (read 'inhuman laws') that we can never quite manage to penetrate. Tlön may well be a labyrinth, but it is a labyrinth forged by men, a labyrinth destined to be deciphered by men. … Spellbound by Tlön's rigor, humanity has forgotten, and continues to forget, that it is the rigor of chess masters, not of angels. (F 24)[27]

Remember that in 'A Comment on August 23, 1944' Borges had written that for Europeans and Americans the only possible order is Western Culture; Nazism is unreal and monstrous, like the first mirror in Ramos Mejía. Borges, of course, wilfully confuses Western Culture, by which he probably means liberalism, with reality, the natural order. In the late thirties, the rival ideologies of Stalinism and Nazism seemed poised to divide the world. State ideologies were set to destroy the individual. By the end of the story, Tlön was well on the way to obliterating the existing order. The history of Tlön was taught in schools and was replacing the pre-existing history, just as the *hrönir* allowed history to be rewritten in Tlön. When the *Second Encyclopaedia of Tlön* comes out, presumably announcing 'Orbis Tertius', which sounds to me

---

25 'Casi inmediatamente, la realidad cedió en más de un punto' (I 442).

26 'Lo cierto es que anhelaba ceder. Hace diez años bastaba cualquier simetría con apariencia de orden – el materialismo dialéctico, el antisemitismo, al nazismo – para embelesar a los hombres' (I 442).

27 'Inútil responder que la realidad también está ordenada. Quizá lo esté, pero de acuerdo a leyes divinas – traduzco: a leyes inhumanas – que no acabamos nunca de percibir. Tlön será un laberinto, pero es un laberinto urdido por hombres, un laberinto destinado a que lo descifren los hombres' (I 442).

very much like the Third Reich, he forecasts: 'French and English and mere
Spanish will disappear from the earth. The world will be Tlön' (F 24–5).[28]

The allegory, if that is what it is, is clear. But it is paradoxical that it is
precisely Borges's favourite philosophical game, idealism, which comes to
articulate the advent of totalitarianism. The world of Tlön in the eleventh
volume is full of enchanting literary teasers and conceits of the sort which
resonate throughout Borges's work. In the *Ursprache* of the planet, given
that reality is a series of independent acts and perceptions in time, nouns
do not have any place and are replaced by impersonal verbs. (Remember
that he elsewhere replaces the Cartesian 'I think' with the impersonal and
collective 'it thinks'.) Significantly, Borges's friend the avant-garde painter
given to inventing new religions and languages such as *neo-criollo*, Xul
Solar, translates the Tlön for 'the moon rose over the river' into Spanish and
English: '*Upward, behind the onstreaming it mooned*' (F 13). The invented
languages that he explores in 'John Wilkins' Analytical Language' cannot be
far from his mind, either. In the northern languages adjectives are the centre
of language, and are combined in its literature into 'ideal objects, called
forth and dissolved in an instant, as the poetry requires' (F 13).[29] He seems
to be thinking of the metaphors of his own early *ultraísmo* or even the poetic
objects of Huidobro's *creacionismo*. Since no one believes in the reality of
verbal objects, nouns proliferate madly, as there are no generalizing categories which would limit their number. Philosophy has no grip on reality, but is
seen as a 'dialectical game', and as such they can proliferate like the nouns
in the northern hemisphere. Truth gives way to astonishment, metaphysics
to play: 'There are systems upon systems that are incredible but possessed
of a pleasing architecture or a certain agreeable sensationalism. The meta-
physicians of Tlön seek not truth, or even plausibility – they seek to amaze,
astound. In their view, metaphysics is a branch of the literature of fantasy' (F
15).[30] This is a pretty good description of Borges's very originality: turning
philosophy into plot, theology into symmetrical literary structures, truth into
aesthetics. Materialism is proposed by some thinkers as a paradox: the fact
that nine coins might continue in being over various days when nobody is
seeing them is a logical scandal that attracts the most ingenious explanations.

---

[28] 'Entonces desaparecerán del planeta el inglés y el francés y el mero español. El mundo
será Tlön' (I 443).

[29] 'objetos ideales, convocados y disueltos en un momento, según las necesidades poéticas'
(I 435).

[30] 'Abundan los sistemas increíbles, pero de arquitectura agradable o de tipo sensacional.
Los metafísicos de Tlön no buscan la verdad ni siquiera la verosimilitud: buscan el asombro.
Juzgan que la metafísica es una rama de la literatura fantástica' (I 436).

A final trait of their concept of literature is a favourite conceit of Borges, an intertextuality generalized to the point that literature is seen as a collective rewriting. As the individual self is basically meaningless, their literary world is that of Pierre Menard. Books are rarely signed, nor does the concept of plagiarism exist: 'It has been decided that all books are the work of a single author who is timeless and anonymous.'[31] Borges returns time and time to this idea.[32] Despite this, they indulge in a very Borgesian game. 'Literary criticism often invents authors: It will take two dissimilar works – the *Tao Te Ching* and the *1001 Nights*, for instance – attribute them to a single author, and then in all good conscience determine the psychology of that most inter-esting *homme de lettres* ...' (F 18).[33] How would the meaning of these works change by this spurious attribution? What would the *Quijote* mean if it were written by a twentieth-century Frenchman?

This is clearly Borges's world. So was the literary culture which led Zur Linde to Nazism in '*Deutsches Requiem*'. The question is very difficult, and may have something to do with the fact that Borges, the very public enemy of pro-Axis Argentinians, greatly admired the culture of Germany, while the Germanophiles whom he so despised, were utterly ignorant of that culture.[34] He is aware, as we see in his review of Russell's *Let People Think*, that Fichte and Carlyle are the remote ancestors of Nazism, not Berkeley and Hume. It may be that any thought or aesthetic, when it hardens into dogma and loses its ironic distance from reality, can become dangerous. One only has to think of his experience with his own gentle and subtle aesthetics of *criollismo* when it hardens into right-wing nationalism verging on fascism after the lead of Lugones in *El payador*.

The final lines of the story have attracted much comment: 'The world will be Tlön. That makes very little difference to me [yo no hago caso]; through my quiet days in this hotel in Adrogué, I go on revising (though I never intend to publish) an indecisive translation in the style of Quevedo of Sir Thomas Browne's *Urne Buriall*.'[35] They have been read as a turning his back

---

[31] 'No existe el concepto del plagio: se ha establecido que todas las obras son obra de un solo autor, que es intemporal y es anónimo' (I 439).

[32] It is perhaps most thoroughly explored in 'Coleridge's Flower', 'La flor de Coleridge'.

[33] 'La crítica suele inventar autores: elige dos obras disímiles – el *Tao Te King* y *Las 1001 Noches*, digamos –, las atribuye a un mismo escritor y luego determina con probidad la psicología de ese interesante *homme de lettres* ...' (I 439).

[34] See, for example, 'Definition of a Germanophile', TL 203–5; *Textos cautivos*, 332–8.

[35] 'Yo no hago caso, yo sigo revisando en los quietos días del hotel de Adrogué una indecisa traducción quevediana (que no pienso dar a la imprenta) del *Urn Burial* de Browne' (I 443).

on reality, as escapism. Borges was a great admirer of Browne, and wrote in
Inquisiciones (1925) of his attitude during the Civil War: even known to be
a fervent Royalist, 'Browne displayed a paradoxical heroism which allowed
him to ignore the insolent war, persisting with his thoughtful pursuits, his
gaze fixed on speculations on pure beauty.'[36] A much more contemporary
essay, 'Our Poor Individualism', refines this attitude. The European, whether
affirmatively, as in Kipling, or tragically, as in Kafka, relates to order, a
cosmos. For the Argentinian the world is chaos; his literary hero is an outlaw.
But in the world of totalitarian states this negative individualism may be a
positive, anarchistic, state of resistance and defiance:

> It may be said that the traits I have pointed out are merely negative or
> anarchic; it may be added that they are not subject to political explanation. I
> shall venture to suggest the opposite. The most urgent problem of our time
> (already denounced with prophetic lucidity by the near-forgotten Spencer)
> is the gradual interference of the State in the acts of the individual; in the
> battle with this evil, whose names are communism and Nazism, Argentine
> individualism, though perhaps useless or harmful until now, will find its
> justification and its duties. (TL 310)[37]

Browne's *Urne-Buriall* was a curious, encyclopaedic review of funeral monu-
ments and rites over history. He ends his discussion dismissively, with an
affirmation of his true Christian faith: 'But all this is nothing in the Meta-
physicks of true belief' (Browne 50). As Marina Kaplan suggests (332),
Borges's 'Yo no hago caso' is his version of Browne's outburst. His defence
is not of Christianity, but of individualism, anarchism, and perhaps his most
treasured virtue, lucidity, freely exercised in the paradox which character-
izes this story.[38] As he wrote in his essay on Valéry in 1945: 'The worthy
mission that Valéry carried out (and continues to carry out) was to propose
lucidity to men in a grossly romantic era, in the melancholic era of Nazism

---

[36] 'Alentó en Browne el heroísmo paradójico de ignorar la insolencia bélica, persistiendo
en empeño pensativo, puesto el mirar en una pura especulación de belleza' (Inq 35).

[37] 'Se dirá que los rasgos que he señalado son meramente negativos o anárquicos; se
añadirá que no son capaces de explicación política. Me atrevo a sugerir lo contrario. El más
urgente de los problemas de nuestra época (ya denunciada con profética lucidez por el casi
olvidado Spencer) es la gradual intromisión del Estado en los actos del individuo; en la lucha
con ese mal, cuyos nombres son comunismo y nazismo, el individualismo argentino, acaso
inútil o perjudicial hasta ahora, encontrará justificación y deberes' (II 37).

[38] Another possible explanation for 'Borges's' *au dessus de la mêlée* attitude lies in the
reviews of 'Two Books'. Theories such as those of Carlyle take many years before they are
applied in reality: 'That is why the true intellectual refuses to take part in contemporary
debates' (TL 209).

and dialectical materialism, of the augurs of the sect of Freud and the traders in *surréalisme*.'[39]

'The Circular Ruins', 'Las ruinas circulares'

In 'The Circular Ruins' the proliferation of writers and commentators, texts and rewritings, footnotes and digressions, erudite listing and discussion of bibliographical and intellectual sources, present in Borges's previous fictions, disappear. Intertextual references are virtually absent beyond the epigraph from Lewis Carroll's *Through the Looking-Glass*: 'And if he left off dreaming you ...', which refers to Tweedledum and Tweedledee explaining to Alice that the Red King is dreaming her and that she would vanish if he woke up. The third-person narration is timeless and rather dream-like, set in a vaguely oriental river and jungle area; it is unencumbered, symmetrical and carried along to its conclusion by a series of prefigurations. A grey man, or sorcerer, comes to a burnt out temple, and sets about dreaming into existence another man. He first conjures up a ghostly amphitheatre of students, chooses one who resembles himself, and proceeds to educate him. Insomnia sets in and his dream is lost. Literature is elsewhere seen as a 'sueño voluntario' ('El escritor argentino', I 274), a 'voluntary dream' (TL 427). Here, however, his inability to give shape to his dreams is expressed in memorable comparisons: 'He understood that the task of molding the incoherent and dizzying stuff that dreams are made of is ... more difficult than weaving a rope of sand or minting coins of the faceless wind' (F 46).[40] In his second attempt he invokes various higher powers and slowly constructs in his dreams a man, organ by organ. A statue at once a tiger and a colt, which turns out to be the deity Fire, brings the dreamed creature to life, and warns that only Fire and the dreamer will know that the man is a ghost. The grey man cancels out the memory of his 'son' so that he will not know the secrets of his genesis, and following the instructions of Fire, sends him down-river to another temple to continue the cult of the deity. He hears that a priest in another temple can tread on fire without being burnt, and fears that his son might discover the

---

[39] 'Proponer a los hombres la lucidez en una era bajamente romántica, en la era melancólica del nazismo y del materialismo dialéctico, de los augures de la secta de Freud y de los comerciantes del *surréalisme*, tal es la benemérita misión que desempeñó (que sigue desempeñando) Valéry' ('Valéry como símbolo', II 65).

[40] 'Comprendió que el empeño de modelar la material incoherente y vertiginosa de que se componen los sueños es ... más arduo que tejer una cuerda de arena o que amonedar el viento sin cara' (I 452).

humiliation and vertigo of being the dream of another man. A fire ravishes his temple; he walks into the fire, and realizes 'with relief, with humiliation, with terror … that he, too, was but appearance, that another man was dreaming him' (F 50).[41] Rather than the regression of pilgrims in search of pilgrims in 'The Approach', we have an endless chain of dreamers and their ghost-like creations.

As in 'The Narrative Art and Magic', where 'every lucid and determined detail is a prophecy' (TL 82), the story is forwarded in a dream-like fashion by a system of prefigurations. The symmetry of the two methods of constructing the son is the largest occurrence of the generalized duplication. The circular shape of the temples suggests a circular process; the grey man knows of the 'ruins of another propitious temple' down-river, and also points to duplication. The importance of fire and also of a process of degeneration or loss of vigour is seen in the temple 'which once had been the color of fire but now was the color of ashes' (like the beard of Herbert Ashe) (F 44).[42] In the first paragraph, the man pushes through the lacerating vegetation 'probably without even feeling', and was not surprised when his wounds were closed on the following morning, prefiguring his immunity to the heat of fire, and thus his ghostly condition. So focused on his task was he that if anyone had asked his name or any detail of his previous life, he would not have been able to answer: this becomes significant when we read how he wipes clean the memory of his son. Later in the story, he has a sense of déjà-vu: 'he was disturbed by a sense that all this had happened before' (F 48).[43] Indeed an adjective in the first line 'la unánime noche', the 'one-souled night', already speaks of a being transcending individual identity.

In the second attempt, various methods of creation, and various authorities are invoked: on two occasions, for example, the 'planetary gods'. The Red Adam of Gnosticism is mentioned, which sends us back to the essay on Basilides, where the demiurge creates a creature which crawls on the ground like a serpent until God 'sends him a spark of his power' (TL 66). His first major breakthrough, however, the dreaming a beating heart, comes when he 'uttered those syllables of a powerful name that it is lawful to pronounce' (F 47).[44] Commentators such as Alazraki pick up on the Kabbalistic connotations of

---

[41] 'Con alivio, con humillación, con terror, comprendió que él también era una apariencia, que otro estaba soñándolo' (I 455).

[42] 'tuvo alguna vez el color del fuego y ahora el de la ceniza' (I 451).

[43] 'lo inquietaba una impresión de que ya todo eso había acontecido' (I 454).

[44] 'pronunció las sílabas lícitas de un nombre poderoso' (I 453).

the power of the name to give life to the golem, which means 'unformed matter':

> We may surmise that he is thinking of the *Shem Hamephorash* or Tetra-grammaton, which the Kabbalists sought by combining the letters of the Hebrew alphabet. Borges himself has paraphrased the Kabbalisitic belief that when the miraculous *Shem Hamephorash* is pronounced over the golem made of clay or mud he must come to life. (Alazraki, *Kabbalah*, 22)

The difference between the golem wrought from clay and the man created by dreaming in the story is obvious, but Borges in the Prologue to the poems of *The Self and the Other, El otro, el mismo*, accepted the link between 'The Circular Ruins' and his long-standing fascination with the golem from his reading Meyrink's novel of the same name in Geneva, to an entry in the *Book of Imaginary Beings*, and to the poem 'The Golem', dated 1958. In the poem, the rabbi who animates the golem by pronouncing 'the Name that is the Key' (SP 193), 'el Nombre que es la Clave' (II 263), is horrified at his crude and sluggish creation unnecessarily added to Creation. An extra dimension is introduced as God looks on his creation the rabbi:

> 'What made me supplement the endless series / of symbols with one more? Why add in vain / to the knotty skein always unraveling / another cause and effect, with not one gain?' / In his hour of anguish and uncertain light, / upon his Golem his eyes would come to rest. / Who is to say what God must have been feeling, / looking down and seeing His rabbi so distressed?
> (SP 195–7)[45]

Talking about the difference between the poem and the story, he mentions that in the former he had also (perhaps) been talking about the relation-ship between the poet and his work. The story also makes more sense if the dreaming of another is partly seen as implying literary creation.

The final waking of the ghost, however, is achieved through another deity, the bastard statue of tiger and colt which in his dream becomes a simulta-neous myriad of religious images: 'those two vehement creatures plus bull, and rose, and tempest, too' (F 48).[46] This living, multiple god's earthy name

---

[45] *¿Por qué di en agregar a la infinita / serie un símbolo más? ¿Por qué a la vana / madeja que en lo eterno se devana, / di otra causa, otro efecto y otra cuita? / En la hora de angustia y de luz vaga, / en su Golem los ojos detenía. / ¿Quién nos dirá las cosas que sentía / Dios, al mirar a su rabino en Praga?* (II 265).

[46] 'a la vez esas dos criaturas vehementes y también un toro, una rosa, una tempestad' (I 453).

is Fire. Fire is a test of reality and unreality in other stories such as 'The Dead Man'. Efraín Kristal mentions a likely, far less numinous source for the story: Giovanni Papini's 'L'ultima visita del gentiluomo malato' ('The last visit of the ill gentleman'), which Borges translated and published in the *Anthology of Fantastic Literature*. In it 'the protagonist knows he is someone else's dream, feels humiliated by this knowledge, wonders about his creator, and longs to vanish' (Kristal, 118).

The dramatically intense prose in which it is described suggests that the humiliation which the grey man fears for the ghost and feels himself in the final lines is traumatic and very disturbing:

> He feared that his son would … discover that he was a mere simulacrum. To be not a man, but the projection of another man's dream—what incomparable humiliation, what vertigo! Every parent [padre] feels concern for the children he has procreated (or allowed to be procreated) in happiness or mere confusion. (F 49)

> With relief, with humiliation, with terror, he realized that he, too, was but appearance, that another man was dreaming him. (F 50)[47]

Williamson argues that the grey man is Borges's father, and I agree that this is one important aspect. In the 'Autobiographical Essay', he wrote 'I had to fulfill the literary destiny that circumstances denied my father' (Aut 211). As Williamson insists, Borges was haunted by the obligation to correct and rewrite Jorge Guillermo's novel *El caudillo*. The word 'vertigo' is a powerful one in Borges, and reappears at the moment when Emma Zunz realizes that her father did to her mother the 'horrible thing' she was suffering, and which, I would add, engendered her. Another similar reading addresses literary originality and the anxiety of influence more generally. A writer creates a work only to realize that it was merely the ghost of a previous work, a previous writer. The word 'ghost', 'fantasma', repeated throughout the story is echoed in the effect that the Library of Babel has on the individual writer: 'The certainty that everything has already been written annuls us, or renders us phantasmal' (F 73).[48]

---

[47] 'Temió que su hijo … descubriera de algún modo su condición de mero simulacro. No ser un hombre, ser la proyección del sueño de otro hombre ¡qué humillación incomparable, qué vértigo! A todo padre le interesan los hijos que ha procreado (que ha permitido) en una mera confusión o felicidad.' (I 454)

'Con alivio, con humillación, con terror, comprendió que él también era una apariencia, que otro estaba soñándolo' (I 455).

[48] 'La certidumbre de que todo está escrito nos anula o nos afantasma' (I 470).

'The Lottery in Babylon', 'La lotería en Babilonia'

'The Lottery in Babylon' and 'The Library of Babel', both written in 1941, are dark and menacing stories of all-powerful and all-encompassing institutions; they, especially the first, verge on being parables of totalitarianism, but speak of personal anguish. They have been insistently linked by criticism to the influence of Kafka, and indeed Borges in the 'Autobiographical Essay' talks of 'my Kafkian story "The Library of Babel" '; in 'The Lottery', a secret latrine where individuals could be denounced is called 'Qaphqa'. Kristal has excellent insights into Borges's relation with Kafka not only in his translations, but also in the stories: 'Notwithstanding Borges's reticence, he owes a great debt to Kafka in those of his tales where a fantastic universe symbolizes dangerous human affairs, sometimes described with resigned stoicism by a narrator who is a victim of the very circumstances he describes' (Kristal 127). Borges moved in his evaluation of Kafka from declaring to Burgin that 'perhaps the strength of Kafka may lie in his lack of complexity' (Burgin, 77), to the 1984 *Personal Library*, *Biblioteca personal*, where he writes: 'Kafka's destiny was to transmute circumstances and agony into fables. He composed sordid nightmares in a limpid style. ... Kafka is the great classic writer of our tormented and strange century.'[49] Borges liked to associate Kafka with the paradox of Zeno, demonstrating the impossibility of movement. In 'Kafka and His Precursors', Zeno is the first precursor:

> A moving body at point A (Aristotle states) will not be able to reach point B, because it must first cover half of the distance between the two, and before that, half of the half, and before that, half of the half of the half, and so on to infinity; the form of this famous problem is precisely that of *The Castle*, and the moving body and the arrow and Achilles are the first Kafkaesque characters in literature. (TL 363)[50]

K in *The Trial* cannot even discover the crime of which he is accused, before the mysterious Court has him executed; K as land surveyor in *The Castle* cannot, in three hundred anguished pages, reach that castle.[51] Rodríguez

---

[49] 'El destino de Kafka fue transmutar las circunstancias y las agonías en fábulas. Redactó sórdidas pesadillas en un estilo límpido. ... Kafka es el gran escritor clásico de nuestro atormentado y extraño siglo' (BP 13).

[50] 'Un móvil que está en A (declara Aristóteles) no podrá alcanzar el punto B, porque antes deberá recorrer la mitad del camino entre los dos, y antes, la mitad de la mitad, y antes, la mitad de la mitad de la mitad, y así hasta lo infinito; la forma de este ilustre problema es, exactamente, la de *El castillo*, y el móvil y la flecha y Aquiles son los primeros personajes kafkianos de la literatura' ('Kafka y sus precursores', II 88).

[51] See also his piece on Kafka in *Textos cautivos*, 182.

Monegal (285) makes the obvious link between the Miguel Cané Library and
the ghetto, the 'infierno burocrático' described by the Czech. Barrenechea
also talks of the 'burocratización del horror' in Kafka and 'The Lottery', but
adds that Kafka and Borges are separated by their attitude towards order:
'[Kafka] feels anguish at being excluded from an order in which he does
not participate but which exists, while [Borges] does not believe in said
order.'[52] Barrenechea is probably referring to Borges's comments in 'Our
Poor Individualism' where, referring to Kafka, he talks of 'the unbearable,
tragic solitude of the individual who lacks even the lowliest place in the order
of the universe' (TL 310).[53] Order in Borges, of course, cannot be dismissed
so easily; in poetry order and adventure are inextricable ('La aventura y el
orden'); in 'The Lottery' order and chance, cosmos and chaos, are also mutu-
ally implied.

If the search for the catalogue of catalogues, indeed for any glimmer of
meaning in 'The Library of Babel' is clearly related to the frustrated search
for access to the Castle by K, 'The Lottery in Babilonia', as Kristal suggests,
is more closely related to Kafka's story 'The Great Wall of China'. The 'high
command' in charge of building the wall is similar in many ways to the
Company in charge of the lottery. The high command is concerned with the
slightest thought of every individual, and yet unknown: 'In the office of the
high command – where it was, and who sat there, no one whom I have ever
asked could tell me, either then or now – in that office there surely revolved
all human thoughts and desires, and counter to them all human goals and
achievements' (Kafka, 62). As with the Company, the high command was
considered eternal: 'My belief is rather that the high command has been in
existence for ever, and the decision to build the wall likewise' (Kafka, 64).
Yet the extraordinary distance between the emperor and his southern provinces means that stories centuries old are received as the latest news, and
thus 'if one were to conclude from such phenomena that basically we have
no emperor at all, one would not be far from the truth' (Kafka, 68).

If Tlön was a world organized by philosophical idealism, Babylon is a
realm where every last act is ruled by a secret lottery and the Company
which runs it. Each sixty days a draw was made in the labyrinths of the god
which dictated the life of every individual initiated into the mysteries of
Baal, until the next draw. This corresponds to what is known of the Assyro-

---

[52] '[Kafka] se siente angustiado por verse excluido de un orden en el que no participa pero
que existe, y [Borges] no cree en dicho orden' (Barrenechea, 40).
[53] 'la insoportable y trágica soledad de quien carece de un lugar, siquiera humildísimo, en
el orden del universo' (II 37).

Babylonian god Bêl Marduk, who decided the fate of the country for one year; decisions were secret and sometimes delivered in dreams (*Larousse*, 63). The story is told by a Babylonian who has recently left his country and is about to embark on a sea trip. This distance for the first time allows him some objectivity: 'until this day I have thought as little about it as about the conduct of the indecipherable gods, or my heart. Now, far from Babylon and its beloved customs, I think with some bewilderment about the Lottery.' But he is at the same time still convinced of the naturalness of the system, and his account is sprinkled with variations on 'naturally', 'as everyone knows'. This may explain the apparent contradictions in his account. The vertiginous changes in his life dictated by the draws are 'that almost monstrous variety', 'esa variedad casi atroz', yet in the same paragraph the local customs are 'beloved'. The Babylonians are 'great admirers of logic and even symmetry' (F 53), but soon after 'are not a speculative people' (F 55). Another reason may be the Babylonian habit of introducing error into any document, a procedure the narrator confesses to have followed: 'I myself, in this hurried statement, have misrepresented some splendor, some atrocity' (F 57).[54] The history of the Company, through chance draws, is no less malleable than that of Tlön, through the production of archeological finds as *hrönir*: 'a paleographic document, unearthed at a certain temple, may come from yesterday's drawing or from a drawing that took place centuries ago' (F 57).[55]

The opening lines are classic: 'Like all the men of Babylon, I have been proconsul; like all, I have been a slave. I have known omnipotence, ignominy, imprisonment.'[56] The Lottery produces the same effect in one life as metempsychosis did in Pythagoras, who in previous lives had been Euphorbus and Pyrrhus. Eternity, in 'The Immortal', has the same effect, but there the annulment of personality is stressed: 'No one is someone; a single immortal man is all men. Like Cornelius Agrippa, I am hero, philosopher, demon, and world – which is a long-winded way of saying that *I am not*' (A 14).[57]

The first part of the story traces the development of the Lottery from the sort of lottery familiar to the reader; the second speculates about the nature

---

54 'yo mismo, en esta apresurada declaración, he falseado algún esplendor, alguna atrocidad' (I 460).

55 'Un documento paleográfico, exhumado en un templo, puede ser obra del sorteo de ayer o de un sorteo secular' (I 460).

56 'Como todos los hombres de Babilonia, he sido procónsul; como todos, esclavo; también he conocido la omnipotencia, el oprobio, las cárceles' (I 456).

57 'Nadie es alguien, un solo hombre inmortal es todos los hombres. Como Cornelio Agrippa, soy dios, soy héroe, soy filósofo, soy demonio y soy mundo, lo cual es una fatigosa manera de decir que no soy' (I 541).

and existence of the Company, and the actual functioning of the Lottery, which is as inconceivable and infinitely complex as is Menard's process of rewriting the *Quijote*. The process of the expansion of the scope of the Lottery is that of a symbolic system which becomes more and more detailed and specific, until it ceases to be symbolic and fades back into reality, like the map in 'On Exactitude in Science', 'Del rigor en la ciencia', in *The Maker*, which is as big as the country it describes, and thus perfectly useless. The primitive, plebeian lottery was modified by the introduction of financial penalties together with cash prizes. Faced with refusal to pay the fines, the Company replaced them with days of imprisonment. *'It was the first appearance of non-pecuniary elements in the lottery'* (F 53), i.e. the first move away from the symbolic, which is completed when money prizes are replaced by concrete rewards such as finding a desired woman in one's bed. 'Terror and hope', 'el terror y la esperanza', become the dominant binary. A tipping point comes when law, i.e. order, and chance dictate the same reality. A slave stole a crimson ticket; the draw specified that his tongue should be burned, and the law prescribed the same sentence. In a parody of Marxist language, which reminds us of the presence of Stalinism in 'Tlön', 'a necessary stage of history' (F 53) had been reached which made the privileged ability of the rich to afford tickets intolerable, and the will of the people (the dictatorship of the proletariat) made the Lottery 'secret, free of charge and open to all' (F 54), 'secreta, gratuita y general' (I 458), and gave all public power to the Company. This is the state described in the opening lines by the narrator.

The Company's doctrinal description of its activity as 'an interpolation of chance into the order of the universe' (F 55), 'una interpolación del azar en el orden del mundo' (I 458), i.e. 'an intensification of chance, a periodic infusion of chaos into the cosmos', led eventually to the introduction of chance into every stage of life. At this moment, *'In reality, the number of drawings is infinite'* (F 56). Zeno and Kafka preside over the process: the ignorant do not understand that time does not need to be infinite to make the draws infinite, it simply needs to be infinitely sub-divisible, 'as in the famous parable of the Race with the Tortoise'. As with Chinese high command, some conclude that the Company is eternal; others that it no longer exists, or never existed. Yet others argue that it makes no difference whether it exists or not, because 'Babylon is nothing but an infinite game of chance' (F 58).[58] Order and chance are two sides of the same coin; symmetry with the appearance of order usher in the totalitarian reality in 'Tlön'; chance the all-powerful

---

[58] 'Babilonia no es otra cosa que un infinito juego de azares' (I 460).

'shadowy corporation', 'tenebrosa corporación'. In so far as the world 'for the Argentine ... is a chaos' (TL 310), for Babylonians, read Argentines.

'The Library of Babel', 'La biblioteca de Babel'

'The Library of Babel' is probably Borges's bleakest and most frightening story. Though there are some good Borges jokes, the feeling of utter nightmare in the descriptions of the visual and physical oppression of the library pretty much dominates. The world is a library: 'the universe (which others call the Library)' (F 65), 'el universo (que otros llaman la Biblioteca)' (I 465). This is the opposite process from 'Tlön' where an encyclopaedia becomes the world. It is composed of a virtually infinite number of identical hexagonal galleries, from where interminable other galleries are visible below and above, with vast ventilation shafts precariously protected by low balustrades. Its inhabitants are librarians; when the narrator librarian dies, he says, 'compassionate hands will throw me over the railing; my tomb will be the unfathomable air, my body will sink for ages, and will decay and dissolve in the wind engendered by my fall, which shall be infinite' (F 66).[59] Its books all have 410 pages, 40 lines per page, about 80 characters per line. It was discovered three hundred years before that the library contains every possible combination, within this format, of twenty-five elements: twenty-two letters, full stop, and comma. As far as the human mind is concerned, this is practically an infinite number of books. Mechanically produced through mathematical combination, the books are not written in any particular language, but contain texts (all texts) in all existing languages, and in any number of imaginary ones, but of course they only coincide with any language by chance, and what one reads in one language could easily be in another language, with which it shares words but not their meaning. The overwhelming majority of the books contain no phrases comprehensible to any of the librarians. The story is the account of the futile search for meaning in the library by librarians, and describes their mythologies and methodologies.

The oppression of the Library echoes the misery of Borges's work day in the Miguel Cané Library, and many physical details are, according to the writer, borrowed from that place. The architecture is reminiscent of Piranesi, the atmosphere of Kafka, but the intellectual affiliation is set out in a piece

---

[59] 'Muerto, no faltarán manos piadosas que me tiren por la barandilla; mi sepultura será el aire insondable; mi cuerpo se hundirá largamente y se corromperá y disolverá en el viento engendrado por la caída, que es infinita' (I 465).

published in *Sur* in 1939, 'The Total Library', and which gives its title to the Penguin anthology of his non-fiction writing. Borges ends that essay stating that 'one of the habits of the mind is the invention of horrible imaginings'. To the notions of Hell and predestination, masks, mirrors, the Sphynx, the teratological Trinity, he 'has tried to rescue from oblivion a subaltern horror: the vast contradictory Library, whose vertical wildernesses of books run the incessant risk of changing into others that affirm, deny, and confuse everything like a delirious god' (TL 216). The last part of this phrase is reproduced in the story; the operation described seems to be a nightmarish version of Borges's own dealings with literature and meaning. He traces the origins of the Total Library to Greek Antiquity, and dwells on Cicero, who muses that if a large number of characters were thrown onto the ground, they were not likely to form the *Annals* of Ennius, and adds: 'I doubt whether chance could possibly create even a single verse to read' (TL 215). Arguing in the opposite direction, Lewis Carroll has noted that the number of words in any language is limited, and thus so are their possible combinations. Foreshadowing Borges's fear of tautology in writing, he adds: 'Soon … literary men will not ask themselves "What book shall I write?" but "Which book?"' Moving from words to characters, it is Kurd Lasswitz who in a collection of science fiction texts (*Traumkristalle*) imagines the total library created by mathematical combination and expanded by Borges in his story.

The Library contains every book written in the universe, and for each one, countless millions of books which may differ from it by a comma, or may be its meticulous refutation. If everything has been said, 'to speak is to commit tautologies' (F 73), 'hablar es incurrir en tautologías' (I 470). The nightmare is redeemed to an extent by a whole series of paradoxes and satirical elaborations. In the midst of all the chaotic babble, one famous text has the lines '*Oh tiempo tus pirámides*' (I 466), '*O Time thy pyramids*' (F 67). Curiously it is a prefiguration of a line from Borges's 1942 poem 'Del cielo y del infierno', which in turn is a translation from Shakespeare's sonnet 123 (Wilson, 103). The title of another book, *Axaxaxas mlö*, is a quotation from an imaginary poem in 'Tlön, Uqbar, Orbis Tertius'. Languages have almost to be re-invented from the scraps of others in a desperate attempt to make the fortuitous glimmer of order in one text comprehensible. It was concluded that the text was written in 'a Samoyed-Lithuanian dialect of Guaraní, with inflections from classical Arabic' (F 68). In the euphoria following the discovery that the Library contained every book, it became common to talk of 'Vindications', texts which would justify the acts of every individual and contain promises for his future. Thousands left their home galleries in search of their own Vindication, not realizing that the chance of their finding it was calculable at zero. Many were thrown down the central shaft, were strangled, or went mad. One 'blasphemous sect' tried, with the use of dice, to construct those canonical books 'through some improbable stroke of chance' (F 70), 'mediante un improbable don del azar' (I 468). The quest of those 'feebly mimicking the divine disorder' (F 70), who 'débilmente remedaban el divino desorden' (I 468), remind the reader of Menard, of the Lottery, perhaps also of Mallarmé's enigmatic (for me) 'Un coup de dés jamais n'abolira le hasard'. More reminiscent of 'The Approach to Al-Mu'tasim' is the search for the 'Book-Man', 'El Hombre de los Libros', who had found and read the ultimate text, the mystical key to the universe, the 'book that is the cipher and perfect compendium *of all other books*' (F 71). The method of the search is much the same as that devised by Mir Bahadur Ali: 'Someone proposed searching by regression: To locate book A, first consult book B, which tells you where book A can be found; to locate book B, first consult book C, and so on, to infinity ...' (F 71). The paradox of Zeno was almost inevitably to figure, and here figures in the final footnote: Letizia Álvarez de Toledo pointed out that the Library was redundant: all that was need was a single volume with 'an infinite number of infinitely thin pages' (F 74).

'A Survey of the Works of Herbert Quain', 'Examen de la obra de Herbert Quain'

Like 'The Approach to Al-Mu'tasim', 'A Survey' discusses and summarizes works by an invented author, at the same time as it invents them. In the case of the first work discussed, his forgetfulness of the work 'impoverishes' it, which, he goes on to clarify, means 'purifies' it. In this story he discusses not one, but four works by Quain. Other critics and rival authors are mentioned, but not developed as in the earlier story. The sources of one of his works are mentioned, Dunne and Bradley, but are not much elaborated on within the story, though they are discussed at length in essays in *Other Inquisitions*. In a sense the story-survey is almost a self-deprecating compendium of experimental literary techniques by a less than first-rate author that Borges himself might use in the future.

In *The God of the Labyrinth*, a pointedly Borgesian title, Quain writes a detective novel where the murder is solved by the detective, only to insert in the final paragraph a sentence which allows the reader to discover that the detective was wrong. This is not very different from 'Death and the Compass', where the detective misreads the original murder by following deceptive clues placed by his criminal enemy. The second project, *April March*, is

related to the thought of English philosophers J. W. Dunne (his thought on
the regression of knowing subjects necessary to know a knowing subject, and
the notion of a pre-existing future towards which many strands of time flow)
and F. H Bradley, where different directions of time might coexist. The series
of nine novels in *April March* take an event, three possible scenarios leading
up to that event, and another three for each of these three. Each novel would
follow one thread in three chapters. As in the editions of 'Al-Mu'tasim', the
nine would belong to different genres or ideologies: symbolic, supernatural,
crime, psychological, communist, anti-communist, etc. This ramification of
plot is taken to greater lengths in 'The Garden of Forking Paths', published
in the same year as the title story of Borges's first collection of fictions.

Quain's play *The Secret Mirror* is also retrospective, but simpler in structure, and, not surprisingly, specular. The first scene is set in an aristocratic
country house. The haughty Ulrica Thrale marries the Duke of Rutland in
preference to the dramatist Wilfred Quales. Subtly suggested contradictions
and sordid details prepare the spectator for the second act, where the same
characters reappear with different names. Quales becomes Quigley who, in
writing the first act, had transformed his modest life in a Liverpool lodging
house, where he had only heard of Ulrica Thrale in the pages of the *Tatler*,
into a more elegant ambience. The plot of the two acts is the same, but in
the second, 'everything is slightly menacing' (F 64), 'todo es ligeramente
horrible' (I 464). Williamson reads Ulrica as Norah Lange and Rutland as
Girondo, with the humiliation reserved for Quigley–Borges (W 220). Be that
as it may, the *mise-en-abyme* and the nightmarish change of tone prefigure
the almost identical structure and content of the play within 'The Secret
Miracle'.

In the eight stories of *Statements*, the roles of reader and writer are blurred.
Borges frequently privileged reading over writing, as in the lines from 'A
Reader': 'Let others boast of the pages they have written; / I am proud of
those I have read.'[60] Here Quain goes a step further: readers are an extinct
species and every European would like to be an author, but the necessary
inventiveness is not available to all. So he writes bungled stories which nevertheless suggest a good plot: 'the reader, blinded by vanity, believes that he
himself has come up with them' (F 64).[61] Borges presents himself as having
availed himself of this self-effacing charity, taking the plot of 'The Rose of
Yesterday' for his story 'The Circular Ruins'. Borges derives a story from

---

[60] 'Que otros se jacten de las páginas que han escrito; / a mí me enorgullecen las que he
leído' ('Un lector', in *Elogio de la sombra*, II 394).

[61] 'El lector, distraído por la vanidad, cree haberlos inventado' (I 464).

a plot suggested by a story by an author invented by Borges, and publishes it in the same collection as the story of the invented author! The genesis of a Borges text often involves a complex and circuitous intertextual history; rarely is it so utterly self-reflexive and solipsistic.

'The Garden of Forking Paths', 'El jardín de senderos que se bifurcan'

'The Garden' marks a new stage in Borges's fictional writing. It involves the sort of examination of a literary text which we have seen before, but this examination is set within a complex political thriller. 'Tlön, Uqbar, Orbis Tertius' and 'The Lottery in Babylon' contained elements of the allegorization of totalitarianism, but 'The Garden' is clearly set in the political cruelty of the First World War. Balderston's recent study has shown the extent of the detailed and important historical references, not only to the war, but to Irish and Chinese history. Its structure is similar to that of 'The Secret Miracle': they start with the brutality of history and historical time, move into a magical or metaphysical timelessness, both as lived experience and as literary artifice, and end by a return to the brutality of history, culminating in the murder of a distinguished intellectual. Like '*Deutsches Requiem*', it is narrated by an individual awaiting execution for a war crime. Just the first paragraph and footnote are apparently written by an English official, who clearly feels distaste for the opinions of the Chinese spy Yu Tsun in the document which constitutes the body of the text. The war is introduced not by direct narration but by reference to a historical study, one of Borges's favourite books (I 276): Liddell Hart's *The History of the World War*. It talks of a British offensive on the Serre–Montauban Line which was postponed for five days because of torrential rain, and proposes a different explanation for the delay: the plot of the story. Balderston points out that the official misreads the month of the offensive, and that it signalled the beginning of the Battle of the Somme, perhaps the bloodiest in human history. Mark Millington correctly remarks that 'the din of history re-enters the story at the very end' (cit. B 55).

The plot is ingenious, and information handled with great dexterity. Yu Tsun knows the position of a British artillery emplacement in France, but does not know how to communicate this information to his masters in Berlin. The telephone directory gives him the name of the person who can help him. We learn that he had met an Englishman, who was as important to him as Goethe, and that he had carried out a terrible act. He travels to the house of a man who we learn is called Stephen Albert, and who turns out to be an eminent Sinologist who has championed the previously discredited work of a famous ancestor of Yu Tsun, and shoots him in the back. Only at the end is his act explained: the artillery emplacement was in Albert in Flanders; the spymaster would understand this on reading about the murder in the English papers.

The symmetries and doublings between the characters are compelling. Yu Tsun is pursued throughout by Captain Richard Madden. Both are in an ambiguous position culturally and nationally. (I take the more detailed historical references from Balderston.) Yu Tsun had been an English professor at a German *Hochschule* in Tsingtao, a virtual German colony before the Japanese invasion, and was now spying for Germany in England. He had not committed the murder for Germany, which he despised:

> I did not do it for Germany. What do I care for a barbaric country that has forced me to the ignominy of spying? ... I did it because I sensed that the Leader looked down on the people of my race – the countless ancestors whose blood flows through my veins. I wanted to prove to him that a yellow man could save his armies. (F 77)[62]

(The tragic paradox is that to honour his ancestors, he kills the man who has returned their honour.) Madden, as an Irishman working for the British, was in a similar position, and he too was forced to be more brutal than his instincts perhaps would have prompted:

> Madden was implacable – or rather, he was obliged to be implacable. An Irishman at the orders of the English, a man accused of a certain lack of zealousness, perhaps even treason, how could he fail to embrace and give thanks for this miraculous favour—the discovery, capture, perhaps death, of two agents of the German Empire? (F 75–6)[63]

Balderston supplies vital contextual information here. The first is the Easter Rising in Dublin of April 1916, only months before the action of the story. One of the executed leaders of that rebellion, Pearse, answering the accusation of collaboration with the Germans, replies 'Germany is no more to me than England is' (B 45). Yu Tsun virtually echoes that statement. The

---

[62] 'No hice por Alemania, no. Nada me importa un país bárbaro, que me ha obligado a la abyección de ser un espía. ... Lo hice, porque yo sentía que el Jefe tenía en poco a los de mi raza – a los innumerables antepasados que confluyen en mí. Yo quería probarle que un amarillo podía salvar a sus ejércitos' (I 473).

[63] 'Madden era implacable. Mejor dicho, estaba obligado a ser implacable. Irlandés a las órdenes de Inglaterra, hombre acusado de tibieza y tal vez de traición ¿cómo no iba a abrazar y agradecer este milagroso favor: el descubrimiento, la captura, quizá la muerte, de dos agentes del Imperio Alemán?' (I 472).

Boxer Rebellion against the English in China, in 1900, links the two spies even further. Balderston also mentions an interesting namesake of Madden's: Richard Robert Madden, an Irishman who was employed by the British Colonial Office in the Caribbean in the 1830s, and who linked British imperialism in Ireland with that in the West Indies. He was well known in Latin American literary circles for having translated and published the autobiography of the black Cuban poet Juan Francisco Manzano.

Curiously, the other main living protagonist in the story has similarly mixed cultural affiliations. Stephen Albert claims to have worked as a missionary in China, before becoming a Sinologist and an expert in the writing of Yu Tsun's ancestor Ts'ui Pên. Balderston reports that the rare Chinese encyclopaedia on Albert's shelves disappeared at the siege of the British legations in 1910, the year of the Boxer Rebellion, which suggests that he too had been involved in the 'Great Game' of espionage (B 48).

Yu Tsun's journey has much of the hallucination. His destination is Ashgrove, both naming the ash tree, which he remarks on, and the ash associated with the greyness of the sorcerer of 'The Circular Ruins' and with Herbert Ashe. Albert's eyes and beard are inevitably grey. The children he meets on a railway platform ask whether he is going to the house of Doctor Stephen Albert, which is the first time the reader hears the name. They advise him to turn left at every crossroad, which he realizes is the common procedure for getting to the centre of certain labyrinths. This leads him to explain that his great-grandfather had been a powerful man who had renounced public life to write a novel and build a labyrinth. He was killed by a stranger; his novel was a meaningless jumble; his labyrinth was never found. When we realize that Stephen Albert was also killed by a foreigner, Ts'ui Pên, we begin to distinguish the real identification between the two men. The sense of unreality and hightened perception as Yu Tsun makes his way through the Staffordshire countryside (the native area of Fanny Haslam) and ponders endless labyrinths gives way to a repetition of the experience of eternity and dissolution of self related by Borges in 'Feeling in Death'. A key phrase is repeated verbatim; circularity and infinity are evoked: '[The road] was of elemental dirt. Branches tangled overhead, and the low round moon seemed to walk along beside me. ... Absorbed in those illusory imaginings, I forgot that I was a pursued man; I felt myself, for an indefinite while, the abstract perceiver of the world. ... The evening was near, yet infinite' (F 79).[64] Networks of repetitions knit together distant people and things. The

---

[64] 'Era de tierra elemental, arriba se confundían las ramas, la luna baja y circular parecía acompañarme. ... Absorto en esa ilusorias imágenes, olvidé mi destino de perseguido. Me sentí,

path 'dropped and forked'; when he finds Albert, the latter says 'I see that [you have] undertaken to remedy my solitude. You will no doubt wish to see the garden? ... The garden of forking paths' (F 80). This is the title of the novel written by Ts'ui Pên: Yu Tsun is walking in a literary landscape. He hears Chinese music coming from a pavilion. The solitude and the pavilion come together when Albert talks of Ts'ui Pên having composed his work in the Pavilion of Limpid Solitude. The circularity is reflected everywhere: the round clock, and the disc on the gramophone. In Albert's garden, 'the dew-drenched path meandered like the paths of my childhood' (F 80),[65] the 'symmetrical garden in Hai Feng' he had mentioned earlier (F 76).[66] Albert says that the Pavilion of Limpid Solitude was 'in the centre of a garden that was, perhaps, most intricately laid out; that fact might well have suggested a physical labyrinth' (F 82).[67] The garden of Yu Tsun's childhood, that of his grandfather (perhaps the same garden), and the garden of Stephen Albert become one garden. Stephen Albert, working in his own secluded pavilion, virtually becomes Ts'ui Pên. In a sense, then, Yu Tsun kills his own ancestor, repeating the gesture of the stranger. The web of timelessness, circularity and dissolution of individual identity woven by Borges's story is further reflected in the text which becomes the burning theme of the conversation between Yu Tsun and Dr Albert.

When Yu Tsun arrives, Albert takes him to be Hsi P'êng, a Chinese consul whom he presumably knew, which, in the light of the subsequent discussion, he might actually be in another bifurcation of time. The name is, of course, very similar to Ts'ui Pên. Yu Tsun curses the monk who had published his ancestor's absurd novel where 'in the third chapter the hero dies, yet in the fourth he is alive again' (F 81), and scornfully talks of the missing labyrinth. Albert dramatically shows him the labyrinth, which is actually one and the same thing as the novel, which Albert possesses and has studied and trans-lated. He mentions the legend that Ts'ui Pên had attempted to create a laby-rinth which was 'truly infinite' (F 82), 'estrictamente infinito' (I 477). Albert had wondered how a novel might be infinite: its last page might be identical to its first; in the *Arabian Nights*, Scheherazade had started to recount the story of the *Arabian Nights*; a novel enlarged or corrected over the genera-tions and passed from father to son. He discovers the truth when he receives

---

por un tiempo indeterminado, percibidor abstracto del mundo. ... La tarde era íntima, infinita' (474–5).

  [65] 'El húmedo sendero zigzagueaba como los de mi infancia' (I 476).

  [66] 'un niño en un simétrico jardín de Hai Feng' (I 472).

  [67] 'se erguía en el centro de un jardín tal vez intricado; el hecho puede haber sugerido a los hombres un laberinto físico' (476–7).

from Oxford a letter from Ts'ui Pên, which reads: 'I leave to several futures (not to all) my garden of forking paths' (F 83).[68] Albert realizes that when characters are faced with a dilemma, the novel chooses not just the one option of traditional fiction, but all the options, simultaneously: '*He creates*, thereby, "several futures," several *times*, which themselves proliferate and fork' (F 83).[69] We are in the world of Herbert Quain, but also in that of the Library of Babel, for to be literally infinite, its pages would have to be infinitely thin like the mythical text read by the Library Man. At this point, the reality of the story we are reading and the novel of Ts'ui Pên merge: 'Once in a while, the paths of that labyrinth converge: for example, you come to this house, but in one of the possible pasts you are my enemy, in another my friend' (F 83).[70]

The novel is a vast riddle, the solution of which, never mentioned, is *time*. The infinite network of Ts'ui Pên's time takes on the nightmarish dimensions of the Library of Babel:

> Unlike Newton and Schopenhauer, your ancestor did not believe in a uniform and absolute time; he believed in an infinite series of times, a growing, dizzying web of divergent, convergent and parallel times. That fabric of times that approach one another, fork, are snipped off, or are simply unknown for centuries, contains *all* possibilities. In most of those times, we do not exist; in some, you exist but I do not; in others, I do and you do not; in others still, we both do. (F 85)[71]

Yu Tsun feels a dizzying pullulation of beings around him, the garden 'was saturated, infinitely, with invisible persons ... Albert and myself – secret, busily at work, multiform – in other dimensions of time' (F 86).[72] The plural nightmare dissolves when Yu Tsun sees just *one* person, Madden who has come to capture him. He uses his one bullet to kill Stephen Albert, and send his message to Germany. In a way he kills the rich multiplicity of his ancestor

---

[68] '*Dejo a los varios porvenires (no a todos) mi jardín de senderos que se bifurcan*' (I 477).

[69] '*Crea, así, diversos porvenires, diversos tiempos, que también proliferan y se bifurcan*' (I 477).

[70] 'Alguna vez, los senderos de ese laberinto convergen: por ejemplo, usted llega a esta casa, pero en uno de los pasados posibles usted es mi enemigo, en otro mi amigo' (I 477–8).

[71] 'A diferencia de Newton y de Schopenhauer, su antepasado no creía en un tiempo uniforme, absoluto. Creía en infinitas series de tiempos, en una red creciente y vertiginosa de tiempos divergentes, convergentes, y paralelos. Esa trama de tiempos que se aproximan, se bifurcan, se cortan o que secularmente se ignoran, abarca *todas* las posibilidades. No existimos en la mayoría de esos tiempos; en algunos exisite usted y no yo; en otros, yo, no usted; en otros, los dos' (I 478).

[72] 'estaba saturado hasta lo infinito de invisibles personas. Esas personas eran Albert y yo, secretos, atareados y multiformes en otras dimensiones de tiempo' (I 479).

by opting for the one outcome, an outcome that damns him to 'endless contrition' (F 86), 'innumerable contrición' (I 480). The Spanish adjective has been carefully chosen.

The story moves brutally out of eternity, timelessness, and infinite bifurcation, into historical reality. Ironically, the two versions of an epic chapter that Albert reads from *The Garden* open up the story to what lies beyond it: war.

> In the first, an army marches off to battle through a mountain wilderness; the horror of the rocks and darkness inspires in them a disdain for life, and they go on to an easy victory. In the second, the same army passes through a palace in which a ball is being held; the brilliant battle seems to them a continuation of the *fête*, and they win it easily. ... I recall the final words, repeated in each version like some secret commandment: 'Thus the heroes fought, their admirable hearts calm, their swords violent, they themselves resigned to killing and to dying.' (F 84)[73]

Balderston picks up on Murillo's observation that labyrinths do not appear in classical Chinese culture, and goes on to show, significantly, that the labyrinth was a term widely used to refer to the chaotic labyrinths of the landscape of trench warfare (B 50). The story has thus been alluding to the horrors of the Great War throughout. In a later poem, Borges describes the battle of Junín as 'the seething labyrinth of cavalries' (SP 169), 'el furioso laberinto de los ejércitos' (II 250). Another labyrinth story, 'Ibn-Hakam al Bokhari, Murdered in his Labyrinth', is set in the early summer of 1914, where the protagonists are ironically and ominously 'weary of a world that lacked the dignity of danger' (A 95).[74]

---

[73] 'En la primera, un ejército marcha hacia una batalla a través de una montaña desierta; el horror de las piedras y de la sombra le hace menospreciar la vida y logra con facilidad la victoria; en la segunda, el mismo ejército atraviesa un palacio en el que hay una fiesta; la resplandeciente batalla les parece una continuación de la fiesta y logran la victoria. ... Recuerdo las palabras finales, repetidas en cada redacción como un mandamiento secreto: *Así combatieron los héroes, tranquilo el admirable corazón, violenta la espada, resignados a matar y a morir*' (I 478).

[74] 'hartos de un mundo sin la dignidad del peligro' (I 600).

Fictions Part II: *Artifices* (1944)

'Funes, His Memory', 'Funes el memorioso'

The unnamed narrator of 'Funes el memorioso' has many of the biographical details of Borges: for example he spends the summer in Uruguay with his relations the Haedo family, and studies Latin. The events he relates, however, are dated 1887, and he writes about them fifty years later, around 1937, at the age of about seventy. He writes a contribution to a collection on Ireneo Funes, who, after a fall from a horse, had acquired total recall. The time lapse and the fallibility of his memory explain the schematic and short account. The charm of the story lies in the almost oxymoronic combination of provincial small-town Uruguay and the grand theme of total memory illustrated with quotes from Pliny and Locke. The older Borges chides his younger version for his snobbery towards the locals, but is not devoid of petty and supercilious sarcasm when referring to Uruguayan writers: 'Unfortunately I am Argentine, and so congenitally unable to produce the dithyramb that is the obligatory genre in Uruguay, especially when the subject is an Uruguayan' (F 91).[1] For the Uruguayan poet Ipuche, Funes was 'un Zarathustra cimarrón y vernáculo' (I 485), 'a maverick and vernacular Zarathustra' (F 91); 'Borges' peevishly replies that he was also a limited, small-time *compadrito*.

'Borges's' first encounter with Funes, who is even then able to tell the time without a watch, comes after a gallop across the pampa with his cousin Bernardo Haedo under a dramatic stormy sky. The literariness of this Güiraldes-like passage is echoed when he next visits Fray Bentos. On the first occasion Funes had been seen on high, on an elevated sidewalk; on the second, he learns that Funes has been thrown down from his horse and is paralysed. The symmetry and magic point to the construction of the short story as outlined in 'Narrative Art and Magic': 'I recall the sensation of unsettling magic that this news gave me. ... [it] struck me as very much like

---

[1] 'Mi deplorable condición de argentino me impedirá incurrir en el ditirambo – género obligatorio en el Uruguay, cuando el tema es un uruguayo' (I 485).

a dream confected out of elements of the past' (F 93).[2] Such literary structuring is, as we shall see, the antithesis of the world of Funes. Funes has asked
to borrow some Latin texts and a dictionary to learn the language; Borges
goes to retrieve them, and spends a whole night talking with him, which is
the basis of the conceptual side to the story. As he approaches Funes's room,
he hears his reciting, from memory, a paragraph about memory from Pliny's
Historia naturalis.

Here the story hits erudite citation and unforgettable philosophical speculation. Borges apologizes for the poverty of his account: 'I will not attempt
to reproduce the words of it, which are now forever irrecoverable. ... Indirect
discourse is distant and weak; I know that I am sacrificing the effective-
ness of my tale (F 95).[3] The apology is ironic. It took Funes twenty-four
hours to recall the events of a day. Such prolixity would not have made for
a gripping short story. It would have given an interminable story written by
Carlos Argentino Daneri. Funes enumerates classical accounts of extraordinary memory before describing his total recall. His memory is the mental
equivalent of the Total Library, where meaning is virtually excluded by infinite detail. Funes describes his memory as a garbage heap, but Borges offers
a classic enumeration to illustrate the difference between normal perception
and that of Funes:

> A circle drawn on a blackboard, a right triangle, a rhombus – all these are
> forms we can fully intuit; Ireneo could do the same with the stormy mane
> of a young colt, a small herd of cattle on a mountainside, a flickering fire
> and its uncountable ashes, and the many faces of a dead man at a wake.
>
> (F 96)[4]

Funes can only perceive difference, not analogy: only one of the two poles
of thought discussed by Emerson. Forgetting as well as memory is essential
to thought: 'I suspect, nevertheless, that he was not very good at thinking.
To think is to ignore (or forget) differences, to generalize, to abstract. In the

---

2 'Recuerdo la impresión de incómoda magia que la noticia me produjo ... tenía mucho
de sueño elaborado con elementos anteriores' (I 486).

3 'No trataré de reproducir sus palabras, irrecuperables ahora. Prefiero resumir con
veracidad las muchas cosas que me dijo Ireneo. El estilo indirecto es remoto y débil; yo sé que
sacrifico la eficacia de mi relato' (I 487).

4 'Una circunferencia en un pizarrón, un triángulo rectángulo, un rombo, son formas que
podemos intuir plenamente; lo mismo le pasaba a Ireneo con las aborrascadas crines de un
potro, con una punta de ganado en una cuchilla, con el fuego cambiante y con la innumerable
ceniza, con las muchas caras de un muerto en un largo velorio' (I 488).

teeming world of Ireneo Funes, there was nothing but particulars' (F 99).[5] So far away from Platonic ideas was he that he considered it absurd that the generic word 'dog' could be applied to the same dog seen from the side at 3.14 and from the front a minute later. The two phenomena were utterly different. His particularized vision is amusingly applied to numbers. Irritated by the fact that the number of the thirty-three famous patriots who liberated Montevideo from the Spaniards needed in Spanish three words, 'treinta y tres', he decides to give every number its own name: 'Instead of seven thousand thirteen (7013), he would say, for instance, "Máximo Pérez"; instead of seven thousand fourteen (7014), "the railroad"; other numbers were "Luis Melián Lafinur," [an uncle of Borges] "Olimar," "sulfur," "clubs", "the whale," "gas," "a stewpot," "Napoleon," ... Instead of five hundred (500), he said "nine"' (F 97).[6] The analytical decimal system is replaced by utter chaos, which he could share with no one. Fittingly, Funes died of pulmonary congestion, asphyxiated by the vast amount of data his mind could not process.

Two Irish tales: 'The Shape of the Sword' and 'The Theme of the Traitor and the Hero'

These two stories, originally published in 1942 and 1944, but placed consecutively in the collection, talk of the ambiguous relationship between cowardice or betrayal and heroism. In the first, two characters, an Irish independence fighter and the person who betrays him to the English, are linked by the narrative in which the traitor assumes the identity of the other in order to recount his story of infamy: the origin of the moon-shaped scar on his face. In the second, an idolized nationalist leader is discovered to have betrayed the cause, and his execution is staged drawing on models from the drama of Shakespeare to present his death as heroic martyrdom.

Both are set in the context of the Irish struggle for independence from England, the first in 1922 and the second in 1824. W. B. Yeats and Charles Stewart Parnell seem to be a real presence in both. 'The Theme' uses as its epigraph lines from *The Tower*: 'So the Platonic Year / Whirls out new right and wrong, / Whirls in the old instead; / All men are dancers and their

---

5 'Sospecho, sin embargo, que no era muy capaz de pensar. Pensar es olvidar diferencias, es generalizar, abstraer. En el abarrotado mundo de Funes no había sino detalles, casi inmediatos' (I 490).

6 'En lugar de siete mil trece, decía (por ejemplo) *Máximo Pérez*; en lugar de siete mil catorce, *El Ferrocarril*; otros números eran: *Luis Melián Lafinur, Olimar, azufre, los bastos, la bellena* ... En lugar de quinientos, decía *nueve*' (I 489).

tread / Goes to the barbarous clangour of a gong.' The Platonic year alludes probably to the cyclical time enacted in the story where Kilpatrick repeats the role of Julius Caesar, becomes him. The scar on Moon's face, the 'half moon of blood' drawn by 'half moon of steel' of the scimitar, would seem to come from Yeats's poem 'My Table' where a sword given to Yeats by a Japanese admirer, Sato, is described as 'curved like new moon, moon-luminous' (Yeats, 248). Moon, speaking as the hero, tells how his group was able to avenge 'our sixteen colleagues fallen to the machine guns at Elphin' (F 104). The executions following the 1916 Easter Rebellion were marked by Yeats in 'Sixteen Dead Men', and in 'Easter 1916', where he wrote famously of the heroes: 'MacDonagh and MacBride / And Connolly and Pearse / Now and in time to be, / Wherever green is worn, / Are changed, changed utterly: / A terrible beauty is born' (Yeats, 230).

Listing the rather literary and mythical things which mattered about Ireland to his group, Moon slips in: 'it was the repudiation of Parnell' (F 102).[7] Parnell was perhaps the most important Irish politician of the nineteenth century, idolized by the people, and referred to as the 'uncrowned king of Ireland'. Working with Gladstone to achieve Home Rule, his dreams were shattered in 1891 when his affair with Katie O'Shea was made public and his party members and the church hypocritically turned against him, and effectively betrayed him, leading perhaps to the many years of bloodshed before full independence was achieved in 1937. I agree with Fishburn and Hughes that the guilt and self-loathing felt by Moon and expressed in his 'Now, despise me' reflects Yeats's similar disgust at the Irish turning on their former hero in the manner of cannibals in 'Parnell's Funeral': 'But popular rage, / *Hysteria passio* dragged this quarry down. / None shared our guilt; nor did we play a part / Upon a painted stage when we devoured his heart. / Come, fix upon me that accusing eye. / I thirst for accusation' (Yeats, 329–30). The notion of the theatricality of Irish history, played out in 'Theme', is also very much present here. In 'The Theme' the identification between Kilpatrick and Parnell is made less explicitly but very clearly. He writes: 'Like Moses, who from the land of Moab glimpsed yet could not reach the promised land, Kilpatrick perished on the eve of the victorious rebellion he had planned for and dreamed of' (F107).[8] This is exactly the comparison made between Moses and Parnell by James Joyce in 'The Shade of Parnell'. Parnell and his life

---

7 'era el repudio de Parnell' (I 492).

8 'a semejanza de Moisés que, desde la tierra de Moab, divisó y no pudo pisar la tierra prometida, Kilpatrick pereció en la víspera de la rebelión victoriosa que había premeditado y soñado' (I 496).

are also copiously woven into the pages of *Ulysses*. Both Parnell and later, allegedly, Sir Roger Casement, executed in 1916, were falsely accused by the English in forged (or in the case of Casement allegedly forged) documents in order to discredit them: Parnell of being involved in the murder of two British officials in 1882, and Casement, of having penned luridly pornographic and homosexual material in the 'Black Diaries'. It is possible to see the reversal of the historical truth in 'The Theme' as a revenge for these English dirty tricks; made all the more ironical by the use of the English national bard.

It is clear that Borges is fascinated by empire, especially the British Empire in India and Ireland, and by the shifting and ambiguous identification and deflection involved, the way in which the colonizers' texts are adopted and diverted from their hegemonic role. Perhaps it is a mirror of Borges's own dual 'colonial' inheritance from Spain and from Edwardian England.

'The Shape of the Sword', 'La forma de la espada'

The theme of cowardice and bravery fascinated Borges. In the sonorously entitled 'The Uncivil Teacher of Court Etiquette Kôtsuké no Suké' from *A Universal History of Iniquity*, the coward is marked by a scar on his forehead. The *samurai* captain who avenges the death ignominiously provoked by this coward, has to pretend for years that he is the opposite of what he really is in order to make his enemy think him inoffensive: he abandons his family, takes up with prostitutes, and allows himself to be trodden on and spat at in a pool of his vomit in the gutter. As Christ notes (76), Borges greatly admired Conrad's *Lord Jim*, the central theme of which, he wrote, was 'the obsession with honour and the shame at having been a coward' (OC 849). The theme is apparently simple but enigmatic in 'Man on Pink Corner', and made far more complex in the sequel 'The Story from Rosendo Juárez'. In story from *The Aleph*, 'The Other Death', cowardice on the battlefield is reversed and turned into heroic death, when God allows history to change. John Vincent Moon, who acted in a cowardly fashion in the Irish Civil War of 1922, and tells the story of his infamy by taking the voice of the man he betrayed, also seems to have taken on his physical appearance. He describes himself in Ireland as 'thin yet slack-muscled, all at once' (F 102), 'flaco y fofo a la vez' (I 492), but the Borges who meets him in his ranch in Uruguay describes him very differently: 'I recall his glacial eyes, his lean energy, his gray mustache' (F 100); 'Recuerdo los ojos glaciales, la enérgica flacura, el bigote gris' (I 491).

The story is introduced and concluded by 'Borges', who was detained by high waters on the river at the ranch, while the main narration is by Moon.

Travestied identity is present from the beginning as Moon apparently allows himself to be known in the area as 'el inglés de la Colorada', when he is Irish, though he betrayed a comrade to the English. After dinner, drunk from drinking much rum, Borges rashly asks, out of 'inspiration or elation or boredom' (F 101),[9] about the scar which traverses Moon's face. Moon's response suggests a sense of threat involved in hearing the story, a moral danger perhaps: he will tell the story on the condition that 'no contempt or condemnation be withheld, no mitigation for any iniquity be pleaded'.[10] This makes more sense of the enigmatic explanation which opens the story. Cardoso, the previous owner of the land, had refused to sell to Moon, who 'had recourse to an unforeseeable argument' (I 491), i.e. to tell him the story of his scar. No more is heard of Cardoso. Moon himself, speaking as if he were the hero, gives us the key to the instability and reversal of identity and roles. As we saw in 'The Nothingness of Personality' and in the accounts of the pantheism of Emerson and Schopenhauer, a continuous and coherent personal identity is a fallacy: repeating or feeling the same thing as another person, fervently reading the words of a writer, means that we *are* that person. On realizing the cowardice of Moon, the heroic patriot feels contaminated by it, feels that he actually becomes the other man:

> I was embarrassed by the man and his fear, shamed by him, as though I myself were the coward, not Vincent Moon. Whatsoever one man does, it is as though all men did it. That is why it is not unfair that a single act of disobedience in a garden should contaminate all humanity; that is why it is not unfair that a single Jew's crucifixion should be enough to save it. Schopenhauer may have been right – I am other men, any man is all men. Shakespeare is somehow the wretched John Vincent Moon.' (F 103–4)[11]

The scar was inflicted by the patriot after he heard Moon denouncing him to the English military, who shot him at dawn. By narrating the patriot's story, Moon, of course, in turn, becomes the other.

---

[9] 'no sé qué inspiración o qué exultación o qué tedio' (I 491).

[10] 'la [condición] de no mitigar ningún oprobio, ninguna circunstancia de infamia' (I 491).

[11] 'Me abochornaba ese hombre con miedo, como si yo fuera el cobarde, no Vincent Moon. Lo que hace un hombre es como si lo hicieran todos los hombres. Por eso no es injusto que una desobediencia en un jardín contamine al género humano; por eso no es injusto que la crucifixión de un solo judío baste para salvarlo. Acaso Schopenhauer tiene razón: yo soy los otros, cualquier hombre es todos los hombres, Shakespeare es de algún modo el miserable John Vincent Moon' (I 493).

'The Theme of the Traitor and the Hero' 'Tema del traidor y del héroe'

'The Theme' is an extraordinarily complex narrative game in which each narration frames another, and is finally framed by it. 'The Circular Ruins' with a twist is written into Irish history. Borges rewrites a story by Chesterton to imagine a novel, the summary of which is the story we read. He is one step away from commenting on the text by an imaginary other author. Ryan is writing a biography of his great-grandfather, a hero of the independence struggle in Ireland, Fergus Kilpatrick. He realizes that the story as it has reached him is very structured and literary, and after receiving various documents deciphers the enigma. Alexander Nolan was a translator of Shakespeare and knowledgeable about *Festspiele*. Nolan discovers the truth about Kilpatrick's treason to the cause (a discovery which suspiciously takes the literary form of Sophocles). He decides to turn Kilpatrick's execution into a vast theatrical performance, following the script of Shakespeare, in which Kilpatrick plays the role of hero and martyr. Nolan also realizes that he, supposedly a historian outside the plot, was somehow a character in it. Nolan had foreseen that he would discover the artifice, and, for love of country and family, decide to silence it. Historicity and literariness slip quickly in and out of focus.

Borges opens the story by claiming to have imagined a plot, which he might one day write up into, presumably, a novel, under the influence of Chesterton and Leibnitz: a nicely characteristic pairing of philosophy and detective literature. Efraín Kristal points out that the Chestertonian hypotext is 'The Sign of the Broken Sword', which does indeed dictate the skeleton of the plot pretty comprehensively. Father Brown investigates the death of the celebrated military officer Arthur St Clare, supposedly hanged by a Brazilian general after a heroic charge. Father Brown is puzzled, because Olivier had the reputation of magnanimity towards his prisoners, and later discovers significant documents. Despite his immaculate reputation St Clare was involved in torture, prostitution and corruption. During a war against the Brazilian general Olivier, he betrayed his side to the enemy. Another officer discovered his deceit, and asked him to resign. St Clare murdered him, breaking his sword in the process. In order to hide the incriminating corpse, he sacrificed numberless men in a suicide attack, which would hide his victim among other corpses. His men, including his son-in-law to be, realized his treachery and hanged him, vowing to keep the treachery and the revenge quiet, allowing it to be attributed to Olivier. Father Brown also decides not to divulge the truth.

Ryan starts the research for his biography on the centenary of his grandfather's death, which had been followed by the victorious rebellion that he had
prepared. (Compare this with Yu Tsun and his great-grandfather Ts'ui Pên,
who rises in his esteem after the revelation of the truth.) He is perplexed
at the coincidences between his death and the circumstances surrounding
that of Julius Caesar, such as the unread letter denouncing the plotters. He
tries to tear himself away from the literary contamination to concentrate on
various theories of circular time, 'some secret shape of time, a pattern of
repeating lines' (F 107).[12] He invokes the 'morphologies of time' expounded
by Vico, Hegel, and Spengler, and notions of metempsychosis, which would
have Kilpatrick as Caesar in a past incarnation. When, however, he realizes
that a beggar had spoken words to Kilpatrick from *Macbeth*, he is astounded:
'The idea that history might have copied history is mind-boggling enough;
that history should copy *literature* is inconceivable …' (F 108).[13] The documents which come into his hands (think of similar ones in 'Tlön' and in 'The
Garden of Forking Paths') disclose Nolan's interest in Swiss *Festspiele*, vast
theatrical performances, on site, of historical events. Another shows Kilpatrick signing a death sentence, when (like the Brazilian general) he was not
wont to do this.

He thus cracks the puzzle: Kilpatrick was killed in a theatre, reflecting
the real and literary death of Caesar and prefiguring the historical death in
a theatre of Abraham Lincoln in Washington in 1865. His death, moreover,
was played out with the whole city as a theatre, a nice *mise-en-abyme*. Yeats
talks of Irish history as a 'painted stage', but Shakepaeare's repeated conceit
as the world as theatre must also have been in Borges's mind. He was fond
of discussing the device in *Hamlet*, and in *Macbeth* we have the well known:
'Life's but a walking shadow, a poor player, / that struts and frets his hour
upon this stage, / and then is heard no more' (Shakespeare, 1024–5). Curiously, the discovery of the truth, which *only later* would be transformed by
literature, is also literary in origin. Kilpatrick orders an investigation into
a suspected traitor and it is revealed that he is the traitor: a reworking of
Oedipus King when Oedipus asks who is responsible for the plague at Thebes.
Ryan 'published a book dedicated to the hero's glory; that too, perhaps, had
been foreseen' (F 110).[14]

---

[12] 'una secreta forma del tiempo, un dibujo de líneas que se repiten' (I 497).

[13] 'Que la historia hubiera copiado a la historia ya era suficientemente pasmoso; que la
historia copie la literatura es inconcebible …' (I 497).

[14] 'Publica un libro dedicado a la gloria del héroe; también eso, tal vez, estaba previsto'
(498).

'Death and the Compass', 'La muerte y la brújula'

If the previous two stories are centred on Irish themes, 'Death and the Compass' and 'The Secret Miracle' are concerned with Jewish culture, which had interested Borges at least from the time of *Discusión*, and which had provided the story of the golem for 'The Circular Ruins'. 'Death and the Compass', Borges's most celebrated detective story, was published in *Sur* in 1942, and in the anthology of the genre, *Los mejores cuentos policiales*, compiled and translated by Borges and Bioy in 1943, before being included in *Artificios* and *Ficciones* in 1944. Kristal argues convincingly that the translation process of stories by Poe, Hawthorne and Jack London contributed much to its gestation.[15] Perhaps the most important of these texts is Poe's 'The Purloined Letter'. Poe's classical combination of sleuth, Auguste Dupin, criminal, Minister D, and the Prefect is reflected in Borges's sleuth Erik Lönnrot, his criminal Red Scharlach, and the police commissioner Treviranus. The Prefect's habit of seeing everything he did not understand as 'odd' is reflected in the first lines of Borges's text; of the many problems solved by Lönnrot, none was 'so odd – so rigorously odd, we might say'[16] as the present case. Borges almost inevitably veers away from the model. In Poe, Dupin had sworn vengeance against the Minister, and achieved it through his brilliance; in Borges it is the criminal Red Scharlach who has sworn vengeance on Lönnrot, and dupes him into following a set of false clues which lead him into a death trap. It is the criminal who finally explains to the detective the mechanism of the plot. The common-sense Commissioner Treviranus is right at key moments, when Lönnrot over-interprets and is both right and fatally wrong. Treviranus's 'no hay que buscarle tres pies al gato', i.e. 'don't invent problems which don't exist', is a decent translation of Poe's pseudo-epigraph from Seneca, which translates into English as 'Nothing is more detestable to wisdom than too much subtlety' (Poe, 330, and 532, note 1). It is Lönnrot's subtlety which weaves the plot in which he becomes the victim.

The story is almost literally a war of readings. Chesterton's Father Brown sadly observes that 'the criminal is the creative artist; the detective only the critic' (Chesterton 15). Piglia, in *El último lector*, refines this scenario. Scharlach and Lönnrot are two modes of writing. Scharlach forces Lönnrot to be a Madame Bovary and Don Quijote, to live out his readings, to read literally, while he uses reading in a criminal, savage way, twisting texts, reading

---

[15] For a detailed consideration of the presence of Poe in Borges's work, see John Irwin, *The Mystery to a Solution: Poe, Borges, and the Analytic Detective Story* (Baltimore: Johns Hopkins University Press, 1994).

[16] 'ninguno tan extraño – tan rigurosamente extraño, diremos' (I 500).

confrontationally. The criminal becomes the model for the literary critic, who
reads against other readers.

> It is a sort of enforced Bovarism, because Scharlach effectively obliges
> Lönnrot to act out what he is reading. Belief is at stake. Lönnrot believes in
> what he reads (he does not believe in anything else); he reads literally, we
> might say. While Scharlach, on the other hand, is a disdainful reader, who
> uses what he reads for his own ends, he twists it and turns it into reality
> (as a crime) ... The reader as criminal, who uses texts to his own benefit
> and makes a deviant use of them, works as a savage hermeneut. He reads
> badly, but only from a moral point of view; he performs a wicked, spiteful
> reading, makes perfidious use of the letter. We might consider literary criti-
> cism as an exercise of that sort of criminal reading ... Scharlach effects
> the delusion of don Quixote, but deliberately. He effects in reality what he
> reads (and he does it for another).[17]

At the beginning of the story Lönnrot and Treviranus face the conjunction
of a dead Hebrew scholar, Yarmolinsky, a set of Jewish religious texts, and a
line on a type-writer: '*The first letter of the Name has been written*' (F 113).[18]
While Treviranus (correctly) declares that the murder was random, a bungled
burglary, Lönnrot counters, with a memorable phrase which is too clever for
his own good: 'Possible, but uninteresting ... You will reply that reality has
not the slightest obligation to be interesting. I will reply in turn that reality
may get along without that obligation, but hypotheses may not' (F 112).[19]
Lönnrot has a dead rabbi and wants a rabbinical solution. To the random
reality of the world he opposes a cultural reading, takes away Yarmolinsky's
books and declares that he will solve the crime by a reading of the mystical
notions contained therein. As the plot unfolds, Lönnrot correctly interprets a
series of kabbalistic clues and attends three murder scenes in the north, west
and east of the city. Predicting the time and place of the fourth by reading a

---

[17] 'Se trata de una suerte de bovarismo forzado, porque Scharlach de hecho obliga a
Lönnrot a actuar lo que lee. La creencia está en juego. Lönnrot cree en lo que lee (no cree en
otra cosa); lee al pie de la letra, podríamos decir. Mientras que Scharlach, en cambio, es un
lector displicente, que usa lo que lee para sus propios fines, tergiversa y lleva lo que lee a lo
real (como crimen). ... El lector como criminal, que usa los textos en su beneficio y hace de
ellos un uso desviado, funciona como un hermeneuta salvaje. Lee mal pero sólo en sentido
moral; hace una lectura malvada, rencorosa, un uso pérfido de la letra. Podríamos pensar a la
crítica literaria como un ejercicio de ese tipo de lectura criminal. ... Scharlach realiza la ilusión
de don Quijote, pero deliberadamente. Realiza en la realidad lo que lee (y lo hace para otro)'
(Piglia, *Lector*, 35–6).
[18] '*La primera letra del Nombre ha sido articulada*' (I 500).
[19] 'Posible, pero no interesante ... Usted replicará que la realidad no tiene la menor obligación de ser interesante. Yo le replicaré que la realidad puede prescindir de esa obligación,
pero no las hipótesis' (I 500).

combination of the mystical clues, he goes to a house in the north, believing he will catch the criminal, but discovers that he has been led into a trap. Scharlach had read of Lönnrot's intent in the *Yidische Zeitung*, reads the same texts, feeds Lönnrot with clues from them, and stages the murders (rather like Nolan later in 'The Theme of the Traitor and the Hero'). The second murder is that of the murderer of Yarmolinsky, and the third is faked.

As in a great many stories a series of texts are cited which are intimately related to the plot: quest, dystopia, intellectual construct, and to the tension between plotting (a heightened form of structured thought and language) and reality. Here the texts are found in the study of the Jewish scholar Yarmolinsky, who was murdered by the drunken Daniel Simón Azevedo in an attempt to steal the jewels of the Tetrarch of Galilee. The first mentioned is a text published by Borges dated 1931, 'A Defense of the Kabbalah', where the world is seen as a creation of Divine language, and the words of the divine Scriptures can be studied and combined in such a way as to reveal the presence of God and the powers of creation. A work on Flood, presumably Robert Fludd, a Kabbalist and Rosicrucian, is an interest shared with Hladík from 'The Secret Miracle', who also translated another work in Yarmolinsky's collection: the *Sepher Yezirah* or *Book of Creation*, where the notion of the ten *sephiroth* or divine emanations is elaborated, which combine with the twenty-two letters of the Hebrew alphabet to form the basis of the world. A biography of Baal Shem, associated with the 'miraculous power of the Sacred Name' (FH), leads to the eighteenth-century Polish movement of Hasidism, often considered heretical by Orthodox rabbis. Crucial to the plot is a monograph on the notion of the Tetragrammaton, the four letters JHVH, which are the revered name of God, only to be uttered by the high priest in the temple. Borges's profane use of the name would be considered at the very least irreverent by the religious.

The number four, here, explicitly associated with Judaism, is played off throughout the story against the 'three' implicitly associated with the Trinity of Christianity, which had always struck Borges as an intellectual monstrosity. Treviranus says he is a poor Christian, and has no time for such Jewish superstitions. Lönnrot suggests that the first crime belongs to the history of Jewish superstitions, to which the reporter from the *Yidische Zeitung* remarks slyly: 'Like Christianity' (I 500). Judaism and Christianity are inseparably intertwined, enemy Siamese twins, ultimately one, like Lönnrot and Scharlach. The threeness of the first murder is absurdly over-determined. It takes place on 3 December; Yarmolinsky's resignation is born of three years of war in the Carpathians, three thousand years of oppression and pogroms. Opposite his room is that of the Tetrarch (ruler of one of four divisions) of

Galilee. The apparent message: 'The first letter of the name of God has been spoken', which is later revealed to be the beginning of an article written by the scholar, is taken up by Scharlach after reading the history of the Hasidim. It is scrawled by his men as 'The second letter ...' when the body of (the person who is later revealed to be) Azevedo, bumped off by Scharlach for bungling the burglary, is found by an abandoned paint factory, on the third of January. It is written over 'the red and yellow rhombuses' (F114), 'los rombos amarillos y rojos' (I 501). The four-sided rhombus becomes one of the most haunting motifs of the story.

On 3 February, Treviranus takes a call from someone calling himself Ginzberg, offering to sell information on the *sacrifice* of Yarmolinsky and Azevedo. It is, of course, Scharlach, planting the notion that the deaths were a ritual or magical religious sacrifice by the Hasidim. He traces the call to a brothel run by Black Finnegan, who tells him of an apparently drunken tall man being dragged away by two carnival harlequins, sporting 'yellow, red, and green lozenges' (F 116), 'losanges amarillos, rojos y verdes' (I 502). In the room he finds a pool of blood, the announcement that the *last* letter of the name had been spoken, and a further, contradictory, clue: a copy of Leusden's *Philologus hebraeograecus* with a passage underlined, which explains that the Jewish day goes from sunset to sunset, not midnight to midnight. The implication of this is that the murders took place effectively on the fourth day of the month. This clue is then apparently contradicted by a letter signed Baruch Spinoza, a philosopher admired by Borges for his combination of intuition and rationality (FH), and use of geometrical theorems. It shows a map of the city where the three murders form a perfect equilateral triangle, and contains the affirmation that there would not be a further murder on 3 March. Lönnrot falls into the trap, set by the four letters of the name of God, the repeated rhombuses, and the Jewish day, of realizing that there would be a fourth murder, at the northern apex of a rhombus. With a pair of compasses and a magnetic compass, 'un compás y una brújula' (I 503), he determines the place: the abandoned mansion Triste-le-Roy. (The name was invented by a friend of Borges's, Amanda Molina Vedia, to whom the story is dedicated.) His joy at having solved the puzzle pushes Lönnrot into a sort of archetypal mode, where the pattern is more important than the individuals involved: 'He had virtually solved the problem; the mere circumstances, the reality (names, arrests, faces, the paperwork of trial and imprisonment), held very little interest for him now' (F 118).[20] This phasing is echoed in one of

---

[20] 'Virtualmente, había descifrado el problema; las meras circunstancias, la realidad (nombres, arrestos, caras, trámites judiciales y carcelarios), apenas le interesaban ahora' (I 504).

Borges's most personal stories, 'Emma Zunz': 'all that was false were the circumstances, the time, and one or two proper names' (A 50).[21]

As Lönnrot approaches Triste-le-Roy, the tone of the story darkens and takes on intensely personal dimensions. In his lecture 'The Argentine Writer and Tradition', Borges explains how a dream-state had allowed him finally to capture, in the cosmopolitan city of this story, the essence of Buenos Aires:

> About a year ago, I wrote a story called 'Death and the Compass,' which is a kind of nightmare, a nightmare in which elements of Buenos Aires appear, deformed by the horror of the nightmare; and in that story, when I think of the Paseo Colón, I call it Rue de Toulon; when I think of the *quintas* of Adrogué, I call them Triste-le-Roy. (TL 424)[22]

Estela Canto points out that the Hotel Las Delicias in Adrogué, where the Borges family summered, and which is so significant to him, contained windows with 'red and blue rhombuses', 'rombos rojos y azules' (Canto, 96). As Lönnrot enters the house, 'The moonlight of the evening shone through the lozenges of the windows; they were yellow, red, and green. He was stopped by an astonished, dizzying recollection' (F 120); 'Lo detuvo un recuerdo asombrado y vertiginoso' (I 505). At this point he is taken by Scharlach. The moment is clearly momentous. In 'Emma Zunz' the protagonist visits a brothel in the infamous Paseo de Julio, where she sees something that reminds her of her childhood home: 'with lozenges identical to those of the house in Lanús' (A 47), 'una vidriera con losanges idénticos a los de la casa en Lanús' (I 566). As she gives herself to the sailor she thinks 'that her father had done to her mother the horrible thing being done to her now … She thought it with weak-limbed astonishment, and then, immediately, took refuge in vertigo' (A 47); 'Lo pensó con débil asombro y se refugió, en seguida, en el vértigo' (I 566). The conjunction of the lozenges with the sensation of *asombro* and *vértigo* is identical in both stories. (Scharlach had intriguingly found it necessary to spend several days in the brothel in Rue Toulon, i.e., according to Borges's commentary, El Paseo de Julio (Com 268), the utter depravity and misery of which he had described in a poem from *Cuaderno San Martín*.) The primal scene directly evoked in the later story might well be seen as haunting this story. In his notes on the story, Borges

---

[21] 'sólo eran falsas las circunstancias, la hora y uno o dos nombres propios' (I 568).

[22] 'hará un año, escribí una historia que se llama "La muerte y la brújula" que es una suerte de pesadilla, una pesadilla en que figuran elementos de Buenos Aires deformados por el horror de la pesadilla; pienso ahí en el Paseo Colón y lo llamo Rue de Toulon, pienso en las quintas de Adrogué y las llamo Triste-le-Roy' (I 270).

adds another dimension: 'Lönnrot is not an unbelievable fool walking into his own death trap but, in a symbolic way, a man committing suicide' (Com 269). It is precisely in the Hotel Las Delicias that, according to María Esther Vázquez (146), Borges attempted to commit suicide in February 1935. I do not wish to draw all these strings together in any conclusive way, but there is clearly a lot going on here.

From fours and threes, the story now starts to work on twos: duality and nightmarish symmetries. Both Lönnrot and Scharlach, waiting for him in the house, are tormented. Lönnrot sees that the house 'abounded in pointless symmetries and obsessive repetitions; a glacial Diana in a gloomy niche was echoed by a second Diana in a second niche ... A two-faced Hermes threw a monstrous shadow' (F119).[23] Scharlach describes the delirious fever he suffered in the house after being shot in the operation in which Lönnrot had arrested and imprisoned his brother, reminiscent of the fever suffered by Borges after his Christmas Eve accident in 1938. The two-faced Janus, said Scharlach, 'lent horror to my deliriums and my sleeplessness. I came to abominate my own body, I came to feel that two eyes, two hands, two lungs are as monstrous as two faces' (F 120).[24] It was then that he planned the labyrinth in which he would imprison his enemy, and kill him. Lönnrot 'looked at the trees and the sky subdivided into murky red, green, and yellow rhombuses' (F 123), and Scharlach shot him, 'hizo fuego'(I 507). The duality points to the fact that the two men are doubles, which had already been suggested by the red in both their names. Borges confirms this reading: 'The killer and the slain, whose minds work in the same way, may be the same man' (Com 269). There is an echo here of the ending of 'The Approach to Al-Mu'tasim', where the student at the end of his quest perhaps simply finds his own face; the forty birds realize that they are the sacred mountain Sīmurg. Lönnrot surprisingly has the energy, as he faces the bullet, to suggest that Scharlach's labyrinth had three sides two many, and suggests that the next time he kills him, his labyrinth should have just one line, like Zeno's paradox of Achilles and the tortoise.

---

[23] 'abundaba en inútiles simetrías y en repeticiones maniáticas: a una Diana glacial en un nicho lóbrego correspondía en un segundo nicho otra Diana ... Un Hermes de dos caras proyectaba una sombra monstruosa' (I 504).

[24] 'el odioso Janus bifronte ... daba horror a mi ensueño y a mi vigilia. Llegué a abominar de mi cuerpo, llegué a sentir que dos ojos, dos manos, dos pulmones, son tan monstruosos como dos caras' (I 505).

'The Secret Miracle', 'El milagro secreto'

'The Secret Miracle' retains much of the nightmarish atmosphere of 'Death and the Compass' and its hints of sexual unhappiness, here combined with paranoia, frustration and fear. It opens memorably with a nightmare: the Jewish writer Jaromir Hladík dreams that he is running through a rainy desert to make his move in a chess game between two enemy families played over generations; he cannot remember the rules of the game, and pounding chimes of clocks remind him that his move is due. He wakes to hear what seems to be a much less threatening sound, 'a rhythmic and unanimous sound', but it is in fact the tanks of the Third Reich moving into Prague at the beginning of the Second World War on 15 March 1939. The structure of the story is similar to that of 'The Garden of Forking Paths'. Both open and close with historical time: the eve of the Battle of the Somme, the German invasion of Czechoslovakia; the murder of the Sinologist, the executions of Yu Tsun and Hladík. In the earlier story, the historical time surrounds two different experiences of time: the timelessness of the garden, and the infinitely divergent times of the novel. Here it surrounds, as in parenthesis, three versions of timelessness: the metaphysical texts of Hladík, the circular time of his play *The Enemies*, and the magic time whereby God concedes to Hladík a year of mental time in the instant between the bullets leaving the guns of his executioners and hitting their target. Various critics have pointed out the similarity between this idea and the many hours of experience lived by the hanged man in Ambrose Bierce's 'An Occurrence at Owl Creek' at the moment of his death.

Hladík is even closer to Borges than Yarmolinsky, as we see from the by now familiar examination of his works. He shares with Yarmolinsky a translation of the *Sepher Yezirah*, but with Borges a *Vindication of Eternity*, which is clearly, from the description of its contents, *A History of Eternity*. He also shares with Borges the youthful and regretted publication of avant-garde poems, which appeared in an anthology, and seemed to haunt him. His unfinished play reflects the same sort of sexual unhappiness and inadequacy as Herbert Quain's *The Secret Mirror*, which it rewrites: the dominant Count of Rutland becomes Baron Roemerstadt; they displace the unfortunate Quarles/Quigley and Kubin in the affections of Ulrica and Julia. Quigley is the author of the first act of the play; in the endlessly circular fantasy of the deranged Kubin he is Roemerstadt, plagued by the machinations of countless enemies. Hladík's situation seems to echo that of Borges at the end of the thirties quite closely:

Hladík was past forty. Apart from a few friends and many routines, the problematic pursuit of literature constituted the whole of his life; like every writer, he measured other men's virtues by what they had accomplished, yet asked that other men measure him by what he planned someday to do.
(F 126)[25]

The completion of his play would 'redeem' Hladík (F 127), rescue 'that which was fundamental to his life' (F 128).[26]

Hladík prays to the God to whom 'the centuries and time' belong, that he grant him a year to finish his masterpiece. He has a dream, set in the Prague library of Clementinum, which sends us back to the Library of Babel and to Al-Mu'tasim. He tells a librarian that he is looking for God, and the librarian replies that He is in one letter in one of the four hundred thousand volumes, and that generations of his family had searched for this letter; he himself had gone blind looking for it. Borges at this time, of course, was a librarian with rapidly failing eyesight. Hladík opens an atlas; he confidently picks one letter from the 'vertiginous' map of India, and his wish is granted. He has a year to compose his play in his mind in easily remembered hexameters. Hladík recommended verse 'because it does not allow the spectators to forget unreality, which is a condition of art' (F 127).[27] Borges's story is hardly unreal in evoking the murder of an intellectual by a totalitarian regime. The unreality of Hladík's story is both pathetically feeble in the face of political brutality, and at the same time heroic and redemptive. The ambiguity is similar to that of Borges at the end of 'Tlön' retiring to complete his indecisive Quevedian translation of Browne. Hladík completes his play, which Borges seems to suggest is pretty awful anyway, not for posterity, for no one will read it, nor for God, of whose literary tastes he knows little.

'Three Versions of Judas', 'Tres versiones de Judas'

'Three Versions of Judas', the story of an imaginary Swedish theologian Nils Runeberg, is a testing combination of breathtaking intellectual and speculative verve (God became man in Judas not in Jesus), an exciting exploration

[25] 'Hladík había rebasado los cuarenta años. Fuera de algunas amistades y de muchas costumbres, el problemático ejercicio de la literatura constituía su vida; como todo escritor, medía las virtudes de los otros por lo ejecutado por ellos y pedía que los otros lo midieran por lo que vislumbraba o planeaba' (I 509).

[26] 'la posibilidad de rescatar (de manera simbólica) lo fundamental de su vida' (I 510–11).

[27] 'Hladík preconizaba el verso, porque impide que los espectadores olviden la irrealidad, que es condición del arte' (I 510).

of tensions at the very heart of Borges's world (the redeemer and the traitor, the punishment for revealing the name of God), and pages of implacable and unrelenting theological argument. The overwhelming weight of quotation in the story – nine real biblical references, some well known authors (T. E. Lawrence, De Quincey), some obviously apocryphal to experienced Borges readers (Jaromar Hladík, from 'The Secret Miracle'), and a host of theologians about whose status and reality many readers will be puzzled – is discussed sensitively by Sylvia Molloy:

> The distance introduced by Borges's quotations is not the distance of prestige, but of suspicious unease. Defying recognition, these quotations refuse nonetheless to be mere games or private jokes. Thus the reader wavers between the temptation to enjoy them for their exoticism and the temptation to decipher, and thus domesticate, the origins of such erudition.
>
> (Molloy, 108)

The footnotes are typical of the game. The first is to Axel Borelius, apocryphal (I believe!). The second is to Euclides da Cunha, certainly a real author, but unknown to Runeberg, and bizarrely exotic in the context. His novelized report *Os Sertões* tells the story of the heretical and charismatic Brazilian rebel leader António Conselheiro. The Argentinian reader would probably see this reference, and certainly that to Almafuerte. A witty quotation in French is supposedly from Maurice Abramowicz, a childhood and lifelong friend of Borges from Geneva. His point is refuted by Erik Erfjord, presumably a relative of the equally imaginary Gunnar Erfjord who appears in 'Tlön', who cites Hladík's *Vindication of Eternity*, modelled on Borges's own *A History of Eternity*, in the story 'The Secret Miracle'.

Borges heartily enjoys heretical theological arguments, a passion he indulges again later in 'The Theologians', lifelong enemies who are mortified to discover that for God they are one and the same person. The early twentieth-century Runeberg would have been at home with Borges's favourite Gnostic Basilides, for whom the world was 'a reckless or maleficent improvisation by angels lacking in perfection' (F 132).[28] Dante would have given him a fiery grave; he would have survived in the paradoxical way Borges enjoys: in the refutations of his enemies. Runeberg argues for the mechanism of redemption and the functioning of the Trinity that Borges found such an intellectual monstrosity in three stages. In the first book, Judas was a necessary and prefigured part of redemption; his infamy mirrored the sacrifice

---

[28] 'una temeraria o malvada improvisación de ángeles deficientes' (I 514).

made by the Word on descending into matter. Judas mirrored Jesus like the
microcosm the macrocosm, where 'the blotches on the skin are a map of the
incorruptible constellations' (F 134).[29] In its revised version Judas acts, not
out of greed, but out of 'limitless asceticism' (F134), mortifying his spirit as
ordinary ascetics mortified the flesh. In the second book, Runeberg takes his
argument to its conclusion. God became man, and it would be blasphemous
to think that he became man only in the brief sacrifice of the crucifixion; he
became man to the human extreme of infamy for all time. God became Judas
and suffers eternal torment, sidelining Jesus to a minor part in the scheme.

Beyond the initially alienating façade of the story, Runeberg's logic is
close to that of many other Borges characters. What he did not like in the
traditional story of Judas's betrayal is the chance element. Going beyond De
Quincey's argument that Judas denounced Jesus to force him into a liberation struggle against Rome, he chooses a metaphysical plot, a beautifully
symmetrical scheme which would eliminate chance:

> To assume an error in the Scriptures is intolerable, but it is no less intoler-
> able to assume that a random act intruded into the most precious event in
> the history of the world. *Ergo*, Judas' betrayal was not a random act, but
> predetermined, with its own mysterious place in the economy of redemp-
> tion. (F 133)[30]

He does exactly the same as Lönnrot in 'Death and the Compass' when
confronted with the random murder of the rabbi: he writes it into a coherent
story. Also, similarly, his arguments 'justified and destroyed his life' (F 133),
'justificaron y desbarataron su vida' (I 514). His position at the end of the
tale is again analogous, because he too has pronounced the ineffable name
of God, here 'el horrible nombre de Dios' (I 517), the 'horrible name of
God': God was Judas. Madness descends on him as he contemplates the
ancient divine curses converging on him: Moses who covered his face so
as not to see God, Isaiah who was terrified by the vision, Saul who was
blinded on the road to Damascus, the wizard Juan de Viterbo who goes mad,
the Midrashim who curse those who pronounce the *Shem Hamephorash*,
the Secret Name of God. In 'The Theme of the Traitor and the Hero', the
traitor is turned into hero by the staging of a mock murder; in 'The Form of

---

[29] 'las manchas de la piel son un mapa de las incorruptibles constelaciones' (I 515).

[30] 'Suponer un error en la Escritura es intolerable; no menos intolerable es admitir un
hecho casual en el más precioso acontecimiento en la historia del mundo. *Ergo*, la traición de
Judas no fue casual; fue un hecho prefijado que tiene su lugar misterioso en la economía de la
redención' (I 515).

the Sword', the traitor becomes hero through the trick of the narration, and the effect of pantheism and contagion. Here the ultimate traitor of Western Culture becomes redeemer through the rigorous but hallucinatory theological dialectic of the Swede Runeberg. The first stage of the argument, where Jesus and Judas are mirror images, both necessary elements in the mechanism of redemption, is decentred and deconstructed as implacably Runeberg's logic develops.

'The End', 'El fin'

Just as Runeberg rewrites the Scriptures, Borges rewrites the Argentine classic poem *Martín Fierro* on two occasions: in 'Biography of Tadeo Isidoro Cruz', published in *El Aleph* in 1949, and in 'The End', originally published in *La Nación* in October 1953, and incorporated with 'The Sect of the Phoenix' and 'The South' into *Ficciones* in 1956. As Williamson points out, 'The End' was the last story Borges published until 1969. The two stories work differently: 'Tadeo Isidoro Cruz' expands on a key episode from the poem, and creates a highly structured but detailed biography of the character known as Sergeant Cruz. 'The End' is a sequel to the poem, recounting an event which Borges in the Prologue to *Artificios* declared was implicit in the original. In Hernández's poem, Fierro had callously killed a black man in a duel after drunkenly insulting his woman. In the second part of the poem, or its sequel, published in 1879, the black man's brother challenges Fierro to a *payada*, or ballad counterpoint contest, which he loses, and then reveals his identity and challenges him to fight. Fierro is reluctant, as he no longer likes to fight; the two are separated, Fierro gives advice to his children, including the injunction never to kill a man, and the poem ends. In 'The End', the black man and Fierro meet again and Fierro is killed in the duel he had tried to avoid. The only element not present in the original is Recabarren, the paralysed owner of the bar–shop, *pulpería*, who presides over and almost seems to dream the fight. His disability means that he is 'a man in the habit of living in the present, as animals do' (F 139).[31] Indeed he is like the cat in 'The South', which presides over the opening of the dreamy, archetypal second part of the story, which also leads to a duel on the pampas: 'man lives in time, in successiveness, while the magical animal lives in the present, in the eternity

---

[31] 'habituado a vivir en el presente, como los animales' (I 518).

of the instant' (F 149).[32] The present is that of the archetypal moment. In a piece in *The Maker*, '*Martín Fierro*', Borges records the importance that the first duel scene has for Argentine readers: 'The thing that was once, returns again; the visible armies have gone and what is left is a common sort of knife fight; one man's dream is part of all men's memory' (CF 312–13).[33] This story is another instant of that return.

The name Martín Fierro is only mentioned in the penultimate paragraph, but Argentine readers will have picked up the references at an earlier stage, when, for example, Fierro recalls the advice given to his children (MF II, line 4733). The duel clearly picks up elements of the fight between Fierro and the Moreno in the poem, inverting the actors. Fierro cuts the Moreno's face, which is what Fierro had done to his brother (I 1226). The Moreno watches the 'laborious agony' of Fierro (MF I, 1238), and cleans his bloody dagger on the grass: 'limpié el facón en los pastos' (MF I, 1249); 'limpió el facón ensangrentado en el pasto' (I 520). As he repeats Martín Fierro's action, as he falls into the archetypal literary pattern, he becomes Martín Fierro, the other person, his enemy, like Tadeo Isidoro Cruz, like the coward in 'The Shape of the Sword'. Moreover, he becomes *no one*: 'His work of vengeance done, he was nobody now. Or rather, he was the other one' (F 141). The grammar of the Spanish is haunting, the normal double negative 'ahora no era nadie' becomes the unfamiliar sounding 'ahora era nadie' as if nobody was a positive role: 'Cumplida su tarea de justiciero, ahora era nadie. Mejor dicho era el otro: no tenía destino sobre la tierra y había matado a un hombre' (I 520).

'The Cult of the Phoenix', 'La secta del Fénix'

'The Cult of the Phoenix' is a curious extended riddle, the solution of which is sex. The first half takes the form of an erudite essay, with real writers evoked from ancient Egypt to the present, who did not, of course, write about the Sect, or its Secret. Christ traces the source of the piece to De Quincey's Secret Society. The phoenix is a symbol of rebirth, perhaps of the phallus, perhaps even a reference to D. H. Lawrence. The second part describes in a circuitous fashion the ritual which ensures eternity for mankind. The smutty way in which children learn of the sacred secret is described in a

---

[32] 'el hombre vive en el tiempo, en la sucesión, y el mágico animal, en la actualidad, en la eternidad del instante' (I 526).

[33] 'Esto que fue una vez vuelve a ser, infinitamente; los visibles ejércitos se fueron y queda un pobre duelo a cuchillo; el sueño de uno es parte de la memoria de todos' (II 175).

lovely parody: 'tradition forbids a mother from teaching it to her children, as it forbids priests doing so; initiation into the mystery is the task of the lowest individuals of the group. A slave, a leper, or a beggar plays the role of mystagogue' (F 144).[34] Bizarre details momentarily throw the reader, or lead to wonderful fantasies: 'The materials used are cork, wax or gum arabic' (F 144).[35] A more personal and anguished tone slips in as he writes, reflecting his own sexual inhibitions: 'A kind of sacred horror keeps some of the faithful from performing that simplest of rituals; they are despised by the other members of the sect, but they despise themselves even more' (F 144–5).[36] Emma Zunz's astonishment and vertigo are re-enacted as he muses that 'they could not bring themselves to admit that their parents had ever stooped to such acts' (F 145).[37]

'The South', 'El Sur'

'The South' is one of Borges's favourite stories, and taps into many aspects of his life and passions. Its specular structure, textured with teasing echoes and symmetries, is pleasurable, and it is unencumbered by erudition. Indeed only three books are cited: *Martín Fierro*, which provides the model for the outcome; the *Arabian Nights*, which serves to illustrate the bookishness of the protagonist and the dreamy literariness of the second part; and an illustration from *Paul et Virginie*, which suggests that the *almacén* where he dies is created from youthful memories. Juan Dahlmann worked like Borges in a municipal library, and considered himself 'profoundly Argentine' (F 146), 'hondamente argentino' (I 524); he knew his *Martín Fierro* well and practised an unostentatious *criollismo*. He also has the same dual lineage as Borges: literary-cum-ecclesiastical and military; Germanic and Hispanic. Johannes Dahlmann was a pastor of the Evangelical Church, and his maternal grandfather Francisco Flores was killed by Indians on the frontier, rather like Borges's grandfather Francisco Borges, who had fought the Indians. At the end of the long first sentence we come across the prediction of Dahlmann's death, a death chosen by him: 'In the contrary pulls from his two lineages,

---

[34] 'el uso no quiere que las madres lo enseñen a los hijos, ni tampoco los sacerdotes; la iniciación en el misterio es tarea de los individuos más bajos. Un esclavo, un leproso o un pordiosero hacen de mistagogos' (I 522).

[35] 'Los materiales son el corcho, la cera o la goma arábiga' (I 522).

[36] 'Una suerte de horror sagrado impide a algunos fieles la ejecución del simplísimo rito; los otros los desprecian, pero ellos se desprecian aun más' (I 522).

[37] 'No se avenían a admitir que sus padres se hubieran rebajado a tales manejos' (I 523).

Juan Dahlmann (perhaps impelled by his Germanic blood) chose that of his romantic ancestor, or that of a romantic death' (F 146).[38] Paradoxically, it is the German romanticism which has him choose a Hispanic destiny. In the South of Buenos Aires province, Dahlmann retained a family house: a 'long pink-colored house that had once been scarlet' (F 146).[39] The dual lineage is reflected in the two plot lines and deaths offered by the story: Dahlmann has septicaemia and dies in a Buenos Aires hospital; Dahlmann (dreams that he) recovers, travels south by train and is killed in a knife duel, like Martín Fierro in 'The End'.

Dahlmann suffered the same accident that Borges had suffered on Christmas Eve 1938, with the added detail that here he rushes up the stairs anxious to examine a rare copy of the *Arabian Nights*, which he had just acquired. Like Scharlach, in the hell of the fever he feels intense self-loathing: 'Dahlmann hated every inch of himself; he hated his identity, his bodily needs, his humiliation, the beard that prickled his face' (F 147).[40] One day, the surgeon announces that he is on the mend and that he can go to his *estancia* to convalesce. I imagine that the surgeon had no reason to know about the estate, and here starts the part of the story which is most likely Dahlmann's dying delirium. The narrator comments rather abruptly that 'reality is partial to symmetries and slight anachronisms' (F 148). Literature, as discussed in 'Narrative Art and Magic', is certainly built on these, and the statement announces the character of the second half of the story. Dahlmann had come to the clinic in a cab, a 'coche de plaza', and leaves in the same vehicle. The South seems to him 'an older and more stable world' (F148), 'un mundo más antiguo y más firme' (I 525), and this impression of the archetypal is confirmed by the magical cat in the café, described as a 'disdainful deity', which lives outside time, 'in the eternity of the instant' (F 149). He carries the same volume as he did at the time of his accident, to assist his recovery. The train journey becomes more and more numinous, and Dahlmann has the impression that he is double: 'it was as though he were two men at once: the man gliding along through the autumn day and the geography of his native land, and the other man, imprisoned in a sanatorium and subjected to methodical attentions' (F 149).[41]

---

[38] 'en la discordia de sus dos linajes, Juan Dahlmann (tal vez a impulso de la sangre germánica) eligió el de ese antepasado romántico, o de muerte romántica' (I 524).

[39] 'la larga casa rosada que alguna vez fue carmesí' (I 524).

[40] 'Dahlmann minuciosamente se odió, odió su identidad, sus necesidades corporales, su humillación, la barba que le erizaba la cara.' (I 525).

[41] 'era como si a un tiempo fuera dos hombres; el que avanzaba por el día otoñal y por la

As he travels not only to the South but back through time, Dahlmann is put off the train at the wrong station, and dines at a store/bar which, like his ranch, 'had once been bright red, but the years had tempered its violent color (to its advantage)' (F 150–1).[42] The owner seemed familiar to him, but perhaps just reminded him of an employee of the clinic. At a nearby table, there were two farm hands and a *compadrito*, a tough who drank with his *chambergo* hat on. Crouching by the bar is the human equivalent of the timeless cat: an old *gaucho* dressed in typical nineteenth-century garb: 'The many years had worn him away and polished him, as a stone is worn smooth by running water or a saying is polished by generations of humankind. He was small, dark, and dried up, and he seemed to be outside time, in a sort of eternity' (F 151).[43] Like the paralysed Recabarren in 'The End' he embodies the timeless repetition of archetypal acts. Dahlmann 'suddenly felt something lightly brush his face' (F 151), repeating the effect of the window which first injured him: 'Something in the dimness brushed his forehead—a bat? a bird?' (F 147).[44] It is a pellet of bred flicked from the nearby table. Dahlmann was keen to ignore the incident, and is about to leave when the owner inexplicably addresses him by name, which obliges him to defend his reputation with his neighbours. When the tough insults him and challenges him to fight, the old *gaucho* throws a dagger at his feet. 'It was as if the South itself had decided that Dahlmann should accept the challenge' (F 152).[45]

As he goes out to face certain death, Dahlmann muses, in a perplexing conditional tense, that this is the death he would have chosen or dreamed; he has in fact both chosen and dreamed it: 'he felt that on that first night in the sanatorium, when they'd stuck that needle in him, dying in a knife fight under the open sky ... would have been a liberation, a joy, and a fiesta' (153).[46] This is the same 'júbilo secreto' (II 245), 'secret and inexplicable joy' (SP 159), which his ancestor Doctor Francisco Laprida feels in 'Conjectural Poem'

---

geografía de la patria, y el otro, encarcelado en un sanatorio y sujeto a metódicas servidumbres' (I 526).

[42] 'El almacén, alguna vez, había sido punzó, pero los años habían mitigado para su bien ese color violento' (I 527).

[43] 'Los muchos años lo habían reducido y pulido como las aguas a una piedra o las generaciones de los hombres a una sentencia. Era oscuro, chico, y reseco, y estaba como fuera del tiempo, en una eternidad' (I 527).

[44] 'sintió un leve roce en la cara' (I 528); 'algo en la oscuridad le rozó la frente ¿un murciélago, un pájaro?' (I 524).

[45] 'Era como si el Sur hubiera resuelto que Dahlmann aceptara el duelo' (I 528).

[46] 'Sintió, al atravesar el umbral, que morir en una pelea a cuchillo, a cielo abierto y acometiendo, hubiera sido una liberación para él, una felicidad y una fiesta, en la primera noche del sanatorio, cuando le clavaron la aguja' (I 528–9).

as he meets his violent death and his 'destiny as a South American', 'mi destino sudamericano'. What in political terms is seen as a barbarous death (Williamson (320) calls it 'his anti-Perón story'), in literary and personal terms is a joy and a liberation.

The Aleph (1949)

The A and Z of lost love and mystical experience in two stories: 'The Aleph' and 'The Zahir'

Though 'El Aleph' was first published in *Sur* in September 1945, and was thus the earliest published story in the collection *El Aleph* (apart from the brief 'The Two Kings and the Two Labyrinths'), it is placed last. The story embodies one of the extremes of Borges's conceptual world, while its twin tale, 'The Zahir', represents the other: everything and the one thing; a chaotic world unaffected by structure or symbolism, and the world reduced to one symbol; difference and unity. Given the importance of the opposition for other stories, I will consider them out of order and before the others. Both involve mystical microcosmic images. The aleph is an inch-round point in space where all space coexists; everything in the world is seen from every angle. The Zahir is a coin which symbolizes the world, is unforgettable, and drives its obsessed owner mad as it replaces the world for him. The starting point of both stories is the death of a woman loved by the narrator 'Borges', and his way of dealing with her memory is reflected in the nature of the microcosmic image involved. In 'El Aleph' Borges wishes to 'consecrate myself to her memory' (A 118) by remembering *all* the images of Beatriz Viterbo. In 'The Zahir', he chooses *one* image of the ever-changing Teodelina Villari. A and Z, reality and plot, omnipotent king and attribute or subordinate, fight for prominence in Emma **Z**unz's duel with **A**aron Loewenthal, and **Z**aid's duel with **A**benjacán (in English unfortunately Ibn-Hakam).

Both stories share the same oxymoronic coexistence of petty, often grotesque, social satire, extreme intellectual intensity and psychological pathos. The beloved dead woman in both is pretty clearly the same woman. Williamson, for example, points out that Beatriz dies in 1929, the same year that Borges receives the Zahir. Much speculation has gone into the identity of the lady in Borges's real life, but it is finally incidental. Williamson argues with much ingenuity that Norah Lange is the woman evoked in both, while Jason Wilson believes that in 'The Zahir', the unforgettable woman is Estela Canto, to whom 'The Aleph' was dedicated, and with whom he was involved at the time of its writing (Wilson, 128). I take it to be Estela's face he sees in the Aleph when he suddenly addresses an individual and says: '[I] saw your face, and I felt dizzy' (A 131); 'vi tu cara, y sentí vértigo' (I 626). María Esther Vázquez (189) claims that Borges told her that the source 'was not one woman, there were three and two have died', while Borges in his Commentary writes that Beatriz 'really existed and I was very much and hopelessly in love with her' (Com 264). Borges was in love with many women, of course, and was finally spurned by them. As Vázquez comments, he would repay the humiliation with biting sarcasm. Neither Beatriz nor Teodelina escape his vituperation. In 'The Aleph', which is driven by a burning sense of humiliation, Borges finds precise and obscene letters written by Beatriz to her lover.

'The Aleph', 'El Aleph'

As Borges explains in the Postscript to the story, the term 'Aleph' comes from the Kabbalah, where it is the most powerful letter in the Jewish alphabet, and from mathematics, in the set theory of Kantor. In his words, 'In the Kabbala, that letter signifies the En Soph, the pure and unlimited godhead; it has also been said that its shape is that of a man pointing to the sky and the earth, to indicate that the lower world is the map and mirror of the higher' (A132).[1] His explanation of set theory or the *Mengenlehre* in the story is brief: 'For the *Mengenlehre*, the aleph is the symbol of the transfinite numbers, in which the whole is not greater than any of its parts' (A 132).[2] In the 1936 essay 'Doctrine of the Cycles', where he uses it to refute Nietzsche's eternal return, he gives a fuller account:

> An infinite collection – for example, the natural series of whole numbers – is a collection whose members can in turn be broken down into infinite series. (Or rather, to avoid any ambiguity: an infinite whole is a whole that can be the equivalent of one of its subsets.) The part, in these elevated numerical latitudes, is no less copious than the whole: the precise quantity of points in the universe is the same as the quantity of points in a meter, or a decimeter, or the deepest trajectory of a star. (TL 117)[3]

---

[1] 'Para la Cábala, esa letra significa el En Soph, la ilimitada y pura divinidad; también se dijo que tiene la forma de un hombre que señala el cielo y la tierra, para indicar que el mundo inferior es el espejo y es el mapa del superior' (I 627).

[2] 'para la *Mengenlehre*, es el símbolo de los números transfinitos, en los que el todo no es mayor que alguna de sus partes' (I 627).

[3] 'una colección infinita – verbigracia, la serie natural de números enteros – es una colección cuyos miembros pueden desdoblarse a su vez en series infinitas. (Mejor, para eludir toda

Borges's fascination in his account is the same fascination as earlier in his career with the paradox of Zeno. As FH (157) explain, the theory 'also talks of a plurality of alephs'. This presumably explains why the aleph can contain the world, which in turn can contain the aleph, and so on, and why 'Borges' can possibly see in Daneri's infinite Aleph, which he maliciously declares to be false, another infinite Aleph, which he prefers to see as the 'true' one. When on a second (or tenth!) reading, we consider the epigraph from Shakespeare, the anachronistic influences of 'Kafka and his Precursors' come to mind, as we read the familiar words of Hamlet, complaining about his bad dreams in Denmark, through the lens of the *Mengenlehre*: 'O God!, I could be bounded in a nutshell, and count myself a King of infinite space.'

Were it not so utterly fascinating, one might share Borges's misgivings about the composition and structure of 'The Aleph': ' "The Aleph" has been praised by readers for its variety of elements: the fantastic, the satiric, the autobiographical, and the pathetic. I wonder whether our modern worship of complexity is not wrong, however. I wonder whether a short story should be so ambitious' (Com 264). It tells three stories, which fluctuate disconcertingly in register, and intertwine suggestively: the death of Beatriz and Borges's quest to maintain and recover her memory; his literary and sexual rivalry with Carlos Argentino Daneri; the account of the Aleph. After Beatriz dies, Borges takes to visiting the house of her father and her first cousin Daneri every anniversary of the death. The pompous and odious Daneri is writing an unspeakably bad poem on the whole of the planet, even more tedious than the fifteen thousand dodecasyllables of Michael Drayton's 1622 *Polyolbion*, which aimed to record the total reality of England. Daneri gives the first of the five enumerations of the story, a pedestrian list of the modern electrical devices, such as the telephone and cinema, which keep the modern-day intellectual well informed. One day he meets Borges to ask for help in procuring a prologue for his work, and on another occasion rings in panic to explain that his landlords Zunino and Zungri (note the hostile Zs) are planning to demolish his house. He explains that in his cellar he has an Aleph, which he needs to write his poem *The Earth*. 'Borges' rushes to see the Aleph, which Borges describes in an enumeration which is perhaps the most sustained and haunting piece of poetry in his career. In the Aleph he sees the obscene letters written by Beatriz to Daneri, who is revealed to have been her lover. In

ambigüedad: conjunto infinito es aquel conjunto que puede equivaler a uno de sus conjuntos parciales.) La parte, en esas elevadas latitudes de la numeración, no es menos copiosa que el todo: la cantidad precisa de puntos que hay en el universo es la que hay en un metro, o en un decímetro, o en la más honda trayectoria estelar' (I 387).

revenge, 'Borges' pretends not to have seen anything, and urges Daneri to see a couple of good doctors and take a long rest away from the pressures of city life. The 'Posdata del primero de marzo de 1943', '1 March 1943 Postscript', is a scholarly and ironic replica of the story, in a sense an embedded subset, or in more familiar terms, *mise-en-abyme*. Borges is humiliated when Daneri wins a literary prize while his own submission does not get a single vote; he offers the intellectual background to the Aleph; he gives an account of an apocryphal document by Captain Richard Burton, discovered by the Dominican critic Pedro Henríquez Ureña, listing a fascinating and erudite series of magical mirrors reported over history, from Alexander of Macedonia to Merlin. He thus echoes and outdoes Daneri's list of electrical gadgets, though his, when compared with the Aleph, are also 'mere optical instruments' (A 133). Finally, he uses Burton's account to posit an Aleph in the column of a mosque in Cairo, which is realer than that of Daneri, thus repeating his earlier, peevish denial.

Carlos Argentino Daneri and 'Borges' cordially detest each other, and Borges puts an enormous amount of satirical energy into describing the other's pedantry, inflated and ridiculous rhetoric, and blindness to the awfulness of his own literature, which he quotes and explicates in florid and boastful terms:

> Application, resignation, and chance had conspired in their composition; the virtues that Daneri attributed to them were afterthoughts. I realized that the poet's work had lain not in the poetry but in the invention of reasons for accounting the poetry admirable; naturally, that later work modified the poem for Daneri, but not for anyone else. (A 122)[4]

The satire comes from the stable of Bustos Domecq, and is very funny, but deeply Argentinian, and can only be fully appreciated in the detail of the Spanish, for example in the snobbery of 'Borges' in registering Daneri's lower middle class expression for afternoon tea: 'tomar la leche' (I 621, see Canto 206). The name Daneri, though Borges pretended to be astonished and grateful for such readings ('unlooked-for gifts' (Com 264)), is generally accepted to be a contraction of DANte AlighiERI, and the *Divine Comedy* to be one model for his total poem. The descent to the cellar would thus be a debased version of Dante's descent to the Inferno. In this light 'Borges's'

---

4 'En su escritura habían colaborado la aplicación, la resignación y el azar; las virtudes que Daneri les atribuía eran posteriores. Comprendí que el trabajo del poeta no estaba en la poesía; estaba en la invención de razones para que la poesía fuera admirable; naturalmente, ese ulterior trabajo modificaba la obra para él, pero no para otros' (I 619).

scornful *criollo* description of Daneri's Italian extraction and pronunciation
is even more ironic: 'At two generations' remove, the Italian *s* and the liberal
Italian gesticulation still survive in him' (A 119–20).[5] Crucially, however,
Daneri is also a double of 'Borges'. His post reflects that of Borges in the
Miguel Cané Library: 'He holds some sort of subordinate position in an illeg-
ible library in the outskirts towards the south of the city' (A 199).[6] The library
is revealed to be the Juan Cristóstomo Lafinur Library, named after Borges's
great uncle, a distinguished professor of philosophy. Daneri also asks Borges
to secure a prologue for his work from Álvaro Melián Lafinur, a combination
of the names of two of Borges's family members. Moreover, later there is
an intriguing and self-humiliating echo between a phrase by Daneri and one
by 'Borges'. Faced with losing his house Daneri exclaims: '¡La casa de mis
padres, mi casa, la vieja casa inveterada de la calle Garay!' (I 622)', 'The
house of my parents, my house, the inveterate old house on Garay Street'
(Hurley misses the rhetoric which 'Borges' reproduces). Left alone in front of
a portrait of Beatriz, 'Borges' pathetically and rather ridiculously exclaims,
with the same anaphora: 'Beatriz, Beatriz Elena, Beatriz Elena Viterbo ...
Belovèd Beatriz, Beatriz lost forever – it's me, it's me, Borges' (A 128).

Daneri's poem, of which we hear the 'Canto Augural' and the title *La
tierra*, has already been linked to Dante's masterpiece and the *Polyolbion*. It
is tempting to relate it also to two collections of poems by a writer disliked
by Borges, Pablo Neruda: his *Residencia en la tierra* and *Canto general*. The
latter is a vastly ambitious poetical account of the whole of Latin American
history and geography. Though the complete work did not come out until
1950, five years after 'The Aleph', its forerunner, *Canto general de Chile*,
was published in 1943. What is almost oxymoronic about Daneri's poetry,
an exploration of 'the possibilities of cacophony and chaos' (A 125), is that
it springs from the ineffable: an incredibly powerful microcosmic image.
Borges's laconic and hilarious enumeration summarizing the necessarily
fragmented nature of Daneri's attempt to 'versify the entire planet'(A 122)[7]
stands in a position towards it similar to that of the brief account of the infinite memory of Funes by another 'Borges':

> by 1941 he had already dispatched several hectares of the state of
> Queensland, more than a kilometer of the curse of the Ob, a gasworks

---

[5] 'A dos generaciones de distancia, la ese italiana y la copiosa gesticulación italiana sobre-
viven en él' (I 618).

[6] 'Ejerce no sé qué cargo subalterno en una biblioteca ilegible de los arrabales del Sur'
(I 618).

[7] 'versificar toda la redondez del planeta' (I 620).

north of Veracruz, the leading commercial establishments in the parish of
Concepción, Mariana Cambaceres de Alvear's villa on the Calle Once de
Setiembre in Belgrano, and a Turkish bath not far from the famed Brighton
Aquarium. (A 122)[8]

In the 1943 Postscript, Borges is again humiliated by Daneri, when the latter
wins the second prize in the National Literature Award. The first was taken by
[Antonio] Aita, then, in reality, secretary of the Argentinian Pen Club, and the
third by Mario Bonfanti, a character invented by Bioy and Borges, and said to
be based on Borges's brother-in-law Guillermo de Torre (Wilson, 115). Freed
from the shackles of the Aleph, Daneri is translating into verse the epitomes
of 'Doctor' Acevedo Díaz, a real writer who famously won the 1941 National
Award, which failed to recognize *The Garden of Forking Paths*.

After reading the *Divina Commedia* through on his tram journey to the
Library in late 1939 or early 1940 (W 241), Borges quickly came to consider
it as the supreme masterpiece of universal literature.[9] The figure of Beatrice
in the work, and the figure of Beatrice Portinari in Dante's life, take on such
importance for Borges that he writes in 'Beatrice's Last Smile' (October
1948) that 'Dante constructed the best book that literature has achieved in
order to interpolate into it a few encounters with the irrecuperable Beatrice.'
Indeed, he continues, the rest of the book is merely an interpolation: 'a smile
and a voice – that he knows to be lost – are what is fundamental' (TL 303).[10]
He describes as hell in paradise the moment when Dante loses her presence
and finds her in her place far above in one of the circles of the ineffable Rose,
from where she smiles at him and then turns away forever. In this essay and in
'Encuentro en un sueño', published in the first edition of *Otras inquisiciones*,
and partially reproduced by Rodríguez Monegal (374), Borges stresses the
humiliation that Dante received from Beatrice in real life, and the construction of the poem to recover her in imagination: 'Forever absent from Beatrice,

---

8   'en 1941 ya había despachado unas hectáreas del Estado de Queensland, más de un
kilómetro del curso del Ob, un gasómetro al norte de Veracruz, las principales casas de
comercio de la parroquia de la Concepción ... y un establecimiento de baños turcos no lejos
del acreditado acuario de Brighton' (I 620).
9   For a detailed account of the relationship, see Humberto Núñez-Faraco's *Borges and
Dante: Echoes of a Literary Friendship* (Bern: Peter Lang, 2006).
10   'Yo sospecho que Dante edificó el mejor libro que la literatura ha alcanzado para inter-
calar algunos encuentros con la irrecuperable Beatriz. ... una sonrisa y una voz, que él sabe
perdidas, son lo fundamental' ('La última sonrisa de Beatriz', in *Nueve ensayos dantescos*, III
373).

alone and perhaps humiliated, he imagined the scene in order to imagine that he was with her' (Rodríguez Monegal 304).[11]

Beatriz Viterbo is clearly Borges's Beatrice, as with Dante, both in his life and in the Aleph where he sees her again. In the past he remembers humiliation: 'I knew that more than once my futile devotion had exasperated her; now that she was dead, I could consecrate myself to her memory – without hope, but also without humiliation' (A 118).[12] He tries to excuse her cruelty by invoking the mad strain in her family: 'Beatriz ... was a woman, a girl of implacable clearsightedness, but there were things about her – oversights, distractions, moments of contempt, downright cruelty – that perhaps could have done with a *pathological* explanation' (A 127).[13] But in the Aleph, Borges's *Comedy*, he does not find a kind guide and a heavenly smile, however cruel, but rather a vilification and further humiliation. Roberto Paoli (87) argues for the extreme double and bisemic quality of the phrase I quoted earlier: 'Beatriz, Beatriz Elena, Beatriz Elena Viterbo ... Belovèd Beatriz, Beatriz lost forever – it's me, it's me, Borges.' He argues that the *querida* in 'Beatriz querida', 'Belovèd Beatriz', can mean 'lover' as well as 'beloved', while 'lost', *perdida* in Spanish, can mean a fallen woman or whore. Be that as it may, in the mystical Aleph, as opposed to the mystical Rose, Borges saw 'in a desk drawer (and the handwriting made me tremble) obscene, incredible, detailed letters that Beatriz had sent Carlos Argentino, saw a beloved monument in Chacarita [Cemetery], saw the horrendous remains of what had once, deliciously, been Beatriz Viterbo' (A 130).[14] He finds (chooses to find) not apotheosis, but lasciviousness and deathly corruption. 'Borges' had claimed to start out to forge a total memory of Beatriz to protect her from the passing of time. In the house he visits every year the wall is covered with endless photographs of Beatriz; Daneri promises that in the Aleph, he 'will be able to begin a dialogue with *all* the images of Beatriz' (A 128). Like the dangerous knowledge acquired by Runeberg in 'Three Versions of Judas' and

---

[11] 'Ausente para siempre de Beatriz, solo y quizá humillado, imaginó la escena para imaginar que estaba con ella.' (III 374) Borges's quirky biographical reading of the Divine Comedy is perhaps parallel to Unamuno's reading of Cervantes's masterpiece in *Vida de don Quijote y Sancho*.

[12] 'alguna vez, lo sé, mi vana devoción la había exasperado; muerta yo podía consagrarme a su memoria, sin esperanza, pero también sin humillación' (I 617).

[13] 'Beatriz ... era una mujer, una niña de una clarividencia casi implacable, pero había en ella negligencias, distracciones, desdenes, verdaderas crueldades, que tal vez reclamaban una explicación patológica' (I 623).

[14] 'vi en un cajón del escritorio (y la letra me hizo temblar) cartas obscenas, increíbles, precisas, que Beatriz había dirigido a Carlos Argentino, vi un adorable monumento en la Chacarita, vi la reliquia atroz de lo que deliciosamente había sido Beatriz Viterbo' (I 625).

by 'Borges' in 'The Other Death' about God modifying the past, Borges is threatened by his vision of totality: having seen everything, he fears eternal déjà-vu. Oblivion thankfully replaces memory: 'Fortunately, after a few unsleeping nights, forgetfulness began to work in me again' (A 131).[15] In the final lines, though he describes forgetting as 'tragic', the impression is rather of one blotting out a memory too horrible to bear: 'Our minds are permeable to forgetfulness; I myself am distorting and losing, through the tragic erosion of the years, the features of Beatriz' (A 133).[16] The moment is of course absolutely ambiguous: 'Borges' has chosen to castigate his cold and indifferent Beatrice, but is at the same time traumatized. At the centre of Borges's vision in the Aleph, and within the fierce and funny satire of the story, lurks a forlorn loneliness or even absence of self: '[I] saw all the mirrors on the planet (and none of them reflecting me) ... [I] saw my bedroom (with no one in it)' (A 130).[17]

'The Zahir', 'El Zahir'

The opening paragraph of 'The Zahir' is one of Borges's most seductive, and the first sentence utterly intriguing: 'In Buenos Aires the Zahir is a common twenty-centavo coin' (A 79).[18] The banality of the coin is set oxymoronically against the exotic-sounding Zahir. Borges then provides six examples of Zahirs from Gujerat to Córdoba, without saying what a Zahir is. Real individuals are invoked to vouch for the truth of the exotic, orientalizing account: '[the Zahir was] in the prisons of Mahdi, in 1892, a small sailor's compass, wrapped in a shred of cloth from a turban, that Rudolf Karl von Slatin touched; in the [aljama, i.e. Mosque] in Córdoba, according to Zotenberg, a vein in the marble of one of the twelve hundred pillars'.[19] The paragraph then returns to an alarming personal present, where 'Borges' is seen to be losing his identity and mind: 'last June 7, at dawn, the Zahir came into my

---

[15] 'Felizmente, al cabo de unas noches de insomnio, me trabajó otra vez el olvido' (I 626).

[16] 'Nuestra mente es porosa para el olvido; yo mismo estoy falseando y perdiendo, bajo la trágica erosión de los años, los rasgos de Beatriz' (I 627).

[17] 'vi todos los espejos del mundo y ninguno me reflejó ... vi mi dormitorio sin nadie' (I 625).

[18] 'En Buenos Aires el Zahir es una moneda común, de veinte centavos' (I 589).

[19] 'en las prisiones de Mahdí, hacia 1892, una pequeña brújula que Rodolf Carl von Slatin tocó, envuelta en un jirón de turbante; en la aljama de Córdoba, según Zotenberg, una veta en el mármol de uno de los mil doscientos pilares'.

hands; I am not the man I was then, but I am still able to recall, and perhaps recount, what happened. I am still, albeit only partially, Borges.'[20]

The next, long paragraph veers unexpectedly to the sort of social satire we saw in 'The Aleph'. 'Borges' is at the wake of Teodelina Villar, the society woman with whom he had been madly in love, moved by another oxymoronic conjunction, 'the sincerest of Argentine passions – snobbery' (A 81).[21] 'Borges' is extraordinarily malicious for someone so in love: 'she was thought to be a very pretty woman, although that supposition was not unconditionally supported by every image of her' (A 79).[22] Teodelina was the very image of mutability and change, and so yet another paradox: 'She sought the absolute, like Flaubert, but the absolute in the ephemeral' (A 80).[23] As a dedicated follower of fashion, she obeyed every dictate emanating from Paris: 'She passed through endless metamorphoses, as though fleeing from herself; her coiffure and the color of her hair were famously unstable, as were her smile, her skin, and the slant of her eyes' (A 80).[24] In a way, she was a living Aleph. During the wake, according to Borges, the dead person's face passes through all her previous faces over time. 'Borges' crucially decides to choose just one of those faces to remember her: 'No version of that face that had so disturbed me shall ever be as memorable as this one; really, since it could almost be the first, it ought to be the last' (A 81).[25]

This choice, the reduction of the multiple to the one, is already the Zahir. As he goes into the street he observes (as often) that night simplifies the streets. On the corner of Chile and Tacuarí Streets, where Estela Canto lived at the time, he went into a bar for a drink (Canto 192). He remarks oddly that 'to my misfortune, three men were playing *truco*' (A 81).[26] As we saw in Borges's pieces on the game, the rigorously codified *porteño* card game *truco* is a ritual which is at one remove from reality and brings its players into the realm of the archetypal and timeless. It is here that he receives the Zahir-

[20] 'el día 7 de junio, a la madrugada, llegó a mis manos el Zahir; no soy el que era entonces, pero aún me es dado recordar, y acaso referir, lo ocurrido. Aún, siquiera parcialmente, soy Borges.'

[21] 'movido por la más sincera de las pasiones argentines, el esnobismo' (I 590).

[22] 'esta plétora [de retratos] acaso contribuyó a que la juzgaran muy linda, aunque no todas las efigies apoyaran incondicionalmente esa hipótesis' (I 589).

[23] 'Buscaba lo absoluto, como Flaubert, pero lo absoluto en lo momentáneo' (I 589).

[24] 'Ensayaba continuas metamorfosis, como para huir de sí misma; el color de su pelo y las formas de su peinado eran famosamente inestables. También cambiaban la sonrisa, la tez, el sesgo de los ojos.' (I 589).

[25] 'Más o menos pensé: ninguna versión de esa cara que tanto me inquietó será tan memorable como ésta; conviene que sea la última, ya que pudo ser la primera' (I 590).

[26] 'para mi desdicha, tres hombres jugaba al truco' (I 590).

coin as change from his drink. Coins, like cards, are a form of discourse, with much in common with language and meaning. In a couple of lovely enumerations, 'Borges' considers three sorts of meaning articulated by coins: connotation, denotation, and the sacred. Firstly, he muses that every coin is the symbol of all the coins of history and fable. This is the rich, fluid cultural world inhabited by Borges, where one text or idea evokes another. Within the eleven examples he gives, are two from *Moby Dick* and *Ulysses*: 'the gold doubloon nailed by Ahab to the mast; Leopold Bloom's unreturning florin' (A 82).[27] The next dimension is the freedom offered by the exchangeability of coins, similar to the polysemia and malleability of language and reading. He gives six fascinating examples of what money can be exchanged for: 'any coin (a twenty-centavo piece for example) is, in all truth, a panoply of possible futures. *Money is abstract*, I said over and over, *money is future time*. It can be ... a Brahms melody, or maps, or chess, or coffee, or the works of Epictetus' (A 82).[28] Money in circulation and exchange is freedom: 'It is unforeseeable time, Bergsonian time ... a coin symbolizes our free will'. The lived, vital and flowing Bergsonian time is opposed to sacred time: 'the hard, solid time of Islam or the Porch' (A 82).[29] He realizes later that these thoughts on freedom and culture were a defence against the Zahir, but already a sign of its influence, the influence of the hard, impersonal time of the sacred.

'Borges' becomes ever more obsessed with the coin, which, to no avail, he contrives to lose. He tries various intellectual exercises to distract himself, but which turn out to be self-defeating. Coins come to be associated with the monstrous and cursed; money is hoarded and guarded, not allowed to circulate. On the first night he had dreamed that he himself was a hoard of coins guarded by a griffon. He wrote a story with a mysterious protagonist who is only gradually revealed to be Fafnir, the dragon, guarding the gold of the Nibelungs, which brings about their downfall. The story ends with the appearance of Sighurd, the hero who slays the monster. In fact Borges had published 'The House of Asterion' in June 1947, a month before 'The Zahir'. The technique of the story is clearly the same, as is the outcome when the Minotaur is slain by Theseus. 'Borges' goes from being the money to being

---

[27] 'en la onza de oro que hizo clavar Ahab en el mástil; en el florín irreversible de Leopold Bloom' (I 591).

[28] 'cualquier moneda (una moneda de veinte centavos, digamos) es, en rigor, un repertorio de futuros posibles. El dinero es abstracto, repetí, el dinero es tiempo futuro. Puede ser una tarde en las afueras, puede ser música de Brahms, puede ser mapas, puede ser ajedrez, puede ser café, puede ser las palabras de Epicteto' (I 591).

[29] 'Es tiempo imprevisible, tiempo de Bergson, no duro tiempo del Islam o del Pórtico' (I 591).

the monster that guards it and who perishes. It is not surprising that an examination of the British sovereign, with the image of St George and the dragon,
does little to help.

As often happens at this stage in a story a document emerges which
provides the key to the mystery. Here it is a book by the fictitious Julius
Barlach, translatable as *Documents Pertaining to the History of the Legend
of the Zahir* (Bell-Villada, 21). Within it real Arab scholars and European
orientalists outline in apocryphal works the nature and history of the Zahir.
'Zahir' is an Arabic word meaning visible or manifest, applied by the people
to people or things which are unforgettable and drive those who come into
contact with them mad. In Shiraz, it had been an astrolabe that the king
ordered to be thrown into the depths of the sea 'in order that men might not
forget the universe' (A 85).[30] Philip Meadows Taylor reported that it had once
been a tiger. In a Mysore prison, a sufferer, thinking he was painting a map of
the world, had done a drawing of 'an infinite tiger': 'It was a tiger composed
of many tigers, in the most dizzying of ways; it was crisscrossed with tigers,
striped with tigers, and contained seas and Himalayas and armies that resem-
bled other tigers' (A 85–6).[31] The Zahir replaces the map of the world; in a
sacred zone beyond the individual, it obliterates individual identity.

The final paragraphs document and project 'Borges's' descent into insanity
and loss of self, as he fantasizes about reaching God beyond the coin. He
learns that Julita Abascal and the chauffeur of another society lady were
raving about a coin, and had to be spoon-fed. He foresees a similar fate for
himself: 'Before the year 1948 ... I will have to be fed and dressed, I will
not know whether it's morning or night, I will not know who the man Borges
was' (A 87).[32] If life is a dream, as for the Idealists, then 'for me, thousands
upon thousands of appearances will pass into one; a complex dream will
pass into a simple one' (A 87).[33] The story is not a political one, of course,
but some of its phrasing reminds us of stories that certainly are. The phrase
'When every man on earth thinks, day and night, of the Zahir, which will
be dream and which reality, the earth or the Zahir?' (A 87–8)[34] is very remi-

[30] 'para que los hombres no se olvidaran del universo' (I 593).

[31] 'Ese tigre estaba hecho de muchos tigres, de vertiginosa manera; lo atravesaban tigres,
estaba rayado de tigres, incluía mares e Himalayas y ejércitos que parecían otros tigres' (I 593).

[32] 'Antes de 1948 ... tendrán que alimentarme y vestirme, no sabré si es de tarde o de
mañana, no sabré quién fue Borges' (I 594).

[33] 'de miles de apariencias pasaré a una; de un sueño muy complejo a un sueño muy
simple' (I 595).

[34] 'Cuando todos los hombres de la tierra piensen, día y noche, en el Zahir, ¿cuál será un
sueño y cuál una realidad, la tierra o el Zahir?' (595).

niscent of the end of 'Tlön, Uqbar, Orbis Tertius': 'The World will be Tlön' (F 25). The Zahir there takes the form of a symmetry hardened into dogma which replaces the world we know. In '*Deutsches Requiem*' the Nazi Zur Linde applies the Zahir turned psychological torture to drive the poet David Jerusalem insane.

'The Writing of the God', 'La escritura del dios'

'The Writing of the God' belongs to the same cycle of stories with a theme of mystical revelation as 'The Aleph' and 'The Zahir', and has much in common with both. The main difference is that the protagonist is not 'Borges', but the sixteenth-century Mayan priest and king Tzinacán. The social satire is missing, and the language is solemn as befits an account of heroic suffering and striving, and finally ecstatic as Tzinacán experiences 'union with the deity' (A 93).[35] Tzinacán, a prisoner of the Spaniards in a deep and dark dungeon, has been looking for a magical phrase which would ward off the calamities attendant on the end of time, but when he does find it, he renounces the omnipotence it conferred on him, and which would have allowed him to free his people from their oppressors because he is no longer himself. 'I no longer remember Tzinacán' (A 93),[36] he says, echoing 'Borges' in 'The Zahir': 'I will not know who the man Borges was' (A 87). The mystical experience of unity with god and the universe transcends the ego, the self, to such an extent that he becomes 'nobody' like the Moreno after killing Martín Fierro in 'The End'; he becomes another to himself:

> He who has glimpsed the universe, he who has glimpsed the burning designs of the universe, can no longer have thought for a man, for a man's trivial joys and calamities, though he himself be that man. He *was* that man, who no longer matters to him. What does he care about the fate of that other man, what does he care about the other man's nation, when now he is no one? (93–4)[37]

Whereas 'Borges' in 'The Zahir' slipped into insanity and incapacity, Tzinacán remains in a state of ecstatic passivity.

---

[35] 'la unión con la divinidad' (I 598).
[36] 'ya no me acuerdo de Tzinacán' (I 599).
[37] 'Quien ha entrevisto el universo, quien ha entrevisto los ardientes designios del universo, no puede pensar en un hombre, en sus triviales dichas o desventuras, aunque ese hombre sea él. Ese hombre ha sido él y ahora no le importa. Qué le importa la suerte de aquel otro, qué le importa la nación de aquel otro, si él, ahora es nadie' (I 599).

Though the story is very powerful, especially in the paradoxical and self-defeating ending, it suffers to an extent from an uneasy combination of mystical traits from different traditions: the Jewish Kabbalah, the Hinduism of the *Bhagavad Gita* and the *Upanishads*, and Mayan traditions extracted from the *Popol Vuh* and the books of *Chilam Balam*. Balderston argues very cogently for a coherent reading of a densely referenced Mayan world, but cannot fully explain away certain extraneous elements. His research on the knowledge about Mayan culture that Borges would have had at his disposal really contributes to bringing the text alive. From the *Popol Vuh* we learn that the historical Tzinacán was the ruler of the second of the main Mayan groups, the Quiché and the Cakchiquels at Iximché. The Spaniards gave him the name Sinacán, from the Náhuatl (Aztec) 'Tzinacán', meaning bat. The burning of his pyramid, which the character mentions, probably was at the time of the razing of Iximché in 1526 by Pedro de Alvarado (B 73) after the general Mayan uprising. The priest's god Qaholom is mentioned in the *Popol Vuh*, and Chilam Balam is revealed to mean 'Jaguar Priest' (B 161). Fourteen, the number of the words in the magical sentence, is the number sacred to the jaguar god. It is, of course, also the number of infinity for Asterion.

Tzinacán in the story is imprisoned in a semi-circular cell, separated into two parts by a wall with a low grill, on the other side of which is a jaguar, which the priest only sees for a brief instant every day as the gaoler winches down his food. He had been tortured by Alvarado to make him reveal the whereabouts of a treasure. He spends his years recovering all the memories of his previous life, and suddenly (and unconvincingly) remembers the sentence written by God on the first day of Creation to ward off the evil accompanying the end of time. Much of the story is his musing on the nature of such divine language, which like the Aleph would be simultaneous and not successive like human language: 'in the language of a god every word would speak that infinite concatenation of events, and not implicitly but explicitly, and not linearly but instantaneously' (A 91–2).[38] As the jaguar is one of the attributes of the god it occurs to Tzinacán that the sentence might somehow be inscribed on the stripes and spots of the jaguar, and he spends many years gradually learning the markings on its coat. The sentence once discovered does give omnipotence, and I am convinced by Alazraki's (and others') arguments suggesting a Kabbalistic reading of the divine text of Creation, derived from the twenty-two letter elements of the Hebrew alphabet. Anyone discov-

---

[38] 'Consideré que en el lenguaje de un dios toda palabra enunciaría esa infinita concatenación de los hechos, y no de un modo implícito, sino explícito, y no de un modo progresivo, sino inmediato' (I 597–8).

ering the correct order of the sections of the Torah 'might create a world, raise the dead and perform miracles' (Scholem, cit. Alazraki, *Kabbalah*, 46). The formula would be thus related to that which allows the Rabbi to create the golem.

One night he dreams that he is moving from one dream to another within the first, and so on to eternity, and being smothered by grains of sand. He screams in defiance and is woken by a 'resplandor' (I 598), a 'circle of light' (A 92), reminiscent of the irridescent sphere of the Aleph. It turns out to be the light from the trap door opened by the gaoler. He emerges from 'that indefatigable labyrinth of dreams' (A 92), as from the 'long night of the soul', the mystical trials of many traditions, to a total acceptance of his circumstance. The anaphora announces the ecstatic visions to follow: 'I returned to my hard prison as though I were a man returning home ... I blessed its dampness, I blessed its tiger, I blessed its high opening and the light, I blessed my old and aching body' (A 92).[39] It is apparently as a result of this sanctification of his miserable reality that Tzinacán experiences the 'union with the deity, union with the universe' (A 93). Taking on the knowledge of Borges, the Mayan lists different symbols for this unity: the *resplandor* of Christianity, the sword of Islam, and the rose of Sufi mystics. The *resplandor*, of course, he has just experienced. Bell-Villada (214) quotes a passage from the *Upanishads* which seems to correspond closely to Tzinacán's experience and his final indifference to his own fate: 'Who sees all beings in his own self, and his own self in all beings, loses all fear. When a sage sees this greater Unity, and his self has become all being – what delusion and sorrow can be near him?' Bell-Villada (215) also quotes the passage from the *Bhagavad Gita* which describes Arjuna's vision of Krishna, whose spirit contains the infinite brightness and beauty of the universe, and Alazraki (48) another passage describing water rushing into a flaming mouth similar to Tzinacán's vision of a Wheel 'made of water, but also of fire' (A 93). The Wheel is a central symbol of the divine in many Hindu, and indeed Buddhist, texts. Tzinacán in the vision of the Wheel understands the infinite interweaving of all the threads of the universe: 'It was made of all things that shall be, that are, and that have been, all intertwined, and I was one of the strands within that all-encompassing fabric, and Pedro de Alvarado, who had tortured me, was

---

[39] 'Del incansable laberinto de sueños yo regresé como a mi casa a la dura prisión. Bendije la humedad, bendije su tigre, bendije el agujero de luz, bendije mi viejo cuerpo doliente, bendije la tiniebla y la piedra' (I 598).

another' (A 93).[40] The suggested identity of the torturer and his victim here is reminiscent of many pantheistic moments in Borges, not all as grand as this particular one, of course. Balderston, with well documented justification, prefers to see the Wheel in the context of the various cycles of time in the Mayan Long Count calendar described by León Portilla: 'The Colonial Maya texts which speak of the twenty-year periods or wheels of the *katuns* confirm this peculiar conception of a universe in which the passage of time consists of arrivals, relays, and departures of divine forces' (B 77).

From the *resplandor*, to the vision of divinity, and to the Wheel, Tzinacán goes on to relive the creation myths of the *Popol Vuh*, before returning to the Kabbalistic cryptogram. In an ecstatic series of phrases beginning, like the vision of the Aleph, with 'I saw', he sees the emergence of mountains from the seas, the first wooden man, the rebellion of the pots against men, and the dogs which eat their faces, all recounted in the Mayan sacred text. After understand everything in this series of total visions, Tzinacán 'also came to understand the writing of the tiger' (A 93), a sentence of fourteen words, and forty syllables. The sentence would give him the power to 'make me immortal, make the jaguar destroy Alvarado, bury the sacred blade in Spanish breasts, rebuild the Pyramid, rebuild the empire', but 'I know that I shall never speak those words, because I no longer remember Tzinacán' (A 93).[41] 'The Writing of the God' was published in February 1949, well into the regime of Perón. It is interesting to compare its end with the equally myste-rious ending of 'Tlön, Uqbar, Orbis Tertius', published in May 1940: 'Yo no hago caso ...'; 'That makes very little difference to me ... I go on revising (though I never intend to publish) an indecisive translation in the style of Quevedo ...' (F 25).

'The Immortal', 'El inmortal'

'The Immortal' is a long and unwieldy, rather over-populated story. The fact that the narrator of the main part of the story is at once Homer, a Roman soldier from the time of Diocletian, Marcus Flaminius Rufus, and an anti-quarian bookseller from Smyrna, Joseph Cartaphilus, is an intriguing notion,

---

[40] 'Entretejidas, la formaban todas las cosas que serán, que son y que fueron, y yo era una de las hebras de esa trama total, y Pedro de Alvarado, que me dio tormento, era otra' (I 598).

[41] 'Me bastaría decirla ... para ser inmortal, para que el tigre destrozara a Alvarado, para sumir el santo cuchillo en pechos españoles, para reconstruir la pirámide, para reconstruir el imperio. ... Pero yo sé que nunca diré esas palabras, porque ya no me acuerdo de Tzinacán' (I 599).

but confusing for the reader, and somehow unconvincing. The ideas are weighty ones which recur in Borges's stories and essays. One of the most important is the notion that all writers are one writer. It is explored most thoroughly in 'Coleridge's Flower': Valéry had written that the history of literature was the history of the spirit and could be written without mentioning a single author; Emerson wrote that a single writer had written all the books in the world; Shelley that all the poems in time are fragments of one infinite poem (II 17). Another is the identity of Homer, the translation and reception of his texts. In 'The Homeric Versions' our ignorance of Homer paradoxically promotes creative freedom:

> That heterogeneous and even contradictory richness is [attributable] to a circumstance that is particular to Homer: the difficult category of not knowing what pertains to the poet and what pertains to the language. To that fortunate difficulty we owe the possibility of so many versions, all of them sincere, genuine, and divergent. (TL 70)[42]

Borges reads in De Quincey's 'Homer and the Homeridae' and Vico's *Scienza Nuova* the debates about how to conceive of a figure called Homer who supposedly wrote texts separated by more years than a man's life. In the story, Homer meets a certain Gianbattista (Vico) and is convinced by his arguments that 'Homer' is a construct. A third preoccupation is immortality, and the effects it would have on the identity of an individual and on morality. One of his sources here, as studied by Ronald Christ in his ground-breaking work on 'The Immortal', is Shaw's *Back to Methuselah*. The notion of totality implied, the idea that an immortal individual could do everything, is parallel to the speculation in 'The Library of Babel' and 'The Lottery in Babylon'. Shakespeare is not mentioned in the story, but the notion in 'Everything and Nothing' that he was everybody in his writing and yet nobody to himself seems to hover over the story. Related to immortality is the idea of not being allowed to die and the figure of the Wandering Jew, cursed for mocking Christ. A final cluster of ideas should be mentioned at this stage: reading, and writing seen as quotation from one's reading. In the story, as in the essay on Coleridge, Ben Jonson gave his judgement on his contemporaries

---

[42] 'Esa riqueza heterogénea y hasta contradictoria [es imputable a una] circunstancia, que debe ser privativa de Homero: la dificultad categórica de saber lo que pertenece al poeta y lo que pertence al lenguaje. A esa dificultad feliz debemos la posibilidad de tantas versiones, todas sinceras, genuinas y divergentes' (I 240).

in fragments of Seneca, Quintilian, etc. In 'Borges and I' he confesses that he recognizes himself less in books by Borges than in many by other writers.

The long main narration, in five chapters, is contained by an epigraph from Francis Bacon on knowledge and memory, a short introduction on Joseph Cartaphilus and the finding of his manuscript, and a final Postscript dated 1950, a year after the story was published, recounting the critical reception of Cartaphilus's text, and Borges's refutation of the criticism. The first chapter recounts how the Roman hears from a blooded and dying horseman of a river whose waters give immortality, and of the nearby City of the Immortals. He sets out from Thebes in search of these things, describing tribes and areas in words borrowed from Pliny's *Historia naturalis*. Almost dead with thirst, he comes to the base of the City. In the second chapter, he finds himself bound in a niche, rolls down the mountain and drinks in a dirty stream, 'unexplainably' then pronouncing words in Greek, which are in fact from the *Iliad*. He is surrounded by naked troglodytes, who seem to have lost the power of speech. He explores the City. The base is a complex labyrinth, but as he emerges into the City above he finds it horrendously chaotic and meaningless, reminiscent of the fantastic visions of Piranesi. In the third chapter, he tries to teach one of the troglodytes, whom he names Argos, after Homer's dog, to speak, and quotes Descartes as he wonders whether they are concealing their ability to speak. One day it rains and Argos speaks in rusty Greek, saying that he remembered little of the *Odyssey* that he had written eleven centuries earlier. The troglodytes are the immortals. The fourth chapter summarizes the story that 'Homer' tells him of the city and the implications of immortality. Ten centuries later, they conceive of a river which would rid them of immortality and set out to find it. The fifth chapter recounts our hero's adventures in modernity: he fought at Stamford Bridge, subscribed to the six volumes of Pope's translation of the *Iliad*, and transcribed the story of the seven voyages of Sinbad. He arrives at the Eritrean coast on board the Patna, which is in fact the steamer of Conrad's *Lord Jim*, and finds the longed-for river.

At this point, the narration, which has seemed more or less epic according to how many quotations and anachronisms have been noticed (most are in fact revealed in the Postscript), suddenly becomes metatextual, as Joseph Cartaphilus re-reads his manuscript. He notices a false note in it, thinking perhaps it might be the 'overemployment of circumstantial details' (A 17), 'abuso de rasgos circunstanciales' (I 542). Borges had discussed this technique of realism in 'The Postulation of Reality', but here I think the point is De Quincey (383) seeing 'circumstantiality', 'the invention of little personal circumstances and details' as a defining characteristic of the *Iliad*. Though Cartaphilus believed he had been telling the story of the Roman tribune, he realizes that '*The story I have told seems unreal because the experiences of two different men are intermingled in it*' (A 17).[43] By an examination of his own writing, as if it belonged to another, he comes to realize that it must have been written by a man of letters not arms, and that he had forgotten over time that he was actually Homer. The obvious clue was that he had used Homeric Greek, already described as 'inexplicable' at the time. More subtly, he had talked of battles but had focused on human destinies, not feats of arms. A note of pathos is introduced when the character reads versions of the *Odyssey* in *Sinbad the Sailor* and Pope's translation of the *Iliad*. As he faces death, he realizes that he will become Nobody, which is what Ulysses gave as his own name to the Cyclops, and as the eternal literary model, everybody – like Shakespeare: 'I have been Homer; soon, like Ulysses, I shall be Nobody; soon, I shall be all men – I shall be dead' (A 18).[44] As time passes and memory fades, words become detached from the circumstances of their uttering, and from the individual who uttered them, which is why he could tell the story of the Roman as his own: 'As the end approaches, there are no longer any images from memory – there are only words. It is not strange that time may have confused those that once portrayed *me* with those which were symbols of the fate of *the person that accompanied me for so many centuries*' (A 18).[45]

As we look back over the text, we see the references to memory, and the instability of personal pronouns. The epigraph from Bacon which contains arguments from two authors who say the same thing as he is saying, and thus in a sense are the same author, stresses the inseparability of memory and forgetfulness in the context of the eternal return and metempsychosis: '*Solomon saith*: "There is no new thing upon the earth". *So that as Plato had an imagination*, that all knowledge was but remembrance: *so Solomon giveth his sentence*, that all novelty is but oblivion.' The first paragraph of Cartaphilus's manuscript contains five uses of the Spanish first-person pronoun *yo*, referring to the Roman soldier, when it is not strictly necessary: 'yo logré divisar apenas el rostro de Marte' (I 533). When describing the troglodyte-immortals, he refers to them with the third-person pronoun: 'it made them immune to pity' (A 14), but shortly afterwards uses the second-person plural:

---

[43] '*La historia que he narrado parece irreal porque en ella se mezclan los sucesos de dos hombres distintos*' (I 543).

[44] 'Yo he sido Homero; en breve, seré Nadie, como Ulises; en breve seré todos: estaré muerto' (I 543).

[45] 'Cuando se acerca el fin, ya no quedan imágenes del recuerdo; sólo quedan palabras. No es extraño que el tiempo haya confundido las que alguna vez me representaron con las que fueron símbolos de la suerte de quien me acompañó tantos siglos' (I 543).

'Let no one imagine that we were mere ascetics.' Cartaphilus's account begins with an implicit reference to the fallibility of memory: 'que yo recuerde' (I 533), 'as far as I remember'. Later experiences distort our memory of the past: 'subsequent events have so distorted the memory of our first days that now they are impossible to put straight' (A 5).[46] Experiences in the City and the dreams produced as they 'infestaron mis pesadillas' ('infested my nightmares') (I 538) become one: 'I can no longer know whether any given feature is a faithful transcription of reality or one of the shapes unleashed by my nights' (A 10).[47] Some experiences were so horrid that they were wilfully banned from consciousness.

We first see Joseph Cartaphilus in 1929 through the eyes of the same Princesse de Lucinge in whose packages artefacts from Tlön had first entered the world, as she buys from him Pope's *Iliad*. The name Cartaphilus is associated with the Wandering Jew, who lived to one hundred and then reverted to being thirty for the rest of eternity (FH). His features were 'singularly vague' and his speech displays a similar mobility and lack of fixity, languages displaced from their origins, rearticulated and rewritten: 'within scant minutes he shifted from French to English and from English to an enigmatic cross between the Spanish of Salonika and the Portuguese of Macao' (A 3).[48] He was from Smyrna, one of Homer's possible birthplaces, and was returning there when he was drowned and buried on the island of Ios, also associated with Homer. In Spanish, Ios conveniently sounds like the plural of *yo*: already the *I* is multiple. The 1950 Postscript principally gives an account of Dr Nahum Cordovero's *A Coat of Many Colours*, which both refers us to the biblical Joseph, and evokes the notion of patchwork. Moses ben Jacob Cordovero was the greatest theoretician of Jewish Kabbalism, and dealt with questions of immortality and transmigration (FH). It reviews various examples of the *cento*, works made up of fragmentary quotations of other texts: a strong tendency, of course, in Borges's literature. He reviews, among others, Ben Jonson, Alexander Ross and Eliot, presumably T. S. Eliot's *The Waste Land*, notoriously an intricate network of quotations, in the early and last lines of which we read: 'Son of man, / You cannot say, or guess, for you know only / A heap of broken images' (Eliot, 51), and 'These fragments have I shored against my ruins' (Eliot, 67). Turning to Cartaphilus's text, he points

---

[46] 'Los hechos ulteriores han deformado hasta lo inextricable el recuerdo de nuestras primeras jornadas' (I 534).

[47] 'no puedo ya saber si tal o cual rasgo es una transcripción de la realidad o de las formas que desatinaron mis noches' (I 538).

[48] 'en muy pocos minutos pasó del francés al ingles y del inglés a una conjunción enigmática de español de Salónica y de portugués de Macao' (I 533).

out the interpolations of Pliny, De Quincey, Descartes and George Bernard
Shaw, concluding that the manuscript is 'apocryphal': according to the *OED*,
sham, counterfeit, of doubtful authenticity. In the context of a Homer already
a construct and rewritten across the centuries, and a notion of literature as
a vast collective intertextual enterprise, the accusation of being apocryphal
is pretty meaningless, or indeed a decent description of literature. Borges
intervenes briefly at the end to stress this in the case of the ex-immortal
Cartaphilus: 'Words, words, words taken out of place and mutilated, words
from other men – those were the alms left him by the hours and the centuries'
(A 19).[49]

The description of the exploration of the City of the Immortals is memorable, frightening almost. First, 'Marcus' enters the labyrinth with its circular
chambers with nine passages, one of which leads to the next chamber. He is
horrified and distraught but as the Borges of 'The South' said: this was simply
the antechamber of hell. When he emerges into the construction above, he
is horrified by the utter meaninglessness and inhumanity of what he sees:
it was built by gods, the gods are dead, the gods were mad. It is radically
different from the maze: 'A maze is a house built purposely to confuse men;
its architecture, prodigal in symmetries, is made to serve that purpose. In the
palace that I imperfectly explored, the architecture had *no* purpose' (A 9).[50]
In Spanish the word correctly translated by 'purpose' is 'fin', which means
both purpose and end. What does not have an end, immortality, for example,
also lacks purpose. Homer soon explains to him that the Immortals had built
a City, but had knocked it down, and he had suggested, nine hundred years
later, rebuilding it as Marcus found it, a 'parody or antithesis of City which
was also a temple to the irrational gods about whom we know nothing save
that they do not resemble man' (A 13).[51] Here lies the major paradox and
tragedy of the story: the expression of the general humanity of collective
literary endeavour is utterly inimical to man. Something similar happens with
the philosophy of idealism in 'Tlön', and with the philosophy of Schopenhauer in '*Deutsches Requiem*'. Homer after all had reputedly written the war
of frogs and mice, the *Batrachomyomachia*, as a parody of his *Iliad*.

Many of the characteristics of the immortals are taken from *Back to Meth-*

---

[49] 'Palabras, palabras desplazadas y mutiladas, palabras de otros, fue la pobre limosna que
le dejaron las horas y los siglos' (I 544).

[50] 'Un laberinto es una casa labrada para confundir a los hombres; su arquitectura, pródiga
en simetrías, está subordinada a ese fin. En el palacio que imperfectamente exploré, la arquitectura carecía de fin' (I 537).

[51] 'suerte de parodia o reverso y también templo de los dioses irracionales que manejan el
mundo y de los que nada sabemos, salvo que no se parecen al hombre' (I 540).

uselah by George Bernard Shaw (S): Adam's despair at immortality, Cain's remark that 'there is nothing new under the sun' (S 374), the forgetting of speech (S 624). The Archbishop has been archbishop three times and also president and general; like Homer he 'persuaded the authorities to knock down all our towns and rebuild them from the foundations' (S 462). The She-Ancient comments that: 'Everything happens to everybody sooner or later if there is enough time. And with us there is eternity' (S 580). The Immortals similarly 'knew that over an infinitely long span of time, all things happen to all men' (A 14).[52] The effect for both communities is indifference. In Shaw: 'Nothing makes any difference to them that I can see' (S 581). In Borges the indifference is moral: 'Viewed in that way all our acts are just, though also unimportant [indiferentes]. There are no spiritual or intellectual *merits*' (A 14). Rather like the Archbishop (Borges puts it more dramatically) an immortal man is all men and nobody: 'No one is someone; a single immortal man is all men. Like Cornelius Agrippa, I am god, hero, philosopher, demon, and world—which is a long-winded way of saying that *I am not*' (A 14).[53]

Death paradoxically defines humanity and confers meaning; individuals are unique, fragile, dream-like:

> Death (or reference to death) makes men precious and pathetic; their ghost-liness is touching; any act they perform may be their last; there is no face that is not on the verge of blurring and fading away like the faces in a dream. Everything in the world of mortals has the value of the irrecoverable and the contingent.

With the Immortals, on the other hand, no act or thought is unique: 'every act (every thought) is the echo of others that preceded it in the past, and the faithful presage of others that will repeat it in the future, *ad vertiginem*. There is nothing that is not as though lost between indefatigable mirrors' (A 15).[54] This is the world of the 'Library of Babel' where everything has been said, and the speech and writing of any individual is tautology. It is the dystopian

---

[52] 'Sabía que en un plazo infinito le ocurren a todo hombre todas las cosas' (I 540).

[53] 'Nadie es alguien, un solo hombre inmortal es todos los hombres. Como Cornelio Agrippa, soy dios, soy héroe, soy filósofo, soy demonio y soy mundo, lo cual es una fatigosa manera de decir que no soy' (I 541).

[54] 'La muerte (o su alusión) hace preciosos y patéticos a los hombres. Éstos conmueven por su condición de fantasmas; cada acto que ejecutan puede ser último; no hay rostro que no esté por desdibujarse como el rostro de un sueño. Todo, entre los mortales, tiene el valor de lo irrecuperable y de lo azaroso. Entre los Inmortales, en cambio, cada acto (y cada pensamiento) es el eco de otros que en el pasado lo antecedieron, sin principio visible, o fiel presagio de otros que en el futuro lo repetirán hasta el vértigo' (I 541-2).

face of the utopia of the pantheistic unity of man and spirit, of Homer as universal author. Homer–Cartaphilus–Marcus resolves to search for the river of mortality.

'The Dead Man', 'El muerto'

'The Dead Man' is a carefully plotted thriller, set like 'The Shape of the Sword' and a scene from 'Tlön' on the frontier between Uruguay and Brazil, a zone seen by Borges as more elementary than Buenos Aires and Argentina, mythical almost. In his commentary on the story he recounts a ten-day stay in the area, which became indelibly impressed on his mind: 'everything I then witnessed – the stone fences, the longhorn cattle, the horses' silver trappings, the bearded gauchos, the hitching posts, the ostriches – was so primitive, and even barbarous, as to make it more a journey into the past than a journey through space [as in 'El Sur']' (Com 271). The setting together with the symmetrical plot of betrayal and punishment, greed, ambition and fall, gives it the air of parable, allegory even. Borges coyly prefers to see it as a 'kind of adventure'. In the epilogue to *The Aleph*, Borges writes that the smuggler boss of the story, Azevedo Bandeira, was from Rivera. This is where Borges goes on the trip mentioned, when he stays at Enrique Amorim's ranch in Tacuarembó (W 210), and sees a man shot in a bar by a *capanga* who, the next day, was casually drinking in the same place. Sylvia Molloy (50) describes the story as 'a distorted picaresque, a parodic *Bildungsroman* in a nutshell'.

In 'Death and the Compass', Lönnrot believes he is confidently reading evidence to solve a murder and capture his enemy until he realizes that his enemy, Scharlach, had been all the time controlling him. Here a young *compadrito*, Benjamín Otálora, fleeing an election rigging murder in Buenos Aires, travels to Uruguay where he enters the employment of Azevedo Bandeira, whom he supplants and whose power he gradually usurps, until he too realizes that his rise to power was a simulacrum allowed and plotted by Bandeira as a preliminary to his punishment and annulment for his presumption. Both Lönnrot and Otálora are eliminated in the last short line by fire, a shooting described in Spanish as 'hacer fuego'. Fire, as in 'The Circular Ruins', shows up unreality. The difference between Otálora and Lönnrot is that Otálora is a subordinate attribute of a semi-divinity, which makes him similar to the vizier who usurps the identity of the king in 'Ibn-Hakam al-Bokhari'. In the Afterword, Borges points to two sources or parallels to his story: Chesterton's *The Man who was Thursday*, and Gibbon's *Rise and Fall*. Bandeira is 'an uncouth sort of deity – a mulatto, renegade version of Chesterton's incomparable Sunday' (A 134).[55] Sunday is as dual, specular and deceitful as anything in Borges: nightmarishly he is at once police chief and the anarchist leader, detective and criminal, traitor and hero in one. There is a sort of monstrosity in him, as Chesterton himself later wrote: 'the mysterious master both of the anarchy and the order was the same sort of elemental elf who had appeared to be rather too like a pantomime ogre' (*The Man*, 185). Azevedo's presence gives the appearance of being 'contrahecho', 'deformed', and combines disparate and sinister elements: 'In his face (which is always too close) there mingle the Jew, the Negro, and the Indian; in his air, the monkey and the tiger' (A 21).[56] This admixture is curiously reminiscent of the monstrously rebuilt City of the Immortals: 'the body of a tiger or bull pullulating with teeth, organs, and heads monstrously yoked together' (A 10).[57] In the episode from Gibbon, a soldier and politician Rufinus had become righthand man to the emperor. An enemy, Stillicho, leads him to believe that a military gathering is in his honour, only to have him surrounded and put to the sword (Bell-Villada, 188).

Otálora's fate is subtly prefigured by Borges in episodes which, blinded by his ambition, he systematically misreads. The story takes on a magical or supernatural character given that Azevedo seems to have been weaving the plot from before the first time that he met Otálora. Otálora, on arriving in Montevideo, had unsuccessfully looked for Bandeira, to whom he had a letter of introduction from an electoral boss in Buenos Aires. In an *almacén*, driven by the taste for danger, he intervenes in a fight between cattle drovers, and saves one man from a low knife thrust, and that man turns out to be Bandeira. The next morning the aggressor wakes him and takes him to Bandeira; he remembers that after the fight Bandeira had sat his attacker on his right and forced him to continue drinking. At least in retrospect one realizes that Bandeira was either in league with the individual, or biding his time to take revenge. As Otálora rises through the ranks, as a 'Bandeira man', from *compadre* to gaucho to smuggler, a series of paradoxes, reversals and oxymora act as destabilizing agents. The fact, for example, that Bandeira was born on the Brazilian side of the river, 'which ought to bring him down a

---

[55] 'una tosca divinidad, una versión mulata y cimarrona del incomparable Sunday de Chesterton' (I 629).

[56] 'da, aunque fornido, la injustificable impresión de ser contrahecho; en su rostro, siempre demasiado cercano, están el judío, el negro y el indio; en su empaque, el mono y el tigre' (I 545).

[57] 'un cuerpo de tigre o de toro, en el que pulularan monstruosamente, conjugados y odiándose, dientes, órganos y cabezas' (I 538).

notch or two in their estimation, lends his aura a vague new wealth of teeming forests, swamps, impenetrable and almost infinite distances' (A 22).[58] The vastness of the connotation, moreover, confers on Bandeira a natural and regal power beyond the individual. When Otálora kills a man to take his place as a *contrabandista* (which points towards *contrabandeirista*), he is moved by ambition and 'obscure loyalty' (A 22), 'una oscura fidelidad' (I 546), a curious combination. One day he is called into the bedroom of the sick Bandeira. A 'distant mirror of cloudy glass' (A 23)[59] warns the reader that Otálora is merely a hazy reflection of Bandeira's essential power. The scantily dressed redhead, Bandeira's prestigious attribute, is also glimpsed through the mirror. Otálora's subsequent possession of her is perhaps not such a big step as he had thought. His most hubristic reading comes when someone says that Bandeira is coming to the ranch because 'there's a foreigner, a would-be gaucho type, that's getting too big for his britches' (A 23).[60] Instead of taking the warning, he is flattered by what he chooses to read as a joke. He takes over Bandeira's three most prestigious attributes: his woman, silver apparel and horse, and seems to gain the support of Bandeira's *capanga*, Ulpiano Suárez (both Otálora and Suárez are Borges's family names). At the New Year's Eve celebrations, Olálora's crowing bombast is menacingly reminiscent of the Tower of Babel raised to challenge the deity: 'Otálora, drunk, builds exultancy upon exultancy, jubilation upon jubilation; that vertiginous tower is a symbol of his inexorable fate' (A 25).[61] Bandeira quietly gets up, and has the redhead dragged from her room, and forced to kiss Otálora, before Suárez 'casi con desdén, hace fuego' (I 549), 'almost disdainfully' shoots him. Otálora the traitor realizes that he has been betrayed, that his power was no more than another's dream:

> Otálora realizes, before he dies, that he has been betrayed from the beginning, that he has been sentenced to death, that he has been allowed to love, to command, and win because he was already as good as dead, because so far as Bandeira was concerned, he was already a dead man. (A 25)[62]

---

58 'eso, que debería rebajarlo, oscuramente lo enriquece de selvas populosas, de ciénagas, de inextricables y casi infinitas distancias' (I 546).

59 'un remoto espejo que tiene la luna empañada' (I 547).

60 'hay un forastero agauchado que está queriendo mandar demasiado' (I 547).

61 'Otálora, borracho, erige exultación sobre exultación, júbilo sobre júbilo; esa torre de vértigo es un símbolo de su irresistible destino' (I 548).

62 'Otálora comprende, antes de morir, que desde el principio lo han traicionado, que ha sido condenado a muerte, que le han permitido el amor, el mando y el triunfo, porque ya lo daban por muerto, porque para Bandeira ya estaba muerto' (I 458–9).

'The Theologians', 'Los teólogos'

'The Theologians', first published in April 1947, involves, like 'Three Versions of Judas', a rather daunting amount of theological and philosophical argument. It has much more of a story, however; it is another duel story, and explores the intellectual rivalry between Aurelian and John of Pannonia, and is more satisfying in the way the plot interacts with the theological conceits, reflecting or inverting them. To a great extent it is a reworking of the ideas of 'History of Eternity', and specifically of 'The Doctrine of Cycles' (1934), and the 1943 essay added later to the collection, 'Circular Time'. In the latter essay, Borges outlines a plot which would develop into 'The Theologians':

> A while ago I imagined a fantastic tale in the manner of León Bloy: a theologian dedicates his entire life to refuting a heresiarch; he bests him in intricate polemics, denounces him, has him burned at the stake. In Heaven he discovers that in God's eyes he and the heresiarch form a single person.
> (TL 228)[63]

The kernel of the story, the model for its functioning, is presented in the first paragraph. The Huns razed a monastery library, but the twelfth volume of the fifth-century *City of God*, where St Augustine explains and refutes Plato's notion of eternal return, is saved. (Attila the Hun razed Aquileia in 452.) It explains that 'in Athens Plato once taught that at the end of time all things will return again to where they once were – that he in Athens, before the same circle of listeners, will one day teach that doctrine once again' (A 26).[64] Augustine perpetuates the heresy, and readers forget that he expounded it solely to condemn it. Augustine, in Borges's paraphrase, wrote that 'Jesus was the straight path that leads men out of the circular labyrinth in which the impious wander' (A 27).[65] Circular time is set against successive time, and the orthodox writer promulgates the heresy he refutes.

Aurelian, theologian and powerful bishop-coadjutor of Aquileia, learns of a heresy professing ideas similar to those of Plato and Pythagoras, a sect known as the Monotoni or Annulari. Ironically they are referred to as

---

[63] 'Yo imaginé hace tiempo un cuento fantástico, a la manera de León Bloy: un teólogo consagra toda su vida a confutar a un heresiarca; lo vence en intricadas polémicas, lo denuncia, lo hace quemar; en el Cielo descubre que para Dios el heresiarca y él forman una sola persona' (I 395).

[64] 'Platón enseñó en Atenas que, al cabo de los siglos, todas las cosas recuperarán su estado anterior, y él, en Atenas, ante el mismo auditorio, de nuevo enseñará esa doctrina' (I 550).

[65] 'Jesús es la vía recta que nos salva del laberinto circular en que andan los impíos' (I 551).

a 'novísima secta', a dubious newness when they repeat a doctrine which
excludes novelty, and claims that 'all things that exist have existed before
and will exist again' (A 26).[66] When he hears that a rival theologian, John of
Pannonia, is writing a refutation of the heresy, he sets about writing his own.
His argument is vastly complex and encumbered with laborious erudition:
'He constructed vast labyrinthine periods, made impassable by the piling
up of clauses upon clauses—clauses in which oversight and bad grammar
seemed manifestations of disdain. He crafted an instrument from cacophony'
(A 27).[67] John's treatise, conversely, was 'limpid, universal' (A 29), and was
chosen to refute the Monotoni at the Council of Pergamon. The heretic
Euphorbus is condemned and burned, and as he dies he cries: '*This has
occurred once, and will occur again … It is not one pyre you are lighting, it
is a labyrinth of fire*' (A 29).[68] This phrase resounds through the remainder
of the story. From this moment the two churchmen fight a 'secret battle'
(A 29), an invisible duel. Aurelian never mentioned the name of John, and
whereas many volumes of his (apocryphal) work were included in the (real)
Patrology of Migne, only twenty words of John's work remained. The number
is important, as we shall see.

A new heresy emerged. Aurelian named its proponents Histrioni, and they,
significantly, inverted the connotation of his name by adopting it themselves.
Their customs were wild, condoning crime, sodomy and incest. They blas-
phemed not only against the Christian God but also against the divinities
of their own pantheon. This allows Borges a nice joke. Sir Thomas Browne
wrote, apocryphally, that their *Histrionic Gospels* had been lost, but not the
'insultes' which condemned them. Erfjord (of 'Three Versions of Judas' fame)
argues that, given their cosmology (of inverted mirrorings), the condemnation of their Gospels was probably the Gospels themselves, thus echoing
Augustine's unwitting propagation of the doctrines of Plato. (Menard too had
been in the habit of writing the exact opposite of his own ideas.) Many of
their doctrines are familiar to Borges's readers: metempsychosis like that of
Pythagoras, while for the Proteans life was as mutable as that of the Immortal
or the inhabitant of Babylon: 'within the period of a single life [they] are
lions, dragons, wild-boars, are water and are a tree' (A 31).[69] Evil can be

---

    66 'nada es que no haya sido y que no será' (I 550).
    67 'Erigió vastos y casi inextricables períodos, estorbados de incisos, donde la negligencia
y el solecismo parecían formas del desdén. De la cacofonía hizo un instrumento' (I 551).
    68 'Esto ha ocurrido y volverá a ocurrir … No encendéis una pira, encendéis un laberinto
de fuego' (I 552).
    69 'en el término de una sola vida son leones, son dragones, son jabalíes, son agua y son
un árbol' (I 553).

eliminated from the world by practising it: '*not* to be an evildoer was an act of satanic arrogance' (A 31),[70] an argument used by Runeberg about Judas. More important for the conclusion of the story is the world view derived from the Gnostics and Kabbalism, about the lower world mirroring the upper. Each man has an opposite and double:

> they imagined that every man is two men, and that the real one is the *other* one, the one in heaven. They also imagined that our acts cast an inverted reflection, so that if we are awake, the other man is asleep; if we fornicate, the other man is chaste; if we steal, the other man is generous. When we die, they believed, we shall join him and *be* him. (A 31)[71]

The form of the heresy in Aurelian's diocese maintained that time does not permit repetitions, that no two moments are alike. To describe the heresy Aurelian casts around for expression until he suddenly comes up with a sentence of twenty words. He realizes that they were the words used by John to counter the belief in circular time of the Monotoni. He publishes it with a half-hearted covering up of John's authorship, which is quickly undone. John is now accused of heresy. He vigorously defends the case that his argument was strictly orthodox. Ironically he fails to apply the notion that no two moments are the same to his own situation: the second time he defends his thesis, its words do not mean the same; times have changed. He is burned at the stake, repeating the death of the heresiarch Euphorbus and confirming the thesis that he had refuted, and his prediction about the labyrinth of fires. In a parallel paradox, the twenty words which survive him were given to posterity by his enemy Aurelian, again repeating the case of St Augustine, and proving the Platonic argument. Aurelian sees his enemy's face for the first time at the execution, and it reminds him of someone: himself most likely. It had rained the previous night and the wood was damp.

Aurelian is left virtually orphaned by the disappearance of his rival, who had been the secret justification for all his work. Many years later, after time in Aquileia, Ephesus, Macedonia, Mauritania, and Rusadirr (Melilla), he is in a monastery in a forest in Hibernia (Ireland). He hears the pattering of the rain, and remembers a similar night in Rome, presumably the eve of John's execution. Lightning strikes the trees and Aurelian dies like John

---

[70] 'no ser un malvado es una soberbia satánica' (I 553).

[71] 'imaginaron que todo hombre es dos hombres y que el verdadero es el otro, el que está en el cielo. También imaginaron que nuestros actos proyectan un reflejo invertido, de suerte que si velamos, el otro duerme, si fornicamos, el otro es casto, si robamos, el otro es generoso. Muertos, nos uniremos a él y seremos él' (I 553).

(and Euphorbus before them), and slips into the pattern of circularity that he too had refuted. In Heaven there is no time, and God is little interested in theology. For 'the unfathomable deity, he and John of Pannonia (the orthodox and the heretic, the abominator and the abominated, the accuser and the victim) were a single person' (34).[72] God sides with the arguments of the Histrioni. The next story takes another classic dichotomy, closer to Argentine reality this time, that of civilization and barbarism, and weaves a chilling political parable.

'Story of the Warrior and the Captive Maiden', 'Historia del guerrero y de la cautiva'

In this story, the barbarian who espoused civilization and the civilized woman who lives a life of barbarism are not enemies, but separated by some thirteen centuries. They were both moved by a 'secret impulse, an impulse deeper than reason' (A 39)[73] to transgress the boundary between their group and another. As in the previous story: 'The obverse and the reverse of this coin are, in the eyes of God, identical' (A 39).[74] What might, however, have been little more than a clever formal game of intriguing symmetries is brought alive, and made more complex and ambiguous, by the very personal voice of Borges and the involvement of his grandmother. In the first sentence he explains that the epitaph and destiny of the Lombard warrior Droctulft who, in the sixth century, seduced by the Roman city of Ravenna, turned against his 'barbarian' allies to defend it against them, had singularly moved him, and only later had he understood why. Droctulft's story, derived from erudite sources in Croce, Paul the Deacon, Tacitus and Gibbon, is followed by the story, recounted in a far more homely way by Borges's grandmother, of a Yorkshirewoman. The latter had been captured by Indians in a *malón* where her parents were killed, had married an Indian chief, had had two children by him, and refused to return to 'civilization'. The story of Droctulft is an intriguing combination of archetype and striking immediacy. On the one hand, the unique individual is irrecoverable in the collaboration of memory and forgetting involved in (history) writing: 'Let us imagine Droctulft *sub specie aeternitatis* – not the individual Droctulft, who was undoubtedly

---

[72] 'para la insondable divinidad, él y Juan de Panonia (el ortodoxo y el hereje, el aborrecedor y el aborrecido, el acusador y la víctima) formaban una sola persona' (I 556).

[73] 'un ímpetu secreto, un ímpetu más hondo que la razón' (I 559–60).

[74] 'El anverso y el reverso de esta moneda son, para Dios, iguales' (I 560).

unique and fathomless (as all individuals are), but rather the generic "type" that tradition (the work of memory and forgetting) has made of him and many others like him' (A 36).[75] And yet the wonder at the city, experienced by this 'type' is fresh and memorable:

> He comes from the dense forests of the wild boar and the urus ... He sees daylight and cypresses and marble. He sees an aggregate that is multiple yet without disorder. ... Perhaps a single arch is enough for him, with its incomprehensible inscription of eternal Roman letters—he is suddenly blinded and renewed by the City. (A 36)[76]

On reading the account in Croce, Borges was 'struck by the sense that I was recovering, under a different guise, something that had once been my own' (A 37).[77]

The second story is set in 1872, which as Balderston points out is also the date of the publication of *Martín Fierro*, which recounts another defection that had long fascinated Borges, that of Sergeant Cruz, who turns on his policemen to defend the outlaw Fierro. In that year his grandmother Fanny Haslam lived with her husband Colonel Francisco Borges, who had fought against the Indians and was the commander of the northern Indian frontier of Buenos Aires, in a remote provincial town. Fanny laments her 'destino de inglesa desterrada a ese fin del mundo' (I 558), 'destiny as an English-woman exiled to that end of the world'. It is pointed out to her that she was not the only Englishwoman there, and was introduced to a blond-haired Indian dressed in red *mantas*, her face painted in fierce colours. Grandmother evokes, very much from her own point of view, and strongly coloured by the literature of the time, a life of utter savagery. She is horrified: 'An English-woman, reduced to such barbarism!' (A 38)[78] Grandmother promises to rescue her and her two sons, but the woman declares herself happy with her life, and disappears. Francisco Borges dies soon after this meeting, in 1974, in the civil war between Sarmiento and Mitre. Fanny and the Yorkshire Indian had perhaps felt sisters for a second; only now does Fanny fully see herself

---

[75] 'Imaginemos, *sub specie aeternitatis*, a Droctulft, no al individuo Droctulft, que sin duda fue único e insondable (todos los individuos lo son), sino al tipo genérico que de él y de muchos otros como él ha hecho la tradición, que es obra del olvido y de la memoria' (I 557).

[76] 'Venía de las selvas inextricables del jabalí y del uro ... Ve el día y los cipreses y el mármol. Ve un conjunto que es múltiple sin desorden ... Quizá le basta ver un solo arco, con una incomprensible inscripción en eternas letras romanas. Bruscamente lo ciega y lo renueva esa revelación, la Ciudad' (I 557–8).

[77] 'tuve la impresión de recuperar, bajo forma diversa, algo que había sido mío' (I 558).

[78] 'A esa barbarie se había rebajado una inglesa' (I 559).

in the terrifying mirror of the other woman. She sees 'that other woman, torn like herself from her own kind and transformed by that implacable continent, as a monstrous mirror of her own fate ...' (38).[79] This intuition is confirmed on the only occasion she sees the 'Indian' again. She had been out hunting at a ranch where a farm-hand had just slit a sheep's throat. Like a flash, and 'as in a dream', the Indian woman jumps from her horse and eagerly drinks the hot blood. She repeats the gesture of the savages in Esteban Echeverría's 1837 Romantic narrative poem *La cautiva*, reflected in our story's title.

Fanny's fate was not in fact particularly monstrous. She missed out, by her husband's death, on the enormous land awards that he would have received in the 1879 campaign against the Indians known as the 'Conquest of the Desert', and was forced to set up a modest lodging house to bring up her two sons, but the 'monstrosity' would seem to evoke rather the time when the story was written: 1949. As Balderston points out, 'La fiesta del monstruo', Bioy and Borges's story of a murder by Peronist thugs, had been written a year earlier; Borges himself had been expelled from his job in the library by the rise of Perón in 1946. Only months before the publication of the story, other female members of Borges's family, his mother and sister Norah, were arrested in Calle Florida for singing the national anthem as a protest against the regime of Perón. The South American destinies of Laprida ('Conjectural Poem') and Dahlmann ('The South') are, of course, also implied in this vibrant tale.

'A Biography of Tadeo Isidoro Cruz (1829–1874)'

This brief story is one of Borges's most complex in its implications, and pregnant with meaning. At the same time, its structure is boldly drawn, with three parallel episodes, leading up to a classic recognition scene and the dissolution of the opposition between outlaw and policeman. The 'impulse deeper than reason' which directed Droctulft and the Yorkshirewoman to change their allegiances is echoed here when Sergeant Cruz realizes that 'every man must accept the destiny he bears inside himself' (A 43),[80] and turns against his own men to fight with the outlaw Martín Fierro. It develops the technique of withholding the identity of the protagonist until the end of the story, but scattering clues that some readers will pick up, while others will only retrospectively discern the pattern. 'The House of Asterion' is the best known example of the

---

[79] 'pudo percibir en la otra mujer, también arrebatada y transformada por ese continente implacable, un espejo monstuoso de su destino ...' (I 559).

[80] 'todo hombre debe acatar el [destino] que lleva adentro' (I 563).

technique, revealing the protagonist to be the Minotaur. Like 'The End' it is a rewriting of Hernández's *Martín Fierro*. The earlier story is a sequel in which the brother of the murdered Moreno returns and kills Fierro in a duel. Here Sergeant Cruz, Fierro's companion in the poem, is given a detailed historical and family past, largely replacing the one that he had in the poem, which goes further to dramatize and add different new layers of meaning to the famous scene mentioned above. Borges in his Commentary on the story says that he had always been puzzled by the behaviour of the policeman and that 'I was moved to write the story out of my personal bewilderment' (Com 270).

In the second paragraph of the story Borges confesses that his story is derived from a classic text, which as such is subject to constant rewriting and re-imagining: 'The adventure is recorded in a very famous book – that is, in a book whose subject can be all things to all men (I Corinthians 9:22), for it is capable of virtually inexhaustible repetitions, versions, perversions' (A 40).[81] The most startling and disruptive change that Borges makes to his famous hypotext is the inclusion of generations of family members: not only the father of Cruz, but also Borges's ancestor Manuel Isidoro Suárez, and others. This latter, of course, echoes the presence of Borges's grandmother and the death of his grandfather Colonel Francisco Borges in 'Story of the Warrior and the Captive'. Detailed references to Argentine history add a political dimension to Borges's story. Borges's great-grandfather Suárez's troops kill Cruz's *montonero* father, placing the struggle between Federalists and Unitarians at the origins of his plot. How far can one project this into the present of the writing of the story? In the light of Borges's association of Rosas and Perón, do Cruz and Fierro become proto-Peronist thugs in any sense?

The climax of Borges's story is the scene where the policeman Cruz, sent to capture Martín Fierro, changes his allegiance and joins Fierro against his own policemen. This is when the clearest quotation from Hernández's poem is reproduced: 'Cruz ... grand gritó que no iba a consentir el delito de que se matara a un valiente (I 563; MF 1625), 'Cruz ... shouted that he would not allow the crime of killing a brave man.' Reproducing the play between domesticated dogs and wild wolves in the poem (MF 1565, 1631), Cruz 'comprendió su íntimo destino de lobo, no de perro gregario' (I 563); he 'realized his deep-rooted destiny as a wolf, not a gregarious dog' (A 43). Borges likes to equate this scene to Don Quixote's liberating of the galley-slaves. In the Commentary on the story, he repeats the knight's judgement that 'an honest

---

[81] 'La aventura consta en un libro insigne; es decir, en un libro cuya materia puede ser todo para todos (1 Corintios 9,22), pues es capaz de casi inagotables repeticiones, versiones, perversiones' (I 561).

man should not go out of his way to be another man's jailer' (Com 271). In the poem Martín Fierro realizes his extreme affinity with Cruz: 'Ya veo que somos los dos / astillas del mesmo palo' (MF 2143–4); 'I see that we are both carved from the same wood.' Borges takes the recognition further, changing it into identity in the metaphysical moment when the ego is transcended: 'Any life, however long and complicated it may be, actually consists of *a single moment* – the moment when a man knows forever more who he is' (A 42).[82] Facing Fierro, he realized 'que el otro era él' (I 563), 'that the other man was he himself' (A 43). Borges draws an analogy between Cruz's realization and rather grander revelations, where history and literature echo each other: 'It is said that Alexander of Macedonia saw his iron future reflected in the fabulous story of Achilles; Charles XII of Sweden, in the story of Alexander' (A 42).[83] Literature and history interact in a rather different way in 'Theme of the Traitor and the Hero', and one wonders here whether the fabulous story of Fierro will be reflected in the iron future of Argentina.

Borges organizes his narrative material in such a way as to make it prefigure the final realization of identity. The three analogous or mirror scenes around which the prefiguration is organized are: the death of Cruz father and his own conception; Cruz's fight against the police *partida*; Cruz's abandoning the *partida* he led to fight with Fierro against it. They are linked by clear motifs, some derived from the text of *Martín Fierro*. These scenes, however, are entwined in a dense web of anecdote and history, which for most will only really come to life with Fishburn and Hughes's dictionary, or a good spell in a library. Cruz's death from small pox, while a captive of the Indians, is recounted in the poem (MF II 910); the circumstances of his birth, however, are invented by Borges. In 1829, during the civil war between Unitarians and Federalists, Lavalle's forces were pursuing the *montoneros* of Manuel Mesa loyal to Rosas. They were routed by Isidoro Suárez, and 'a man perished in a ditch, his skull split by a saber from the wars in Peru and Brazil' (A 40),[84] i.e., from the wars of Independence when Suárez fought at Junín and from the war with Brazil (1825–8). The night before he had slept with a woman named Isidora Cruz in an *estancia* near Pergamino. The child she bore him was called Tadeo Isidoro. Curiously his second name comes from his mother Isidora, from Isidoro Suárez, the man responsible for his father's death, and

---

[82] 'Cualquier destino, por largo y complicado que sea, consta en realidad *de un solo momento*: el momento en que el hombre sabe para siempre quién es' (I 562).

[83] 'Cuéntase que Alejandro de Macedonia vio reflejado su futuro de hierro en la fabulosa historia de Aquiles; Carlos XII de Suecia, en la de Alejandro' (I 562).

[84] 'el hombre pereció en una zanja, partido el cráneo por un sable de las batallas del Perú y del Brasil' (I 561).

from Borges himself. Another maternal grandfather, Isidoro Acevedo, also shared the name, and was the son of Judas *Tadeo* Acevedo. Cruz is curiously both a victim of Borges's forebear and, by name, an adopted or illegitimate son. Borges comments, fusing his own character with that of Hernández: 'those who have commented on the story of Tadeo Isidoro Cruz, and there are many, stress the influence of the wide plains on his formation ... He did live in a world of monotonous barbarity' (A 40–1).[85] Borges here is surely slipping slyly from Hernández's character to the classic *gaucho malo* Facundo Quiroga, immortalized by Sarmiento in his 1845 *Facundo: civilización y barbarie*, which has famous passages on the influence of the pampa landscape on the mind-set of the *gaucho*.

In 1849 Borges has Cruz as a cowhand employed by a relative of Borges on his mother's side: Francisco Xavier Acevedo. He inserts him into a story he had written back in *Evaristo Carriego*: 'Historias de jinetes', 'Stories of Horsemen', where a *gaucho* was lodged in a Buenos Aires inn for some days, but never left his lodgings, such was his indifference to the city, or his fear of it (I 152). He kills a man who mocked him (not in the poem), escapes, hides in a *fachinal*, swampy ground, and is surrounded by the police. His fight repeats nothing corresponding to Cruz in the poem, but reproduces Martín Fierro's preparation to fight the policemen of Cruz. The fight in Hernández is thus played out twice in the story, with Cruz and then Fierro as protagonists. Readers of *Martín Fierro* will quickly identify textual fragments: the cry of a bird called a *chajá* (MF 1472), his trying his knife on a bush (MF 1503), and his taking off his spurs (MF 1499). His punishment also corresponds to that of the Fierro of the poem, as he is sent to serve in a fort on the Frontera Norte (which Francisco Borges would later command), echoing the injustice done to Fierro at the beginning of his poem, which causes him to lose his wife, home and family. (In 1856, in an episode alien to the poem, he fights at Las Lagunas del Cardoso under the historical Eusebio Laprida, who shares the surname of Borges's ancestor Francisco de Laprida, the hero of his 'Conjectural Poem'.)

In 1868 he is back in Pergamino where he was born, and in 1869 is made sergeant of the rural police force. In the poem, shortly after killing two people, Cruz gains this post through contacts made by a woman friend. In 1870 he was ordered to capture an outlaw who had deserted, on the Southern Frontier (echoing Cruz's time on the Northern Frontier), forces under the historical

---

[85] 'Quienes han comentado, y son muchos, la historia de Tadeo Isidoro, destacan la influencia de la llanura sobre su formación ... Vivió, eso sí, en un mundo de barbarie monótona' (I 561).

Benito Machado, and who had murdered a black man in a brothel. Fierro in the poem does desert the Frontier (but there is no mention of Machado) and kills the Moreno (MF 1230). The echoes and déjà-vus become almost dream-like at this point. The outlaw was coming from Laguna Colorada, which was where his father's skull, repeating an earlier line, 'was split by a saber from the battles of Peru and Brazil' (A 42). Cruz had forgotten the place name, which he must have learned from his mother, and recognizes it with an uncanny and 'slight but inexplicable sense of uneasiness' (A 42).[86] He meets Fierro in a battle which is another version of his own fight with the police. He had to take refuge in a *fachinal*, swampy ground, 'hubo de guarecerse en un fachinal' (I 562), while Fierro 'se había guarecido en un pajonal' (I 563), he had taken refuge in a *pajonal*, a reed-bed. (Hurley's translation misses the repetition.) A *chajá*, a bird which famously warns of intruders, called out as it had in the previous encounter, and 'Tadeo Isidoro Cruz had the sense that he had lived the moment before' (A 43).[87] He had, of course, because it was a repeated rewriting of the scene from *Martín Fierro*. The repetitions, however, effectively produce a sense of the uncanny, something once familiar, forgotten and remembered. For example both Cruz and later Fierro 'gravely wound', 'malhirió' (I 562, 563) a number of their assailants.

The parallels confirm and make almost redundantly clear the identity between Cruz and Fierro. What is more uncanny, and disruptive of the symmetry of the story, is the haunting presence of Cruz's father. The crucial encounter with Fierro takes place where Cruz was conceived and his father killed. If we flick back to the first paragraph, we see that his death was already a prefiguring of the two fight scenes. His 'confuso grito' (I 561), 'confused cry', which woke his partner as he had a nightmare, is echoed in the cries of the *chajá*. He was pursued and killed in the gloomy *pajonales*, prefiguring the *fachinal* of his son, and the *pajonal* of Fierro. The literary symmetry between the two heroes of Hernández is consolidated in the story only to be disturbed and disrupted by a traumatic echo from the turbulent and fratricidal historical past of Argentina. That the echo should involve Borges's family history suggests that he is at once reclaiming the texts from the nationalists, with great-grandfather as key character, and great-grandson as irreverent rewriter, and investing it with a menacing predictive force.

---

[86] 'con leve pero inexplicable inquietud lo reconoció' (I 562).

[87] 'Gritó un chajá; Tadeo Isidoro Cruz tuvo la impresión de haber vivido ya ese momento' (I 563).

'Emma Zunz'

'Emma Zunz' is a remarkably personal story in so far as it deals with sexual inhibition, a character in whom men inspire 'an almost pathological fear' (A 45),[88] and unique in that its protagonist is a working-class woman. I wonder whether Emma Zunz's monotonous toil at the 'Tarbuch & Loewenthal weaving mill' (A 44) reminded Borges of the Miguel Cané Library. The story is an intriguing crime thriller, with a rigorously symmetrical plot. Emma's father Emanuel had been framed by Aaron Loewenthal for embezzlement, and had committed suicide. Emma prostitutes herself with a Scandinavian sailor, shoots Loewenthal, and absolves herself by framing him for rape. Emma Zunz joins Scharlach in 'Death and the Compass' and Nolan in 'Theme of the Traitor and the Hero' in passing off as true a spurious reading of an incident, indeed of a death. Scharlach and Nolan provide texts, Kabbalistic tracts, and Shakespeare's tragedies, which induce their opponents into misreading the random death of the rabbi Yarmolinsky and the execution for treason of Kilpatrick. Emma does not have texts, indeed she tears up a letter and money; her explanation is pretty unbelievable, but the intensity of her emotions imposes itself in one of Borges's most famous passages:

> The story was unbelievable, yes – and yet it convinced everyone, because in substance it was true. Emma Zunz's tone of voice was real, her shame was real, her hatred was real. The outrage that had been done to her was real, as well; all that was false were the circumstances, the time, and one or two proper names. (A 49–50)[89]

Her truth is of an archetypal or legendary nature. If the Aleph is the cipher of all the infinite complexity of reality, and the Zahir that of reduction of the real by symbol, the two *z*s of Zunz impose their plot on the banal reality of the two *a*s of Aaron.

The symmetrical scheme of revenge is disturbed by more embedded motivations. Emma presumably sells herself to the sailor to lose her virginity and thus prepare herself for a medical examination, but even before the days of DNA testing, the ploy was unlikely to stand up to forensic investigation. Neither would her removing Loewenthal's blood-specked glasses before disordering his clothes and placing them on a filing cabinet. Perhaps it is

---

[88] 'un temor casi patológico' (I 565).

[89] 'La historia era increíble, en efecto, pero se impuso a todos, porque sustancialmente era cierta. Verdadero era el tono de Emma Zunz, verdadero el pudor, verdadero el odio. Verdadero también era el ultraje que había padecido; sólo eran falsas las circunstancias, la hora y uno o dos nombres propios' (I 568).

a basic honesty which will allow her to tell a lie which is a fundamental truth that only she can know; certainly without her genuine revulsion and horror, she would not have been believed. Her original purpose of avenging her father, however, is perverted by the experience: 'Sitting before Aaron Loewenthal, Emma felt (more than the urgency to avenge her father) the urgency to punish the outrage she herself had suffered' (A 49).

Embedded in the second motive, lies a more complex one which inverts the surface logic of the story. Recalling her childhood in the house in Lanús, which had been auctioned off after the trial, she remembers 'the yellow lozenges of a window' (A 45).[90] When she enters the labyrinthine brothel in the Paseo de Julio, she sees identical lozenges. The brothel becomes the childhood house, and with astonishment and vertigo 'she thought (she could not help thinking) that her father had done to her mother the horrible thing being done to her now' (A 47).[91] The thought momentarily endangers her goal. Her father's marital sex with her mother, the sailor's mercenary sex with Emma, and Loewenthal's alleged criminal sex with Emma are the same act. Without fully realizing it (she 'took refuge in vertigo'), Emma finally does not avenge her father; she takes revenge on him. This reading scuppers the neat, if paradoxical, thriller plot into altogether murkier waters.

'The House of Asterion', 'La casa de Asterión'

'The House of Asterion' is composed of a five-paragraph monologue by Asterion and a brief epilogue with a rather puzzled comment by Theseus. Those who know that the epigraph from Apollodorus ('*And the queen gave birth to a son named Asterion*') refers to Queen Pasiphae, who after intercourse with the red bull gave birth to the Minotaur which her husband Minos enclosed in the labyrinth designed by Daedalus, will miss what for most people, I imagine, is a surprise ending: the revelation that Asterion is the Minotaur. The clues are in fact increasingly obvious, like the beginning of his last paragraph: 'Every nine years, nine men come into the house so that I can free them from all evil' (A 53).[92] The reference is to the seven Athenians sacrificed to the half-man/half-bull, but disguised by the change of number

---

[90] 'los amarillos losanges de una ventana' (I 564).

[91] 'Pensó (no pudo no pensar) que su padre le había hecho a su madre la cosa horrible que a ella ahora le hacían. Lo pensó con débil asombro y se refugió, en seguida, en el vértigo' (I 566).

[92] 'Cada nueve años entran en la casa nueve hombres para que yo los libere de todo mal' (I 570).

and the curious use of the phrase from The Lord's Prayer to describe killing. A second reading offers a different sort of pleasure as one understands what had seemed quirky or bizarre phrases. Words like 'misanthropy' take on a different meaning: not hatred of other men, but hatred of the human race as different. Once Asterion ventures out into Knossos, and on the second reading we realize why he had found the faces of the people so frighteningly different from his own muzzle: 'I did so because of the terrible dread inspired in me by the faces of the people – colorless faces, as flat as the palm of one's hand' (51).[93] And we realize why he calls them in Spanish 'la plebe' (I 569), the plebs: he was, of course, himself of partly royal blood.

The attraction of the piece is far from being exhausted by the puzzle and solution. The first reading, before we know the protagonist is a monster, allows us to grasp the pathos of a lonely character without the baggage that an early identification with the monster would have brought with it. Asterion is lonely, proud and defensive. He is aware of his uniqueness and his power but naïve and pathetically ignorant: 'there are two things in the world that apparently exist but once – on high, the intricate sun, and below, Asterion. Perhaps I have created the stars and the sun and this huge house, and no longer remember it' (A 53).[94] Borges radically reverses the conventional understanding of the figure, when Asterion talks of the coming of his redeemer (as Bell-Villada points out (150), quoting Job 19:25), whom he hopes will take 'me to a place with fewer galleries and fewer doors' (A 53).[95] The redemption is death, the release from solitude and difference, as a rather smug Theseus reveals in the last line: 'Can you believe it, Ariadne? ... The Minotaur scarcely defended itself' (A 53).[96] The death is a sort of suicide, which reminds us of Borges's conceit in 'A Comment on August 23, 1944', that Hitler wished to be defeated just as 'the metal vultures and the dragon (which must have known that they were monsters) collaborated, mysteriously, with Hercules' (II 211). In the Afterword to The Aleph Borges claims that he owes the story and 'the character of its poor protagonist' (A 134) to an 1896 painting by Watts. The painting, reproduced in Jason Wilson (88), depicts a Minotaur described by Bell-Villada (151) as a 'wrinkled, lonesome, and rather pitiful creature leaning on his rooftop walls'. In the context of his speculation on Borges's bodily self-disgust, Wilson (87) reports the

---

[93] 'lo hice por el temor que me infundieron las caras de la plebe, caras descoloridas y planas, como la mano abierta' (I 569).

[94] 'dos cosas hay en el mundo que parecen estar una sola vez: arriba, el intricado sol; abajo, Asterión' (I 570).

[95] 'Ojalá me lleve a un lugar con menos galerías y menos puertas' (I 570).

[96] '¿Lo creerás, Ariadna? —dijo Teseo—. El minotauro apenas se defendió' (I 570).

psychoanalyst Julio Woskoboinik's view that 'Borges was Asterion, autistic, introverted and solitary.'

Curiously, the other great Argentinian writer of the twentieth century, Julio Cortázar, also published a version of the Minotaur myth in 1949, with equally bold inversions: *Los reyes*. In Cortázar's version the Minotaur represents music and the poet, in opposition to the authoritarian power of Minos and the thuggery of Theseus. Cortázar clearly seems to be aligning the king with Perón and the generals who preceded him. Cortázar's Ariadne is in love with her half-brother, and gives Theseus the thread so that the Minotaur will kill him and escape. The Minotaur chooses to die, however, to gore the throne of Minos from the realms of the subconscious.[97]

'The Other Death', 'La otra muerte'

'The Other Death' tells the story of Pedro Damián, a peasant farmer from Entre Ríos who acted as a coward in the 1905 battle of Masoller during the nationalist rebellion of Saravia against the government of Uruguay, fervently dreamed in 1942 after years of shame that he died in the battle, and in fact did die as he had dreamed because God changed the past for him. There are various antecedents to the story. In the poem published in 1929, 'Isidoro Acevedo', Borges's grandfather was dying at home, like Pedro Damián, of 'pulmonary congestion' (I 86, I 571), when he dreamed in his delirium that he was actually dying with the soldiers with whom he had fought at Cepeda and Pavón. A past of cowardice is changed by narrative deceit and identification in 'The Shape of the Scar'; a past of treachery is changed in popular memory by the staging of the murder of Kilpatrick in 'Theme of the Traitor and the Hero'; the historical and archaeological past is changed by the invoking of *hrönir* in 'Tlön', and by lottery draws in Babylon. The status of reality in the story is brilliantly modulated. Like other stories it slips tantalizingly between lively realistic anecdote, citing real historical campaigns and real friends of Borges, and theological arguments from which it might have been invented. It slips between the self-conscious account of the genesis of a fantastic story, which might be the story we are reading, and a supposedly factual account of a string of events. In the future, moreover, 'Borges' will remember it not as the factual account that it was initially presented as being, but as a fantastical story based on ideas of Pier Damiani, so as to avoid the consequences of the dangerous knowledge that he has acquired.

---

[97] See my introduction to volume II of Cortázar's *Obras completas*, 15–16.

The story is set on the Argentine–Uruguayan border, which fascinated Borges, between the sonorous Gualeguay and Paysandú. In the first sentence, most of the dimensions of the story are presented. 'Borges' received from a real friend, Patricio Gannon, the announcement of his translation of Emerson's poem 'The Past', and the news of the death of a mutual acquaintance Pedro Damián. The poem elaborates on the common-sense position that the past cannot be changed: 'Not the gods can shake the past, nor the devil can finish what is packed / Alter or mend eternal Fact' (cit. FH). This notion, backed later in the story by the authority of Aristotle and Aquinas, is contested by the Italian theologian Pier Damiani, Peter Damian. As in 'The Theologians' we have two warring concepts of time. Gannon tells 'Borges' of Damián's final delirium of heroism.

There follows a series of episodes in which the memory of witnesses of Damián's life seems to fluctuate and change. 'Borges' is inspired to write a fantastic tale about the final moments of Damián, and the Uruguayan critic Emir Rodríguez Monegal introduces him to the presumably fictional Colonel Dionisio Tabares, who embarrasses 'Borges' and shatters his high opinion of Damián by revealing that under cannon fire at Masoller, his courage had failed him. That same winter, he returned to see Tabares to gather material for his fantastic story. Tabares had forgotten that he ever knew Damián, and another veteran of Masoller, Juan Francisco Amaro, remembers him dying while leading a cavalry charge. 'Borges' meets Gannon in a Buenos Aires bookshop, and he too has now forgotten that he ever knew Damián, or had written about him. Tabares writes to say that he now perfectly remembers Damián's heroic death. 'Borges' visits Damián's region, but his house seems to have disappeared; Abaroa, who had witnessed his death, has died. Here we see 'Borges's' memory waver, or a falsity introduced into his account, as he later confesses to have done. Gannon had sent 'Borges' a photograph of Damián, which, twice in the first paragraph, 'Borges' claims to have lost, saying that he had not looked for it because he was afraid of finding it. Now he claims that he had confused his memory of Damián's face with the image of the tenor Tamberlik singing in Rossini's *Otello*.

As in many stories at this stage, Borges introduces various conjectures about the nature of the phenomenon, reaches a startling conclusion, and expands on its consequences. He first thinks that there were two Damiáns; his friend Ulrike von Kühlmann suggests that he died in the battle and that God, who cannot change the past, but can change the appearance of the past, had allowed him to return home as a ghost. 'Almost magically' he comes across Pier Damiani's argument that God can in fact change the past. Any change of the past would have created two universal histories with infinite and unforeseeable consequences. For the tear in time to be healed, the divergence mended, the memories of Tabares and Gannon had to change; more threateningly, Abaroa had to be eliminated. (The school teacher who witnessed the change in the past effected by the *hrönir* in Tlön had also died.) 'Borges' is aware of the danger, as Runeberg was when he discovered God's terrible secret that he had become human not as Jesus but as Judas: 'I have guessed at and recorded a process inaccessible to humankind, a sort of outrage to rationality' (A 60).[98] He hopes for various reasons that he will be spared the fate of Abaroa. For one thing he has lied (like the inhabitant of Babylon). Also, he has changed the name of the main character to assist his own memory to change appropriately for his own safety. As he formulates this, he already starts to doubt the actual existence of Pedro Damián: 'I suspect that Pedro Damián (if he ever existed) was not called Pedro Damián, and that I remember him under that name in order to be able to believe, someday in the future, that his story was suggested to me by the arguments of Pier Damiani' (A 60).[99] That hope is fulfilled when we read in the Afterword to *The Aleph*, which is an integral part of the story: '"The Other Death" is a fantasy about time, which I wove under the suggestion of some of Pier Damiani's arguments' (A 134).[100]

'Deutsches Requiem'

'*Deutsches Requiem*' was a very bold story for Borges to write only two years after the end of the Second World War. Echoing the case of Yu Tsun in 'Garden of the Forking Paths' and his murder of Stephen Albert, the story is the testimony of a Nazi, Christophe zur Linde, on the eve of his execution for war crimes, in justification of a career which led him to kill the person he most admired, the Jewish poet David Jerusalem. The interpretative tact it demands is made greater by the fact that Zur Linde has many of the family and intellectual characteristics of Jorge Luis Borges. Borges was a prominent ant-Nazi during the war, but also a great admirer of German culture and scornful of the Argentine Germanophiles who were utterly ignorant of that

---

[98] 'He adivinado y registrado un proceso no accesible a los hombres, una suerte de escándalo de la razón' (I 575).
[99] 'Sospecho que Pedro Damián (si existió) no se llamó Pedro Damián, y que yo lo recuerdo bajo ese nombre para creer algún día que su historia me fue sugerida por los argumentos de Pier Damiani' (I 575).
[100] '"La otra muerte" es una fantasía sobre el tiempo, que urdí a la luz de unas razones de Pier Damiani' (I 629).

culture. Borges bravely tries to get into the skin of an educated and civilized Nazi to understand the German tragedy:

> During the last war, no one could have wished more earnestly than I for Germany's defeat; no one could have felt more strongly than I the tragedy of Germany's fate; '*Deutsches Requiem*' is an attempt to understand that fate, which our own 'Germanophiles' (who know nothing of Germany) neither wept over nor even suspected. (A 134)[101]

Zur Linde is basically mad: 'Those who heed my words shall understand the history of Germany and the future history of the world' (A 63).[102] He is a Germanic Don Quijote who has gone mad by reading too much Spengler, Schopenhauer and Nietzsche, or by reading it too naively and literally. Absolutely everything in the world for him is justified, pre-willed, and part of a scheme of delirious determinism: the destruction of Judaism and that malady of Judaism, Christianity, and the abolition of pity in the name of the new man, the Nazi, the *übermensch*. Reading Borges's favourite philosopher Schopenhauer convinces him that every last act of a man has been willed and predetermined by him, which creates a topsy-turvy, oxymoronic logic: 'every humiliation is an act of penitence, every failure a mysterious victory, every death a suicide'. Such a philosophy renders the individual godlike: 'that individual [teleology] reveals a secret order, and in a marvelous way confuses ourselves with the deity' (A 65).[103] Zur Linde had been badly wounded and, being unfit for combat service as he had wished, was put in charge of Tarnowitz concentration camp in Poland, which was clearly odious to him. According to his Schopenhauerian scheme, he must have willed this mutilation. His logic is that of Runeberg in 'Three Versions of Judas' arguing why God should have chosen to become incarnate in Judas in eternal torment in Hell, a fate and sacrifice more rigorous than the brief agony of Jesus on the cross. The examples he gives are different, but the logic is identical:

---

[101] 'En la última guerra nadie pudo anhelar más que yo que fuera derrotada Alemania; nadie pudo sentir más que yo lo trágico del destino alemán; "*Deutsches Requiem*" quiere entender ese destino, que no supieron llorar, ni siquiera sospechar, nuestros "germanófilos", que nada saben de Alemania' (I 629).

[102] 'Quienes sepan oírme, comprenderán la historia de Alemania y la futura historia del mundo' (I 576).

[103] 'toda humillación [es] una penitencia, todo fracaso una misteriosa victoria, toda muerte un suicidio ... esa teleología individual nos revela un orden secreto y prodigiosamente nos confunde con la divinidad.' (I 578)

> To die for a religion is simpler than living that religion fully; battling
> savage beasts in Ephesus is less difficult … than being Paul, the servant of
> Jesus Christ; a single act is quicker than all the hours of a man. The battle
> and the glory are *easy*; Raskolnikov's undertaking was more difficult than
> Napoleon's. (A 65)[104]

His acceptance of the vilifying task is an act of humility, a subjection to the
logic of the cause. Hence the epigraph from Job 13:15: '*Though he slay me,
yet will I trust in him.*' Ironically, for a man dedicated to eliminating Christianity and Judaism, his references are remarkably biblical.

His personal fate is an image of the destiny of Germany. Quoting the
aphorism of the enemy Englishman Coleridge, he argues that the dialogue
between men born Aristotelian and men born Platonists resounds through the
centuries. With a slightly strained analogy, he sees a 'secret continuity' in the
history of peoples. The secret logic of history can be paradoxical, and involve
the same sort of sacrifice as seen above:

> Luther, the translator of the Bible, never suspected that his destiny would
> be to forge a nation that would destroy the Bible forever … Hitler thought
> he was fighting for *a* nation, but he was fighting for *all* nations, even for
> those he attacked and abominated. … There are many things that must be
> destroyed in order to build the new order; now we know that Germany was
> one of them. (A 68)[105]

What matters is the destruction of Christian servility and the reign of
violence, not individuals or nations: 'What does it matter that England is the
hammer and we the anvil?' Repeating the logic of Judas, he concludes: 'Let
heaven exist, though our place be in hell' (A 68).[106] But again more biblical
examples are summoned up. When David in II Samuel 12:2 is told of a rich
man who had stolen his neighbour's only sheep, he judges that that man
should be killed. His interlocutor replies: 'Thou art that man', for his stealing
Bathsheeba. We are reminded here of Lönnrot in 'Death and the Compass',

---

[104] 'Morir por una religión es más simple que vivirla con plenitud: batallar en Éfeso contra
las fieras es menos duro … que ser Pablo, siervo de Jesucristo; un acto es menos que todas
las horas de un hombre. La batalla y la gloria son *facilidades*; más ardua que la empresa de
Napoleón fue la de Raskolnikov' (I 578).

[105] 'Lutero, traductor de la Biblia, no sospechaba que su fin era forjar un pueblo que
destruyera para siempre la Biblia … Hitler creyó luchar por *un* país, pero luchó por todos, aun
por aquellos que agredió y detestó. … Muchas cosas hay que destruir para edificar el nuevo
orden; ahora sabemos que Alemania era una de esas cosas' (I 580).

[106] '¿Qué importa que Inglaterra sea el martillo y nosotros el yunque? … Que el cielo
exista, aunque nuestro lugar sea el infierno' (I 580–1).

who is a similarly manic reader and constructs his own death trap: 'we are like the wizard who weaves a labyrinth and is forced to wander through it till the end of his days' (A 68).[107]

Intriguingly, Borges gives the Nazi Zur Linde many of his own traits. The most obvious is an ancestry split between arms and letters. One of his ancestors died in a cavalry charge in the battle of Zondorf during the Seven Years' War against Russia, evocative of Isidoro Suárez's leading the cavalry charge at Junín. His maternal great-grandfather was killed by snipers during the Franco-Prussian war of 1870, and his father distinguished himself at the siege of Namur during the Great War. An 'editor's note' is an useful device to point out that Zur Linde has censored one half of his genealogy, omitting his most distinguished forebear, the theologian and Hebraist Johannes Forkel. The name Forkel, of course, suggests forking and duality. The schematic account of his intellectual development suggests an opening out and a dramatic narrowing of vision. An early interest in metaphysics and theology was erased by contact with Schopenhauer, and by 'Shakespeare and Brahms with the infinite variety of their worlds' (A 63).[108] As we have seen, however, the mind of the theologian, and the Calvinist at that, persists in his account. The rich world of Shakespeare, who was everything, is in turn suffocated by Nietzsche and Spengler, or at least by the version of them forged by Nazi ideology: radically German values, exaltation of violence, and scorn for weakness and pity. Very schematically indeed, Aristotle is replaced by Plato, the individual and particular by the Idea.

In March 1939, just about the time when Borges was hospitalized with septicaemia, during anti-Jewish riots in Tilsit, Zur Linde received two bullet wounds as a consequence of which one of his legs was amputated. (Colonel Francisco Borges is hit by two bullets at La Verde.) A euphemistic footnote from the editor, and the fact that in hospital he is accompanied by 'un gato enorme y fofo' (I 578), 'an enormous, soft cat', suggests that zur Linde is rendered impotent by the shooting. The physical mutilation of one side of the fork reflects the mutilation of his genealogy, and that of his intellect. A compassionate man at heart, his Nietzschian destruction of his own pity is put to a serious test when the poet David Jerusalem, a symbolic name and an individual, enters his camp. Jerusalem was a Whitmanesque poet who 'se alegra de cada cosa con minucioso amor' (I 578), 'takes delight in every smallest thing, with meticulous and painstaking love' (A 65–6). He seems to

---

[107] 'somos comparables al hechicero que teje un laberinto y que se ve forzado a errar en él hasta el fin de sus días' (I 580).

[108] 'Shakespeare y Brahms, con la infinita variedad de su mundo' (I 577).

be an echo of Zur Linde in his Shakespearian days, which is why he vows to
destroy him, for he is destroying the old man in himself: 'In my eyes he was
not a man, not even a Jew; he had become a symbol of a detested region of
my soul. I suffered with him, I died with him, I somehow have been lost with
him; that was why I was implacable' (A 66–7).[109] He sends Jerusalem mad,
reflecting his own ideological lunacy. Though the editor censors the actual
method, Zur Linde gives us a good clue:

> I had realized many years before I met David Jerusalem that everything in
> the world can be the seed of a possible hell; a face, a word, a compass, an
> advertisement for cigarettes – anything can drive a person insane if that
> person cannot manage to put it out of his mind. Wouldn't a man be mad
> if he constantly had before his mind's eye the map of Hungary? (A 66)[110]

This is the madness that befalls 'Borges' in 'The Zahir', where he receives a
coin which he cannot forget. The coin or Zahir is an utterly radical schema-
tization of the world, its reduction to a minimal symbol; a map of course is
a radical impoverishment of the richness and 'infinite variety' of a country.
The induction of madness in Jerusalem is a sadistic intensification of Zur
Linde's own intellectual and ideological trajectory, his move from the variety
of liberalism to the dogma of Nazism. Jerusalem kills himself on the first
of March 1943, the anniversary of Zur Linde's wounding and subsequent
mutilation. (The reduction also echoes the reduction of Stephen Albert's rich
mental world to one word, Albert, which kills him.)

'Averroës' Search', 'La busca de Averroes'

'Averroës' Search' is an atmospheric story set in twelfth-century Al-Andalus
about the Arab physician and philosopher, born in Córdoba, whose commentaries on Aristotle became the principal source of Greek thought for medieval
Christian and Jewish theology (FH). The Spanish title can mean both 'The
Search *of* Averroës', i.e. his search for the meaning of the terms 'comedy' and
'tragedy' in Aristotle's *Poetics*, and 'The Search *for* Averroës', i.e. Borges's

---

[109] 'Ante mis ojos, no era un hombre, ni siquiera un judío; se había transformado en el
símbolo de una detestada zona de mi alma. Yo agonicé con él, yo morí con él, yo de algún
modo me he perdido con él; por eso, fui implacable' (I 579).

[110] 'Yo había comprendido hace muchos años que no hay cosa en el mundo que no sea
germen de un Infierno posible; un rostro, una palabra, una brújula, un aviso de cigarrillos,
podrían enloquecer a una persona, si ésta no lograra olvidarlos. ¿No estaría loco un hombre
que continuamente se figurara el mapa de Hungría?' (I 579).

attempt to capture in writing the presence of the man Averroës. Borges describes the story as a description of 'the process of failure' (A 77). Averroës did not know Syriac or Greek, and worked from a translation of a translation of Aristotle; moreover in his own Arabic culture there was no notion of the theatre. The limits of his own culture made his attempt to understand another destined to failure. Borges, similarly, approaches his subject with just a few pieces from nineteenth-century orientalists: 'no more material than a few snatches from Renan, Lane, and Asín Palacios' (A 77). What may be a failure of representation on the literal or denotative level is a success on the connotative level in so far as Borges's writing signifies and echoes the story and writing of Averroës: 'I felt, on the last page, that my story was the symbol of the man I had been as I was writing it' (A 77–8).[111] More generally, in the long conversation which forms the central part of the story, we also see how the limitation of language is, paradoxically, at the same time its strength.

Questions of connotation, displacement, familiarity and unfamiliarity, cultural limitation and translatability, are accentuated by the fact that Averroës is in Moorish Europe, at one remove from the origins of his culture in Cairo or Damascus. The story begins and ends in a beautifully evoked house in Córdoba where the murmuring fountains and the Guadalquivir outside contrast with the sandy deserts of his ancestors. The central section is a conversation about language and literature at the house of the Koranist Farach, and Borges intervenes briefly to comment on his own story in an unmarked one-paragraph epilogue. As Averroës struggles with the notions of comedy and tragedy, without the concept of drama and theatre, and consults the most authoritative cultural texts, there are two lovely pieces of irony. Through his window, he witnesses three boys, speaking the incipient romance language of the Peninsula, playing in turn at being the muezzin, the minaret, and the worshippers. He has the reality of theatre before his very eyes, and words describing it, but is blind to the link between them. Similarly, over dinner, the traveller Abu-al-Hasan uncomprehendingly recounts a visit to a theatre in China. His account very effectively produces an uncanny sense of defamiliarization in the reader:

> One evening, the Muslim merchants of Sin-i Kalal conducted me to a house of painted wood in which many persons lived. It is not possible to describe that house, which was more like a single room, with rows of cabinet-like contrivances, or balconies, one atop another. ... These masked

---

[111] 'Sentí, en la última página, que mi narración era el símbolo del hombre que yo fui, mientras la escribía' (I 588).

ones suffered imprisonment, but no one could see the jail; they rode upon
horses, but the horse was not to be seen; they waged battle, but the swords
were of bamboo; they died, and then they walked again. (A 73–4)[112]

One listener, Faraj, promptly concludes that they are mad. When it is explained
to him that they were representing acts, he exclaims that in that case a single
speaker could have told the story.

The quirky, amusing, and rather rambling conversation on language
between the dinner-guests tangentially but significantly casts light on the
dilemmas of the story. Abu-al-Hasan, who had never taken the trouble to
look at them, declared that the roses of the Andalusian villas, or *cármenes*,
were unique. Language and perception are again out of kilter. Faraj countered
by offering an account of a permanent rose in Indostan the petals of which
have the inscription '*There is no God but Allah*' (A 71); another, an account
of a tree which produced green birds. Averroës counters that birds and fruit
belong to the natural world whereas writing is an art: he has already encoun-
tered the artificial and arbitrary nature of words, signifying only within a
cultural system. Almost inevitably, the notion of divine language is invoked
by another: the Koran, like the Scriptures for the Kabbalists, was a divine
substance which antedated the Creation, and was infinitely meaningful. On
the other hand, when asked to recount a marvel from his travels, Abu-al-
Hasan finds language too weak and abstract to describe the subtly nuanced
reality of experience: 'the marvelous was perhaps incommunicable: the moon
of Bengal is not the same as the moon of Yemen, but it deigns to be described
with the same words (A 73).[113]

As the conversation turns to poetry, it seems at times to be more related to
the role of metaphor in Argentinian *ultraísmo* than to Arabic literature. Abd-
al-Malik criticizes poets in Damascus and Córdoba who reuse the old metaphors derived from Bedouin experience, such as the comparison between fate
and a blind camel: 'five hundred years of admiration had worn it very thin'
(A 75).[114] Averroës–Borges replies that he himself had argued this in the past
(in many *ultra* manifestos and publications), but that only someone who has

---

[112] 'Una tarde, los mercaderes musulmanes de Sin Kalán me condujeron a una casa de
madera pintada, en la que vivían muchas personas. No se puede contar cómo era esa casa, que
más bien era un solo cuarto, con filas de alacenas o de balcones, unas encima de otras. ... [las
personas] Padecían prisiones, y nadie veía la cárcel; cabalgaban, pero no se percibía el caballo;
combatían, pero las espadas eran de caña; morían y después estaban de pie' (585).

[113] 'la maravilla es acaso incomunicable: la luna de Bengala no es igual a la luna del
Yemen, pero se deja describir con las mismas voces' (584).

[114] 'esa figura pudo suspender a la gente, pero ... cinco siglos de admiración la habían
gastado' (I 586).

professed an erroneous opinion can be free of it in the future. The surprise
factor in new metaphors is of little importance: 'if the purpose of the poem
were to astound, its life would not be measured in centuries but in days, or
hours, or perhaps even minutes' (A 75).[115] Anything can be compared to
anything, but lasting metaphors transcend and pre-exist the individual poet
as a sort of archetype: 'a famous poet is less an inventor than a discoverer'
(A 75).[116] Reflecting Borges's classicism, for Averroës, something that could
only be invented by one man is irrelevant: 'the image that only a single
man can shape is an image that interests no man'.[117] Time, through successive readings, and layers of connotation, enriches classical verses and tropes
which 'are all things to all men' (A 76).[118] Borges had already explored this in
'Pierre Menard' and many other places, but here he gives the idea a classical
expression: 'time, which ravages fortresses and great cities, only *enriches*
poetry' (A 76), or in the more elegantly balanced Spanish phrase: 'el tiempo,
que despoja los alcáceres, enriquece los versos' (I 586). He gives various
examples of the richness accrued in classical verses over time. Zuhair's image
of the camel and destiny originally had just two terms and now has four as
it is also a reminder for the reader, of the poet who wrote them and allows
him to 'conflate our tribulations with those of that dead Arab' (A 76).[119] The
arbitrariness of words, earlier seen as an impoverishment, now allows great
freedom and richness. Abd-al-Rahmān wrote '*Tú también eres, ¡oh palma!, /
en este suelo extranjera ...*' (I 587), '*Thou too art, oh palm!, a foreigner
on this soil ...*', to express his nostalgia for the Orient. The same verses
comforted Averroës when in Africa, Marrakesh, he was missing his home-
land Spain. The weakness of language, its sober abstraction which cannot
express the particular difference between two moons, is paradoxically its
richness as it can gain in universality and resonance over time and in the
reading process. Thus it is that the failure of Averroës to translate the terms
from Aristotle, and of Borges to recover the immediacy of Averroës in his
prose, is transcended by the universality of their shared destiny, the identity
of the writing process and the subject of that writing.

Borges paraphrases Ernest Renan (FH) to document Averroës's only very
partial success in translating his problematical terms, assimilating them to his
own Islamic culture: '*Aristu* [Aristotle] *gives the name "tragedy" to pane-*

---

[115] 'si el fin del poema fuera el asombro, su tiempo no se mediría por siglos, sino por días
y por horas y tal vez por minutos' (I 586).

[116] 'un famoso poeta es menos inventor que descubridor' (I 586).

[117] 'La imagen que un solo hombre puede formar es la que no toca a ningno' (I 586).

[118] 'todo para todos los hombres' (I 586).

[119] 'confundir nuestro pesares con los de aquel árabe muerto' (I 586).

gyrics and the name "comedy" to satires and anathemas. There are many admirable tragedies and comedies in the Qur'ān and the mu'llaqat *of the mosque'* (A 77).[120] As he looks into a mirror Averroës and his surrounding reality 'disappeared, as though annihilated by a fire without light' (A 77).[121] The 'fuego sin luz' which would fulminate reality if the attention of God were diverted for a second had been evoked in 'History of Eternity' (TL 134, I 363) and in '*Deutsches Requiem*'. Here it is Borges as creator, rather like the wizard in 'The Circular Ruins', who takes the role of God: 'And just when I stop believing in him, "Averroës" disappears' (A 78).[122]

'Ibn-Hakam al-Bokhari, Murdered in His Labyrinth', 'Abenjacán el Bojarí, muerto en su laberinto', togther with 'The Two kings and the Two Labyrinths', 'Los dos reyes y los dos laberintos'

'Ibn-Hakam al-Bokhari, Murdered in His Labyrinth' is a highly entertaining and exoticizing detective story, and at the same time a wild parody of a detective story, set in Cornwall and Sudan. Its two young protagonists, as they walk through a labyrinth on the Cornish coast, and later in a London pub, offer rival versions of the dramatic events concerning King Ibn-Hakam al-Bokhari and his vizier Sa'īd. (In Spanish, the first letter of his name, Abenjacán, highlights the contrast with the Z of Zaid.) Dunraven recounts the events as he recollects them from his childhood, while, by pure logic (like Auguste Dupin, and Isidro Parodi), Unwin deduces his version from inconsistencies in the former account. Neither, in fact, is fully satisfactory. According to Dunraven, Ibn-Hakam had built the labyrinth to defend himself from the ghost of his vizier, whom he had murdered; in Unwin's version it is Sa'īd who built the labyrinth as a trap to attract the king, who he had not dared to kill in Sudan, to England, and murder him there. The names of the two friends and rivals, one a poet and the other a mathematician, already suggest a certain identity. Unwin, with the initial D of Dunraven, becomes *unwind*, leaving his friend, as Unraven, very close to *unravel*, both reflecting Poe's view in 'The Murders in the Rue Morgue' that the role of the analyst is to *disentangle* (Poe, 189). Indeed, both are aware of the literary tradition

---

120 'Aristú (Aristóteles) denomina tragedia a los panegíricos y comedias a las sátiras y anatemas. Admirables tragedias y comedias abundan en las páginas del *Corán* y en las mohalacas del santuario' (I 587).
121 'desapareció bruscamente, como si lo fulminara un fuego sin luz' (I 587).
122 'En el instante en que yo dejo de creer en él, "Averroes" desaparece' (I 588).

in which they are inserted by Borges, and almost aware of themselves as characters, belated characters in a mystery story. Unwin interrupts the florid Dunraven to admonish him: 'Please – let's not multiply the mysteries ... Mysteries ought to be simple. Remember Poe's purloined letter, remember Zangwill's locked room' (A 96).[123] He takes the role of Treviranus warning Lönnrot not to 'buscarle tres pies al gato', i.e. not to overcomplicate matters. Dunraven counters that mysteries can also be complex, 'like the universe'. The simple plot is opposed, in classic Borges style, to the vastness of reality.

There is an enormous irony in the position of the two young men, one the author of a grand epic, yet to be commenced, and the other the author of a study of a theorem that Fermat had not written: 'It was the first evening of the summer of 1914; weary of a world that lacked the dignity of danger, the friends prized the solitude of that corner of Cornwall' (95).[124] Right at the cusp of the Great War, they blithely weave insubstantial labyrinthine plots, before being inevitably cast into the more universal labyrinth of battle and slaughter. Their position is not dissimilar to that of Yu Tsun learning of his great-grandfather's labyrinth-novel at just about the same date in 'Garden of the Forking Paths', or of Hladík imagining his play while facing a hail of Nazi bullets in 'The Secret Miracle'.

At once inside and outside the story is the short, parable-like piece, 'The Two Kings and the Two Labyrinths', originally published at an equally emblematic time in *El Hogar*, in June 1939. In the Postscript to the collection, Borges suggests that 'Ibn-Hakam' should be read as a 'variation' of the short piece that he presents, apocryphally, of course, as having been 'interpolated into the *1001 Nights* by the copyists yet passed over by the prudent Galland' (A 135). It is placed directly after 'Ibn-Hakam' in the collection, and has a footnote explaining that it is the story recounted by vicar Allaby in the previous story. It serves as a sort of external *mise-en-abyme*. The King of Babylon has constructed a labyrinth and left the visiting king of the Arabs within it. After escaping with the aid of his gods, he vows to show his tormentor a better labyrinth. He invades and sacks Babylonia, and abandons the first king in the middle of a vast desert, where he dies of thirst. Here we have the human labyrinth set against the divine labyrinth of reality in a way which reflects on the plight of the young thinkers. Allaby glosses and strengthens a suggestion made in the parable: 'Most unseemly was the edifice

---

[123] 'No multipliques los misterios —le dijo—. Éstos deben ser simples. Recuerda la carta robada de Poe, recuerda el cuarto cerrado de Zangwill' (I 600).
[124] 'Era la primera tarde del verano de 1914; hartos de un mundo sin la dignidad del peligro' (I 600).

that resulted, for it is the prerogative of god, not man, to strike confusion and inspire wonder' (A 105).[125] Allaby's sermon becomes 'the story of a king punished by the Deity for having built a labyrinth' (A 97).[126] When Dunraven, as a youth, named Ibn-Hakam 'King of Babel' (Babel and Babylon being the same word), implicitly the labyrinth was associated with that other challenge to Divinity, the Tower of Babel.

Dunraven's version of events is highly literary, re-elaborated from scraps of reading, dream, and cultural bric-a-brac. Unwin realizes that he has told it many times, 'with the same self-conscious gravity and the same paucity of effect' (A 100).[127] He cites Nicholas de Cusa on the geometry of circles; sees Ibn-Hakam, his black slave and his lion, through the lens of illustrations in his Bible; he describes the ship not from memory, because he had not seen it, but from 'some forgotten print of Aboukir or Trafalgar' (A 99), adding that the 'elaborately carved vessels' seemed 'less the work of shipwrights than of carpenters, and less that of carpenters than of cabinetmakers' (A 99).[128] Dunraven elaborates the story of Ibn-Hakam from the account given to Allaby by Ibn-Hakam himself. After cruelly oppressing his people, he was defeated by an uprising and escaped with his cousin and vizier Sa'īd with the fruit of his plundering. In hiding and during the night he was woken by a dream of a web of serpents, provoked by the brush of a spider's web, and felt humiliated to see that Sa'īd, who was considered a coward (a fact confirmed by Allaby in *The Times*) slept soundly. He murdered Sa'īd, destroyed his face with a stone, and left with the treasure, but dreamed that the dead man warned him: 'Como ahora me borras te borraré, dondequiera que estés' (I 602); 'Wherever you are, I will erase you as you now erase me.' (The word *borrar* is important but missed by Hurley's translation.) Faced with the threat, he built the labyrinth over the ocean so that Sa'īd's ghost would not be able to reach him. The locals see the slave going down to the visiting African boats to see whether 'the ghost of the vizier' is abroad, whereas in the 1957 edition of the story, he looks for 'the ghost of the king' (Al 128). The earlier version possibly leaves a clue which would confirm the version of Unwin, i.e. that Ibn-Hakam was actually Sa'īd. The last time Allaby sees Ibn-Hakam, he is inexplicably struck by a terror inappropriate to such a brave and cruel king, and tells the vicar

---

[125] 'Esa obra era un escándalo, porque la confusión y la maravilla son operaciones propias de Dios y no de los hombres' (I 607).

[126] 'la historia de un rey a quien la Divinidad castigó por haber erigido un laberinto' (I 601).

[127] 'con idéntico aplomo y con idéntica ineficacia' (I 603).

[128] 'esos barcos muy trabajados que no parecen obra de naviero, sino de carpintero y menos de carpintero que de ebanista' (I 603).

that (the ghost of) Sa'īd has returned and has already killed his slave and his lion. When Allaby goes to the labyrinth, he finds the bodies of the slave, the lion and the king, all with their faces destroyed, i.e. erased.

Unwin is not convinced by Dunraven's account, and bluntly, without measuring his words, describes it as a lie. There are clear parallels between the pair of the poet and mathematician and the pair of king and vizier. Dunraven is introduced in the opening lines as a distinctly regal figure: ' "This," said Dunraven with a vast gesture that did not blench at the cloudy stars, and that took in the black moors, the sea, and a majestic tumbledown edifice ... "is my ancestral land" ' (A 95).[129] Unwin seems the subordinate figure: he 'uttered modest sounds of approbation' (A 95).[130] The uncomfortable night they spend in the central chamber of the labyrinth echoes that spent by Ibn-Hakam and Sa'īd in the tomb of a saint. Whereas the cowardly Sa'īd slept soundly, the brave Ibn-Hakam was awakened by a dream. Similarly, Unwin sleeps, while Dunraven is kept awake by two haunting lines of poetry. Their rival versions of events echo the more bloody rivalry between the Sudanese, in a similar way to how Borges's narration of Averroes echoes Averroes's attempt to write his commentary on Aristotle. In Unwin's version Sa'īd is the inhabitant of the labyrinth, posing as Ibn-Hakam, whom he hopes to lure there to his death. Cowardice and bravery are opposed here as they have been since the time of 'Man on Pink Corner', but are as ever difficult to locate in any stable fashion. The first time Allaby met Sa'īd-Ibn-Hakam, he had not been able to reconcile the king's fear of his vizier's ghost with the 'enérgica impresión' (I 602), 'energetic impression' he left. We are reminded of the bland traitor in 'The Shape of the Sword' who takes on the vigour of his victim, and impresses Borges with his 'enérgica flacura' (I 491), 'energetic leanness', when he meets him on the Uruguayan border.

Unwin's version wins over Dunraven, but is not entirely waterproof, and within the logic of Borges's stories, can be readily inverted. A crimson labyrinth on a sea cliff, he argues, is not a good place to hide; London would be a better labyrinth (again, the normal labyrinth set against a vaster reality). He had been convinced of his theory by thinking of the labyrinth of Crete inhabited by a man with a bull's head. Dunraven quickly inverts the form of the Minotaur: Dante had imagined a bull's body with a man's head. Moreover, the Minotaur kills many Athenians, but is finally killed by Theseus, and in 'The House of Asterion', welcomed his own death as redemption. He interprets the dream of the spider's web to suggest the labyrinth as a trap to catch

---

129 'Ésta ... es la tierra de mis mayores' (I 600).
130 'emitió sonidos modestos y aprobatorios' (I 600).

the fly Ibn-Hakam. The epigraph to the story, from the Koran, concerns a spider's house, but when one consults the whole sentence, the connotation is far from that of a powerful trap: 'The false gods which the idolators serve besides Allah may be compared to the spider's cobweb. Surely the spider's is the frailest of all dwellings, if they but knew it' (cit. FH 134). According to Unwin, it was the brave Ibn-Hakam who slept while Sa'īd considered killing him but did not dare, and then fled to England with half the treasure, hoping to trap and kill the king in the labyrinth. On the other hand, Sa'īd seems to be cleverer than Unwin credits him with being. If Unwin is right about the identity, then the story about the rubbing out the face in Africa and the dead man's threat was invented by Sa'īd, and told to Allaby to explain the return of 'Sa'īd's' ghost, and the triple murder and erasing. He feigns fear when he sees Allaby, not because he has just killed three people, as Unwin argues, but to pretend that he will be the next victim, and thus turn Allaby into his homophone *alibi*, as he escapes back to Africa.

Unwin sums up Sa'īd's life as a pretence which becomes reality: 'He pretended to be Ibn-Hakam, killed Ibn-Hakam, and at last *was* Ibn-Hakam' (A 104).[131] This would fit in with certain instances in the stories of pantheism and identification with the other, as in 'Tadeo Isidoro Cruz', but in other stories, taking someone else's name, as in 'The Wait', or taking the position and attributes of a superior as in 'The Dead Man', leads to death. The death is by fire in 'The Dead Man' ('Suárez hizo fuego'), and by fire significantly described as an erasing (*borrar*) in 'The Wait': 'lo borró la descarga' (I 611), 'he was rubbed out by the revolver's fire' (A 11). The logic of these last two stories would suggest that the dead man should be the subordinate Sa'īd, as would the notion of being punished for weaving a labyrinthine plot to supplant the deity (Bandeira, remember, was a 'deidad cimarrona'). The battle between the symbol, Zahir, Zaid, over totality, the Aleph, Abenjacán is ultimately undecided here, as far as I can see. The final sentence reminds us of the Shakespeare of 'Everything and Nothing': 'He was a wanderer who, before becoming no one in death, would recall once having been a king, or having pretended to be a king' (A 104).[132] Dreaming, playing, and being are synonymous. In the early summer of 1914, Dunraven and Unwin were likely soon to be no one in death.

---

[131] 'Simuló ser Abenjacán, mató a Abenjacán y finalmente fue Abenjacán' (I 606).
[132] 'Fue un vagabundo que, antes de ser nadie en la muerte, recordaría haber sido un rey o haber fingido ser un rey, algún día' (I 606).

'The Wait', 'La espera'

'The Wait' is the simple, haunting story of a man on the run, waiting in an anonymous room in Buenos Aires for his inevitable death at the hand of an enemy who is hunting him down. His situation is that of Emma Zunz waiting for the next day to carry out her murder, and that of Hladík, Zur Linde, and Yu Tsun waiting for their execution in 'The Secret Miracle', '*Deutsches requiem*', and 'The Garden of the Forking Paths'. It is also a dry, crime-fiction version of 'Ibn-Hakam al-Bokhari, Murdered in His Labyrinth', where two men are inextricably locked together by their enmity, and one takes the name of the other. Though keenly aware of the need not to call attention to himself, the hunted man seems unconsciously to acquiesce to his fate: he gives the driver a Uruguayan coin, left over from his stay in Melo, and when asked for his name answers 'Villari', the surname of his enemy, Alejandro Villari. He gives the name because 'le fue imposible pensar en otro' (I 608); 'it was impossible for him to think of another': 'he said Villari – not as a secret act of defiance, not to mitigate a humiliation that quite honestly he didn't feel, but rather because that name haunted him, he couldn't come up with another one' (A 108). Very effectively, the text then uses this name for him, without quotation marks, suggesting a strong identification with the other. He scours the newspaper obituaries for his only hope of release: the death of Alejandro Villari. He suddenly comes upon a thought which disturbs him so much that he bans it from his mind: 'It was also possible that Villari *was already dead*, and then his life was a dream. That possibility disturbed him, because he couldn't quite figure out whether it felt like a relief or a misfortune' (A 109).[133] His life, like that of Aurelian in 'The Theologians', when his enemy John of Pannonia dies, becomes meaningless, here a 'dream', which is perhaps the major motif in the story. In a way he is the dream of the other man, like the wizard in 'The Circular Ruins'.

Separated from his past in the limbo of the lodging house, not by time but by 'two or three irrevocable acts', he is left with a life reduced to the desire to 'endure'. He trains himself to live in the mere present, and finally 'he was not a great deal more complex than the dog' he had befriended (A 109).[134] He reaches the timeless state of the cats in 'The End' and 'The South', and of Homer–Argos in 'The Immortal', and is roused like Homer from that timeless dream by a sharp stimulus: in the latter story, rain. The oxymoronic

---

133 'También era posible que Villari *ya hubiera muerto* y entonces esta vida era un sueño. Esa posibilidad lo inquietaba, porque no acabó de entender si se parecía al alivio o a la desdicha' (I 609).
134 'en momentos así, no era mucho más complejo que el perro' (I 609).

'horrible miracle' (A 109), 'horrible milagro' (I 610), which brings him back to life is a tooth-ache described as an 'íntima descarga' (I 610). The word *descarga*, meaning shooting, unloading, or unleashing, occurs at three key moments, not marked by Hurley's translation. The second occasion it occurs is in the endlessly recurrent dream of 'Villari' who, each time, shoots his pursuers: 'sacaba el revólver del cajón ... y lo descargaba contra los hombres' (I 610); 'he would take the revolver out of the drawer ... and fire it at the men' (A 110). When Villari and another man do actually come into the room at dawn, 'Villari' asks them to wait a second and turns to face the wall. In the Spanish he turns 'como si retomara el sueño' (I 610), which Hurley translates 'as though going back to sleep' (A 111), but can also mean: 'as if he were continuing his dream'. The second version fits in better with the meaning of Borges's third and preferred explanation for his action: 'so that his murderers would become a dream, as they had already been so many times, in that same place, at that same hour' (A 111).[135] As the two men become one, 'Villari' perhaps dreams that he is Villari shooting his enemy. The shot is another *descarga*: 'En esa magia estaba cuando lo borró la descarga' (I 611), 'That was the magic spell he was casting when he was rubbed out by the revolver's fire' (A 111). (Note the term *borrar*, to 'erase' or 'rub out', carried over from 'Ibn-Hakam al-Bokhari'.) The repetition of the term *descarga* causes the physical reality of pain, dreaming, and death to coalesce into a continuum.

In 'Ibn-Hakam al-Bokhari', the sophisticated Dunraven and Unwin are pretty much aware that they are living in a detective story with well codified rules for writing and readerly expectation: 'Such metamorphoses, you will tell me, are classic artifices of the genre – conventions that the reader insists be followed' (A 104).[136] 'Villari' has no such awareness, and Borges plays the ironic game throughout the story of confronting him with literature and literary elaboration, in which mirror he uncomprehendingly fails to see himself. Borges might have expected 'Villari', he records, to process the crimson peacocks on the wallpaper into 'a monstrous gazebo of living birds all intertangled' (A 110) (as Ibn-Hakam processed the brush of the spider's web into a tangle of serpents), but he does no such thing.[137] He was not 'seduced by the literary error of imagining that adopting the name of his

---

[135] 'para que los asesinos fueran un sueño, como ya lo habían sido tantas veces, en el mismo lugar, a la misma hora' (I 611).

[136] 'Tales metamorfosis, me dirás, son clásicos artificios del género, son verdaderas *convenciones* cuya observación exige el lector' (I 606).

[137] 'el señor Villari no soñó nunca con una glorieta monstruosa hecha de inextricables pájaros vivos' (I 610).

enemy would be the astute thing to do' (A 108),[138] because 'unlike people who had read novels, he never saw himself as a character in a book' (A 108).[139] He is a character in a book, of course, derived by Borges from other artistic sources, and confronted with these sources. He went to see crime movies, which reflected his previous life, but he did not notice, because 'the notion that there might be parallels between art and life never occurred to him' (A 108).[140] In a similar, slightly more complex incident, we come across the same dilemma as in 'The Other Death', where 'Borges' hesitates between seeing his story as the transcription of real experience, or as elaborated from the figure and arguments of Pier Damiani in the *Divina Commedia*. Borges claims in the Postscript that he had taken the story from a police report read to him ten years before by Alfredo Doblas, but it also clearly derives from the famous scene in Dante's Comedy where Ugolino is buried in ice with his enemy Ruggiero and endlessly gnaws at his neck. Ugolino had been accused of betraying Florence, and his friend Archbishop Ruggieri betrayed him by imprisoning him with his family in a tower where they all died of hunger. In Dante they are sentenced to an eternity in the circle of the traitors. Out of his patriotic duty as an Italian, 'Villari' reads the copy of the Comedy that he finds in the room, but does not recognize himself as deserving the infernal circle of the traitors: 'He did not think of the infernal torments as improbable or excessive, nor did it occur to him that Dante would have condemned him, Villari, to the farthest circle of Hell' (A 110).[141] This is, of course, exactly where he is in the lodging house, and as inseparable from the enemy he betrayed as Ugolino and Ruggiero. Though 'hard-boiled' and understated, 'The Wait' is perhaps Borges's ultimate story of betrayal, in the line of 'The Shape of the Sword', and 'The Dead Man'.

'The Man on the Threshold', 'El hombre en el umbral'

'The Man on the Threshold' revisits the paradoxes and ambiguities generated by the cultural complexity of Empire and colonialism, explored so memorably in the Irish context in 'Theme of the Traitor and the Hero' and 'The Shape

---

[138] 'No lo sedujo, ciertamente, el error literario de imaginar que asumir el nombre del enemigo podía ser una astucia' (I 608–9).

[139] 'A diferencia de quienes han leído novelas, no se veía nunca a sí mismo como un personaje del arte' (I 609).

[140] 'la idea de una coincidencia entre el arte y la realidad era ajena a él' (I 609).

[141] 'No juzgó inverosímiles o excesivas las penas infernales y no pensó que Dante lo hubiera condenado al último círculo' (I 610).

of the Sword'. As in the first of these stories, where classic English Shakespearian texts are turned against the colonial master, here the Indian knowingly turns the Englishman's prejudiced view of him to his own advantage,
arguably mimicking his own stereotype. It was first published in *La Nación*
in 1952, five years after the independence of India in 1947, and returns to
the world of 'The Approach to Al-Mu'tasim', published in 1935. According
to Balderston in his detailed historicizing study, the story is a critical revisiting also of Kipling's 'On the City Walls', an important source of the earlier
story. Whereas in Kipling the Anglicized Indian Wali Dad acts hysterically
after murdering a fellow Indian, in this story the dead man is a corrupt and
unjust English administrator, judged and executed by a popular Indian court,
which uses a madman to judge the English judge. In Borges's story, a rather
stupid British colonial official, Christopher Dewey, investigating the disappearance of a powerful and feared administrator in the inter-war years, is
duped by an old Indian man who recounts the trial and execution of a British
judge as if it had happened before 1857, when it was actually taking place
at that very moment and only a few yards away. His story entertains Dewey
for the time vital for the execution to take place. His discourse, disguised
as a confused oriental fable for the supercilious English listener, is in fact a
powerful political weapon. The irrationality attributed by the Europeans to
the Eastern other, turns against them as a madman sits in judgement over
their administration.

The status of the narration is complex. There are three narrations,
embedded one within the other. The first narrator is Borges in so far as he
is introduced as a friend of Bioy Casares, and has knowledge of Kipling
and a taste for *The Arabian Nights*, but his voice is far from transparent.
The second is a British Council worker in Buenos Aires, Christopher Dewey,
who tells Bioy and Borges about his experiences in India. Borges promises
to reconstruct his narration in a faithful fashion. Much of Dewey's story is
his account of the story told by an old Indian who sits at the entrance to a
deep native house. The Indian's story is thus filtered twice: through the voice
of an English colonial official, and then through that of an intellectual of the
ex-colonial Argentina. This ambiguity is accompanied by a double focus of
temporality. The double focus is accentuated considerably when the story is
read in conjunction with Balderston's account, which sets it precisely in the
detailed historical context of the struggle of the Indians against British colonial rule. Borges–Dewey's account, on the other hand, stresses the timelessness of India. They describe the old man in the same way as the archetypal
gaucho in 'The South' and Recabarren in 'The End': 'His many years had
reduced and polished him in the way water smoothes and polishes a stone

or generations of men polish a proverb' (A 114).[142] How far this reflects the naïve, orientalizing, and patronizing vision of the English colonialist, ironized by Borges, and how far Borges's own taste for the archetypal is tantalizingly undecidable.

The authority of Dewey is seriously undermined in the first paragraph, where he is shown to have badly misquoted Juvenal's Latin. 'Borges' adds, confusingly:

> My text will be a faithful one; may Allah prevent me from adding small circumstantial details or heightening the exotic lineaments of the tale with interpolations from Kipling. Besides, it has an antique, simple flavor about it that it would be a shame to lose – something of the *1001 Nights*.
>
> (A 112)[143]

'Borges's' invocation of Allah, uncharacteristic of Borges, is already a clear element of exoticism. The 'circumstantial details' are a favourite technique of Borges's discussed as far back as 'Postulation of Reality', and Kipling is alluded to in the ambience and the references to the time of Nikal Seyn/ Nicholson. The exoticism of *The Arabian Nights*, of course, as Borges demonstrated in a key essay, depends on the translator. The antique simplicity expected from the archetypal old man is not recognizable in the tumultuous, exoticizing enumeration attributed to him:

> Scholars of the Qur'ān, doctors of the law, Sikhs who bear the names of lions yet worship God, Hindus who worship a multitude of gods, monks of the master Mahavira who teach that the shape of the universe is that of a man with his legs spread wide open, worshippers of fire, and black Jews, composed the tribunal, but the ultimate verdict was to be decided by a madman. (A 116)[144]

---

[142] 'Los muchos años lo habían reducido y pulido como las aguas a una piedra o las generaciones de los hombres a una sentencia' (I 613).

[143] 'Mi texto sera fiel: líbreme Alá de la tentación de añadir breves rasgos circunstanciales o de agravar, con interpolaciones de Kipling, el cariz exótico del relato. Éste, por lo demás, tiene un antiguo y simple sabor que sería una lástima perder, acaso el de *Las 1001 Noches*' (I 612).

[144] 'Alcoranistas, doctores de la ley, *sikhs* que llevan el nombre de leones y que adoran a un Dios, hindúes que adoran muchedumbres de dioses, monjes de Mahavira que enseñan que la forma del universo es la de un hombre con las piernas abiertas, adoradores del fuego y judíos negros, integraron el tribunal, pero el último fallo fue encomendado al arbitrio de un loco' (I 614).

Dewey is repeatedly shown to be ignorant and brutal in a way in which his own unfiltered account was unlikely to show. He punches liars in the face, confuses the trial with 'some sort of Muslim celebration' (A 114),[145] and believes that the old man's incredibly astute speech confirms that he is out of touch with present reality.

Balderston's background research clearly suggests that the writer Borges had a detailed knowledge of Indian history derived from the Britannica, Kipling and other sources. He situates the story in Amritsar because of the important 1919 massacre there, and points out the import of Dewey's judgement of the old man's timeless mind: '*News of the Mutiny or the latest word of Akbar, this man might have* (I thought) *but not of Glencairn*' (A 114).[146] Experience of the 1857 Mutiny and of the Mogul leader Akbar (1556–1605) did not fit in the life-span of any individual. He also shows that David Alexander Glencairn is based on the historical figure of the notoriously cruel colonial administrator John Nicholson, who died by the city walls of Delhi in 1857. Borges's story thus superimposes different periods to create the impression of timelessness attributed to the old man. His story moves as deftly between the planes of historical specificity and recurring patterns as it does between the mind games of colonial master and subject, and their ironic, unreliable, and none too impartial observers in South America.

---

[145] 'no sé qué fiesta musulmana' (I 613).
[146] '*Nuevas de la Rebelión o de Akbar podría dar este hombre* (pensé) *pero no de Glencairn*' (I 613).

SUGGESTIONS FOR FURTHER READING

Borges's primary texts are widely available. Alianza/Emecé has convenient paperback editions of individual collections, while the *Obras completas* by Emecé has three volumes of his works and another of work done in collaboration with writers such as Bioy Casares. In English, the US Penguin volume *Collected Fictions* is a handy and attractive collection of most of his stories, while in the UK individual Penguin volumes such as *Fictions* and *The Aleph* are more readily to be found.

Borges's own essays are an excellent way into the intellectual and referential world of the stories, and often set out his concerns in a less paradoxical fashion than the stories, which tend to hold together contradictory takes on any issue. Many of the essays of the original *Discusión* and *Otras inquisiciones*, together with a good selection of others, can be found in English translation in the Penguin volume edited by Eliot Weinberger, *The Total Library. Non-Fiction 1922–1986*.

Of the biographical studies, Edwin Williamson's *Borges. A Life* is a thorough and outstanding piece of research, and a mine of information on Borges's life and its wider context in Buenos Aires, while Jason Wilson's Reaktion volume is shorter, informative and very readable. Estela Canto's *Borges a contraluz* and María Esther Vázquez's *Borges: Esplendor y derrota* offer more personal testimonies, and are very entertaining.

There are a number of good introductions and surveys of Borges's work. Gene Bell-Villada's *Borges and His Fiction* has full, lively and informative analyses, while Sylvia Molloy's *Signs of Borges* offers a sophisticated account of his dealings with meaning and discourse. Alan Pauls's *El factor Borges* is a stimulating excursion though Borges's key words and *topoi*. Evelyn Fishburn and Psiche Hughes's *A Dictionary of Borges* is a gem, saving hours, days and weeks of slog, and opens up the connotations of the most innocuous looking references.

On the Argentine intellectual setting to Borges, various studies can be highlighted. John King's excellent study of the journal *Sur* is most helpful, and Beatriz Sarlo's works offer a firm grasp of the intellectual groupings of the time. Other scholars have indispensable studies on particular aspects. Daniel Balderston's *Out of Context* is a ground-breaking attempt to contextualize many stories historically. On intertextuality and allusion, Ronald Christ's early *The Narrow Act* is pioneering but still essential reading, while Michel Lafon's *Borges ou la réécriture* formalizes the field following the lead of Gérard Genette. Efraín Kristal's *Invisible Work* is extraordinarily revealing, as he follows up the related theme of translation. As a model of the study of the referential world of one single story, Eduardo Ramos-Izquierdo's *Contrapuntos analíticos a 'El acercamiento a Almotásim'* is exemplary. On the presence of Jewish mysticism in Borges's texts, Jaime Alazraki's *Borges and the Kabbalah* has much of the information one needs. The journal *Variaciones Borges* offers a constant flow of new research on Borges.

BIBLIOGRAPHY

Helft, Nicolás, *Jorge Luis Borges: Bibliografía completa*. Mexico City: Fondo de
  Cultura Económica, 1997

Principal works by Borges, by order of publication in Spanish

1923: *Fervor de Buenos Aires*
1925: *Luna de enfrente* (*Moon Across the Way*)
1925: *Inquisiciones* (*Inquisitions*)
1926: *El tamaño de mi esperanza* (*The Size of my Hope*)
1929: *El idioma de los argentinos* (*The Language of the Argentines*)
1929: *Cuaderno San Martín* (*San Martín Copybook*)
1930: *Evaristo Carriego*
1932: *Discusión*
1935: *Historia universal de la infamia* (*A Universal History of Iniquity*)
1936: *Historia de la eternidad* (*A History of Eternity*)
1941: *El jardín de senderos que se bifurcan* (*The Garden of Forking Paths*)
1943: *Poemas (1923–43)*
1944: *Ficciones* (*Fictions*)
1949: *El Aleph* (*The Aleph*)
1952: *Otras inquisiciones* (*Other Inquisitions*)
1958: *Poemas (1923–1958)*
1960: *El hacedor* (*The Maker*)
1969: *Elogio de la sombra* (*In Praise of Darkness*)
1970: *El informe de Brodie* (*Dr Brodie's Report*)
1974: *Obras completas* (*Complete Works*)
1975: *El libro de arena* (*The Book of Sand*)
1982: *Nueve ensayos dantescos* (*Nine Dantean Essays*)
1989: Four-volume edition of *Obras completas* (*Complete Works*)

Biographies of Borges

Canto, Estela, *Borges a contraluz*. Madrid: Espasa Calpe, 1999
Jurado, Alicia, *Genio y figura de Jorge Luis Borges*. Editorial Universitaria de
  Buenos Aires, 1964

Rodríguez Monegal, Emir, *Borges: una biografía literaria*. Mexico City: Fondo de Cultura Económica, 1987
Vázquez, María Esther, *Borges: esplendor y derrota*. Barcelona: Tusquets, 1996
Williamson, Edwin, *Borges. A Life*. New York: Viking, 2004
Wilson, Jason, *Jorge Luis Borges*. London: Reaktion, 2006

Interviews with Borges

Burgin, Richard, *Conversations with Jorge Luis Borges*. London: Souvenir Press, 1973
Charbonnier, Georges, *Entretiens avec Jorge Luis Borges*. Paris: Gallimard, 1967
Christ, Ronald, 'Interview', in *The Narrow Act*, 247–89
Milleret, Jean de, *Entretiens avec Jorge Luis Borges*. Paris: Pierre Belfond, 1967
Solares, Ignacio, 'Soy tan escéptico que ahora dudo de que no exista Dios', in Brescia and Zavala, *Borges múltiple*, 327–39
Vázquez, María Esther, *Borges: sus días y su tiempo*. Barcelona: Javier Vergara, 1984

Select Bibliography on Borges

Alazraki, Jaime, *Versiones. Inversiones. Reversiones. El espejo como modelo estructural en los cuentos de Borges*. Madrid: Gredos, 1977
——, *Borges and the Kabbalah, and Other essays on his Fiction and Poetry*. Cambridge: Cambridge University Press, 1988
Balderston, Daniel, *El precursor velado: R. L. Stevenson en la obra de Borges*. Buenos Aires: Sudamericana, 1985
——, *Out of Context. Historical Reference and the Representation of Reality in Borges*. Durham, NC, and London: Duke University Press, 1993
Barrenechea, Ana María, *La expresión de la irrealidad en la obra de Borges*. Buenos Aires: Centro Editor de América Latina, 1984
Bell-Villada, Gene, *Borges and His Fiction. A Guide to His Mind and Art*. Chapel Hill: University of North Carolina Press, 1981
Bioy Casares, Adolfo, *Borges*. Barcelona: Destino, 2006
Bloom, Harold, ed., *Jorge Luis Borges*. New York: Chelsea House, 1986
Brescia, Pablo and Lauro Zavala, eds., *Borges múltiple: cuentos y ensayos de cuentistas*. Mexico City: UNAM, 1999
Cahiers de l'Herne, Jorge Luis Borges. Paris: Editions de l'Herne, 1964
Christ, Ronald, *The Narrow Act. Borges' Art of Allusion*. New York: Lumen Books, 1995
Fishburn, Evelyn and Psiche Hughes, *A Dictionary of Borges*. London: Duckworth, 1990
Fishburn, Evelyn, ed., *Borges and Europe Revisited*. London: Institute of Latin American Studies, 1998

Kaplan, Marina, ' "Tlön, Uqbar, Orbis Tertius" y "Urn Burial" ', *Comparative Literature*, 36:4 (1984), 328–42

Kefala, Eleni, *Peripheral (Post)Modernity. The Syncretist Aesthetics of Borges, Piglia, Kalokyris and Kyriakidis*. New York: Peter Lang, 2007

Kristal, Efraín, *Invisible Work. Borges and Translation*. Nashville: Vanderbildt University Press, 2002

Lafon, Michel, *Borges ou la réécriture*. Paris: Seuil, 1990

Molloy, Sylvia, *Signs of Borges*. Durham, NC: Duke University Press, 1994

Paoli, Roberto, 'Ambigua Beatriz', in Julio Ortega and Elena del Río, eds, *'El Aleph de Jorge Luis Borges: edición crítica y facsimilar*. Mexico City: El Colegio de México, 2001

Pauls, Alan, *El factor Borges*. Barcelona: Anagrama, 2004

Piglia, Ricardo, 'Ideología y ficción en Borges', in Brescia and Zavala, *Borges múltiple*, 177–85

———, *El último lector*. Barcelona: Anagrama, 2005

Ramos-Izquierdo, Eduardo, *Contrapuntos analíticos a 'El acercamiento a Almotásim' Op. I.* Mexico City and Paris: Rilma 2 and Adehl, 2006

Sarlo, Beatriz, *Borges. A Writer on the Edge*. London: Verso, 1993

Shaw, Donald, *Borges's Narrative Strategy*. Liverpool: Francis Cairns, 1992

Sturrock, John, *Paper Tigers. The Ideal Fiction of Jorge Luis Borges*. Oxford: Clarendon Press, 1977

Other

Avellaneda, Andrés, *El habla de la ideología: modos de réplica literaria en la Argentina contemporánea*. Buenos Aires: Sudamericana, 1983

Bianco, José, 'Borges', in *Ficción y reflexión*. Mexico City: Fondo de Cultura Económica, 1988, 351–4

Browne, Thomas, *Hydriotaphia. Urne-Buriall*, in *Works*, vol. 4, London: Faber & Gwyer, 1929

Cervantes, Miguel de, *Don Quijote de la Mancha*, Barcelona: Instituto Cervantes. Crítica, 1998

Chesterton, G. K., *The Man Who Was Thursday*, London: Penguin, 1975

———, *Father Brown. Selected Stories*. London: Collector's Library, 2003

Cortázar, Julio, *Obras completas*, vol. II, *Teatro, Novelas I*, ed. By Saúl Yurkievich. Barcelona: Galaxia Gutenberg/Círculo de Lectores, 2004

De Quincey, Thomas, 'Homer and the Homeridae', in *Works*, vol. 5. Edinburgh: Adam and Charles Black, 1880

Eliot, T. S., *Selected Poems*. London: Faber & Faber, 1970

Emerson, Ralph Waldo, *Essays and Lectures*. New York: The Library of America, 1983

Fernández Retamar, Roberto, *Calibán*, in José Enrique Rodó, *Ariel*, Roberto Férnandez Retamar, *Calibán*. Mexico City: SEP/UNAM, 1982

Genette, Gérard, *Palimpsestes: la littérature au second degré*. Paris: Seuil, 1992

Hernández, José, *Martín Fierro*. Madrid: Cátedra, 1990

Kafka, Franz, *The Great Wall of China and Other Stories*, trans. by Malcolm Pasley. London: Penguin, 1991

King, John, *Sur. A Study of the Argentine Literary Journal and its Role in the Development of a Culture, 1939–1970*. Cambridge: Cambridge University Press, 1986

Larousse Encyclopedia of Mythology. London: Batchworth Press, 1959

Marechal, Leopoldo, *Adán Buenosayres*. Buenos Aires: Sudamericana, 1966

Poe, Edgar Allan, *Selected Writings*. London: Penguin, 1975

Rimbaud, Arthur, *Oeuvres complètes*. Paris: Gallimard, 1988

Sábato, Ernesto, *Sobre héroes y tumbas*. Buenos Aires: Sudamericana, 1970

Sarlo, Beatriz, *Una modernidad periférica: Buenos Aires 1920 y 1930*. Buenos Aires: Nueva Visión, 2003

Shakespeare, William, *The Complete Works*, London and Glasgow: Collins, 1979

Shaw, George Bernard, *Back to Methuselah*, in *Collected Plays with Their Prefaces*. London: Max Reinhardt, The Bodley Head, 1972

Valéry, Paul, *Monsieur Teste*, in *Oeuvres*, II. Paris: Gallimard, 1992

Yeats, William Butler, *The Poems*. London: Everyman's Library, 1992

INDEX

Abramovich, Maurice, 19, 121
Acevedo, Leonor Rita (mother of Borges)
   see under Borges, family
Acevedo Díaz, Arturo, 36, 134
Acevedo Laprida, Isidoro de *see under*
   Borges, family
Achilles, 160
Adam, 149
Adrogué, 18, 26, 79, 85, 117
Aita, Antonio, 134
Alazraki, Jaime, 88, 89, 141
Albert, Stephen, 172
Alem, Leandro Nicebro, 54
Alexander of Macedonia, 132, 160
Allende, Salvador, 42
Almafuerte (Pedro Bonifacio Palacio),
   121
Alvarado, Pedro de, 141, 142
Álvarez de Toledo, Letizia, 97
Amorim, Enrique, 82, 150
Anales de Buenos Aires, Los, 37
anarchism, 11, 17, 42, 73, 86
Andreä, Johannes Valentinus, 79
Annick, Louis, 5
anti-Semitism, 37, 39–40, 74, 83
Apollinaire, Guillaume, 20
Apollodorus, 164
Aquinas, Thomas, 167
Arabian Nights see A Thousand and One
   Nights
Arabic culture, 73, 172–6
Aramburu, General Pedro, 23, 41
Argentina, history of
   Civil War between Unitarians and
      Federalists, 159, 160
   Conquest of the Desert, 158
   Dirty War after 1976 Revolution, 43
   Falklands/Malvinas War, 43
   Independence, 9, 160

   military coup of Rawson and Ramírez,
      13
   Revolución Libertadora, 1955, 41
   war with Brazil (1825–8), 160
   see also battles, Irigoyen, nationalism,
      Radical Party, Rosas, Unitarians
      and Federalists
Ariadne, 166
Aristotle, 167, 172–3, 175
   Poetics, 172
Aristotelianism,
   see Platonism and Aristotelianism
Arlt, Roberto
   El juguete rabioso, 23
'Arms and Letters', 12, 73, 75, 76, 146,
   171
arrabal, 46, 53
Ashbury, Herbert
   The Gangs of New York, 29
Asín Palacios, Miguel, 173
Attār, Farīd al-dīn
   Conference of the Birds, 65, 68–9
Attila the Hun, 153
Augustine, Saint, 154, 155
   City of God, 153
avant-garde, 19, 20, 21, 22, 26, 84
Avellaneda, Andrés, 35

Baal, 92
Baal Shem, 115
Bacon, Francis, 145, 146
Balderston, Daniel, 4, 99, 100, 101, 104,
   141, 143, 157, 158, 184, 186
Banchs, Enrique, 6
   Los parques abandonados, 35
barbarism, 8, 13, 38, 128, 150, 160
   see also Civilization and Barbarism
Barrenechea, Ana María, 92
Barthes, Roland, 4, 71

Lightning Source UK Ltd.
Milton Keynes UK
UKOW05f2327061013

218565UK00003B/6/P